Madame Bo

DATE DUE

FAUX TITRE

325

Etudes de langue et littérature françaises
publiées sous la direction de

Keith Busby, M.J. Freeman,
Sjef Houppermans et Paul Pelckmans

Madame Bovary at the Movies
Adaptation, Ideology, Context

Mary Donaldson-Evans

Rodopi

AMSTERDAM - NEW YORK, NY 2009

Cover design: Andrew Donaldson-Evans

The paper on which this book is printed meets the requirements of
'ISO 9706: 1994, Information and documentation - Paper for documents -
Requirements for permanence'.

Le papier sur lequel le présent ouvrage est imprimé remplit les prescriptions
de 'ISO 9706: 1994, Information et documentation - Papier pour documents -
Prescriptions pour la permanence'.

ISBN: 978-90-420-2504-2
© Editions Rodopi B.V., Amsterdam - New York, NY 2009
Printed in The Netherlands

For Lance, Catherine, and Andrew

Contents

Acknowledgements

This has been a long-haul project, and if the debts I've incurred to the people who have helped me along the way had been monetary, the bank would have repossessed my house by now. Let me begin by thanking Laurence M. Porter. In the last decade of my career, I would not have had the pluck to embark upon a book-length study in a field doubly removed from my own (twentieth-century cinema as opposed to nineteenth-century literature) had Larry not intervened three times to nudge me along. The first intervention came as an invitation to contribute an essay to the MLA's *Approaches to Teaching Flaubert's* Madame Bovary (1995). My essay, "Teaching *Madame Bovary* through Film," brought two further invitations, the first, to write entries on Renoir, Minnelli and Chabrol for *The Gustave Flaubert Encyclopedia* (2001); and the second, to speak on film adaptations at the 2001 NCFS colloquium. All of these assignments propelled me along on the path towards this book. I had reached the point of no return. I also "outed" Larry as an anonymous reader of the manuscript, a task he accomplished with truly impressive thoroughness. I am most grateful to him. Suggestions made by another consultant reader, whose cloak of anonymity I have been unable to remove, have also been most helpful.

Two other close friends read the entire manuscript in an earlier version. Graham Falconer, whose acumen as a critic of the nineteenth-century French novel is of the highest order, didn't wait to be asked. His keen insights and gentle mentoring have helped me to improve my manuscript. Gerald Krell, a film director accustomed to crying "Cut!" on the set, approached my manuscript with the same concern for fluidity that he exhibits in making his remarkable documentaries. Although I could not bring myself to excise many of the passages he would have left on the cutting room floor, I did take most of his suggestions for less painful changes, and if my book is more sensitive to the director's viewpoint, it is largely because of him.

At the University of Delaware, my research has been supported by an Elias Ahuja Professorship since 2002, an honor for which I was nominated by my chair, Richard Zipser. Thanks also to Professor Zipser, I have had the incalculable advantage of a steady supply of research assistants. Julia Brunner, Kate Copeland, Heike Gerhold, Loïc Marie-Magdelene, Fatima Mhinat, Kate Stark, and Thomas Chapman Wing have all been part of the production team for this book. In my courses, students have played supporting roles by asking provocative questions, thereby encouraging me to examine my own assumptions about adaptation.

No scholarly work can be accomplished without access to a good library and a helpful staff. I have been fortunate indeed to enjoy such facilities at the Morris Library of the University of Delaware, where a faculty study has been made available to me. Closer to my home, I have for several years found refuge from the summer heat in the air-conditioned comfort of the John D. Vairo Library at the Brandywine Campus of Penn State University. I am grateful to the staff for their hospitality.

During the time that this project has been under construction, I have been given many opportunities to give tours of the work-in-progress. Colleagues at conferences as well as scholars met on-line have helped me in myriad ways. Let me thank Anne-Marie Baron, Ross Chambers, Lucienne Frappier-Mazur, Kate Griffiths, Tomoko Hashimoto, Delphine Jayot, Martine Mesureur-Ceyrat, Judith Moortgat, Marshall Olds, Allan Pasco, Gerald Prince, Maurice Samuels, and Lawrence Schehr. Barbara Cooper deserves a sentence of her own, for she has pointed out many relevant articles to me through the years and has been a reliable source of friendly encouragement. To those colleagues who have invited me to speak on the *Bovary* films, I am also deeply beholden: Sonya Stephens, Tim Unwin and Robert Lethbridge (Leeds, UK, 2003); Jacques Neefs (Cerisy, 2006); Anne Herschberg-Pierrot (Paris, 2008). At these venues, I would have been seriously handicapped without the film clips that Tom McCone and Rae Stabosz of UD's Foreign Language Media Center patiently helped me string together. Additionally, the illustrations that enhance this volume would not be there without the technological expertise of Tom McCone.

Several of my colleagues at the University of Delaware have taken more than a casual interest in this book. Peter Feng became an indispensable source of information in the early stages of this project when he allowed me to audit two of his film courses. More recently, he read the Renoir chapter and offered pertinent suggestions. His ready answers to my technical questions have been most appreciated. To my good friend Gary Ferguson, who has been especially encouraging and helpful, I owe my awareness of *Beyond the Forest*. To him also goes the credit for coming up with the title that I have finally chosen for this study. Bruno Thibault has kindly shared the fruit of his own research on French film with me. Bonnie Robb's recently published book on Félicité de Genlis served as a model for details of format when the *MLA Handbook* was silent. Monika Shafi, finally, with whom I have had a steady dialogue through the years about things both professional and personal, has been wonderfully steadfast in her support of this and all of my endeavors.

I am indebted to Laure Marchaut for projecting the 35 mm. Renoir adaptation at the Cinémathèque archives; to Joan Dejean who graciously tried to locate the scenario of this same adaptation at the Bibliothèque de l'Arsenal; to my neighbor Jacki Bishop, cat-sitter extraordinaire, who upon receiving a panicked call from Paris, dug through my files for information needed for a film paper I was about to read; to my son, Andrew, who designed the cover for this book; to my daughter, Catherine, who viewed *Maya Memsaab* and gave me the benefit of her insights; to Keith Busby, of the Faux Titre editorial board, who served as my liaison with Rodopi, generously presenting my manuscript to the other editors; to Amy Ralston, who meticulously prepared the camera-ready copy and the index for this book; to Christa Stevens of Rodopi who responded quickly to every query; to Bob Mitchell, who has played a vital role in my career and whose optimism feeds my own; to Margaret Kinetz and Susan Johnson, whose life-long friendship and concern for my welfare make them major players in any project I undertake.

But it is above all to my husband Lance that this book owes its existence. Leaving aside the extra time I have had for my work thanks to the domestic tasks he has so cheerfully shared, he has been part of this project in so many ways that no written acknowledgement can give the measure of his role. My unofficial research assistant, he has on countless occasions returned home from the Van Pelt library bent under the weight of books on film, has good-naturedly sat through viewings of every one of the *Bovary* adaptations, has read and re-read every page of this manuscript, listened to endless recitals of every idea. After re-playing a single scene from the Renoir adaptation dozens of times, he was the one, finally, who deciphered a snippet of dialogue that even had the subtitle writers stumped.

It is to Lance and to our wonderful adult children that I dedicate this book.

Note on the translations: Unless otherwise noted, all translations from the French are my own. Page references to *Madame Bovary*, given parenthetically in the text, are to the 1999 Livre de Poche edition listed in the bibliography. I have also listed the most authoritative and readily available translations in the hope that this information will be helpful to the non-French-speaking reader.

Introduction

The year 2007 marked the 150th anniversary of the publication, by the Parisian publishing house Charpentier, of the first edition of Gustave Flaubert's classic novel *Madame Bovary*. To argue that this novel has become a cultural icon is to belabor the obvious. A search of the on-line bibliography of the Modern Language Association conducted in the summer of 2008 revealed 590 subject entries for the novel since 1933 (555 since 1980 alone). Of these, some thirty-five are books; the rest of the entries are journal articles, book chapters, and dissertations. These numbers do not include the vast majority of studies published in languages other than English or French. Whatever their individual worth, these commentaries testify to the timeless critical appeal of Flaubert's masterpiece. A singularly protean text, Flaubert's novel differs from most works in the canon of world literature in that critical reaction to it has undergone not one, but several shifts (one of them seismic) since it first appeared. Although, right from the beginning and up to the present day, it has found favor with other novelists (Henry James, among many others, considered it indispensable reading, and more recently, Mario Vargas Llosa and Julian Barnes have had an interest in the novel that borders on the obsessive), it is no longer pigeon-holed as a quintessentially realist novel, as had been the case for roughly the first one hundred years after its publication. Successively labeled "immoral," "a masterpiece of French literary realism," "the first modern novel," and "the ancestor of post-modernism," *Madame Bovary* has proven susceptible to a myriad of critical approaches, from Marxist to feminist to deconstructionist. Today, it holds special appeal for those engaged in the field of Cultural Studies.

Literary critics are not alone in what amounts to a quasi-fetishization of *Madame Bovary*. In anglophone countries, the novel's enduring popularity with the reading public and the challenges it continues to pose for translators can be measured by the numerous translations it has undergone. From each generation of readers, a translator seems to emerge, determined to "get it right" once and for all.[1] Now, it is true that language and culture are in constant evolution and thus that new translations will always be necessary in order to communicate with the public of the moment. Nevertheless, the fact that so many translators have applied themselves to the task of making this complex text available to the Anglophone reader is in itself impressive. Impressive, too, are the numerous spin-offs. As with any classic of world literature, the novel, itself an important *hypertexte* (to use Gérard Genette's term)[2] inspired by and incorporating elements from earlier literary traditions (most notably romanticism), is in its turn a model (an *hypotexte*), having spawned a vast number of *hypertextes* of its own, re-writings that vary from sequels and transpositions to parodies, pastiches, caricatures, and modernizations.[3] Among the numerous *hypertextes* published in the nineteenth century, several novels tend to be mentioned by literary scholars, among them the Portuguese *O primo Basílio* (1878), by José María Eça de Queirós; the Spanish *La Regenta* (1884-85) by Leopoldo Aldas (pseud. "Clarín"); and the German *Effi Briest* (1895) by Theodor Fontane. *Les Incarnations de Madame Bovary*, a collection of five short stories that "up-date" episodes from the novel, appeared in 1933.[4] More recent examples include Raymond Jean's *Mademoiselle Bovary* and Laura Grimaldi's *Monsieur Bovary* (both 1991), Posy Simmond's *Gemma Bovery* (2001), Elke Schmitter's *Frau Sartoris* (2002), and Cathleen Schine's *She is Me* (2003). However, perhaps the most notable of the

---

[1] Translators include Mildred Marmur, Lowell Bair, Eleanor Marx Aveling, Paul de Man, Margaret Mauldon, Geoffrey Wall, and many others. For a list of translators up to 1997 and a provocative discussion of the stakes of translation, see Graham Falconer, "Madame Bovary and the translators."

[2] Gérard Genette, *Palimpsestes, la littérature au second degré*. For Genette, a hypertext is a text "dérivé d'un texte antérieur par transformation simple (dit, ailleurs, 'directe') ou par transformation indirecte" [derived from an existing text by way of a simple transformation (called direct) or by an indirect transformation] (14). Today, scholars of book history and computer scientists use the term "hypertext" in entirely different ways.

[3] See Annick Bouillaguet's *L'Ecriture imitative. Pastiche, Parodie, Collage* for a full discussion of the various ways in which a text can be "rewritten."

[4] For a list of these stories and a brief discussion of them, see Alain Buisine, "Emma c'est l'autre," 27.

twentieth century's re-workings of *Madame Bovary* have been its film adaptations. There is some irony in this fact, given that Flaubert himself, despite his acute awareness of the poverty of mere words to represent even the most mundane reality, refused to allow his novel to be illustrated and thereby fixed in the reader's imagination by the mediation of pictorial images:

> Jamais, moi vivant, on ne m'illustrera, parce que la plus belle description littéraire est dévorée par le plus piètre dessin. Du moment qu'un type est fixé par le crayon, il perd ce caractère de généralité, cette concordance avec mille objets connus qui font dire au lecteur: "J'ai vu cela" ou "Cela doit être." Une femme dessinée ressemble à une femme, voilà tout. L'idée est déjà fermée, complète, et toutes les phrases sont inutiles, tandis qu'une femme écrite fait rêver à mille femmes. Donc, ceci étant une question d'esthétique, je refuse formellement toute espèce d'illustration. (Letter to Ernest Duplan, 12 June 1862, *Correspondance III*, 221-22.)

> [As long as I live, I will never allow my books to be illustrated, because the most beautiful literary description is swallowed up by the most wretched little drawing. As soon as something is represented pictorially, it loses its general nature, that resemblance with a thousand familiar objects that makes the reader say, "Oh yes, I've seen that" or "It must be like that." A woman in a drawing looks like one particular woman, case closed. The idea is already classified, complete, and all words are useless, whereas a woman described in writing makes the reader dream of a thousand different women. Because this is a question of esthetics, I categorically reject any kind of illustration.]

Since 1932, when the first film adaptation of *Madame Bovary* was released, filmmakers have ignored Flaubert's prejudice against the iconic in their attempts to translate his words into visual images. Indeed, the filmmaker Claude Chabrol persuaded himself that Flaubert would have approved of this activity, because what the nineteenth-century author found objectionable in illustrations—their static quality—would not apply to moving pictures. In a "God is my co-pilot" expression of faith, Chabrol even insisted that he made his adaptation of *Madame Bovary* exactly as Flaubert would have done, had the author had at his disposal a camera instead of a pen. The filmmaker, grappling with the problems he encountered in attempting to produce a visual equivalent of Flaubert's style, claims that he had to accept Flaubert as his "co-scénariste" [screenwriting partner] (Chase 8).

Counting only those films that have either named or alluded to *Madame Bovary* as their source, one can identify eighteen screen adaptations of Flaubert's chef d'œuvre.[5] From France to the United States and Italy to Argentina, filmmakers have found this novel irresistible. However, like Rodolphe who, smitten by the health officer's wife and eager to appropriate her for himself in spite of what he suspected might be complications later on, they have often gotten both more—and less—than they bargained for. Why does *Madame Bovary* continue to seduce filmmakers? Like James Rampton (n.pag.), one is tempted to answer flippantly: because, like Mount Everest, it is *there*. In fact, though, art is as complex as life, and there are compelling aesthetic reasons for the stubborn desire to scale this particularly rugged summit, reasons I shall examine in due course.

In this study, I have decided to focus on four of the best-known adaptations, the studio films of Jean Renoir (1934-35), Vincente Minnelli (1949), and Claude Chabrol (1991); and the *Masterpiece Theatre* adaptation of Tim Fywell (2000). There seemed little point in undertaking an in-depth analysis of a film such as Albert Ray's *Unholy Love* (1932) which is accessible only to those who travel to the UCLA Film and Television Archives in Hollywood, California.[6] Nor did I feel qualified to analyze film adaptations in languages other than those in which I have native (English) and near-native (French) abilities. Quite aside from the fact that sub-titles in the other

---

[5] The adaptations, in chronological order, are as follows: *Unholy Love*, d. Albert Ray (USA, 1932); *Madame Bovary*, d. Jean Renoir (France, 1934); *Madame Bovary*, d. Gerhard Lamprecht (Germany, 1937); *Madame Bovary*, d. Carlos Schlieper (Argentina, 1947); *Madame Bovary*, d. Vincente Minnelli (USA, 1949); *Madame Bovary*, d. Rex Tucker (U.K., 1964); *Madame Bovary*, d. Hans-Dieter Schwarze (Germany, 1968); *Die Nackte Bovary* [transl. *Les Folles Nuits de la Bovary* and *Play the Game or Leave the Bed*] d. Hans Schott-Schöbinger [alias: John Scott] (Germany/Italy, 1969); *Madame Bovary* d. Pierre Cardinal (France, 1974); *Madame Bovary*, d. Rodney Bennett (U.K., 1975); *Pany Bovary, to ja* [transl. *Madame Bovary, That's Me*], d. Janusz Kaminski (Poland, 1976); *Madame Bovary*, d. Daniele D'Anza (Italy, 1981); *Spasi i sokhrani* [transl. *Sauve et Garde*] d. Alexandre Sokourov (USSR, 1990); *Madame Bovary*, d. Claude Chabrol (France, 1991); *Madam Bovari ot Sliven* [transl. *Madame Bovary from Sliven*], d. Emil Tsanev (Bulgaria, 1991); *Maya Memsaab* [transl. *Maya: The Enchanting Illusion*], d. Ketan Mehta (India, 1992); *Vale Abraão* [transl. *Val Abraham* and *Abraham's Valley*], d. Manoel de Oliveira (Portugal, 1993); *Madame Bovary*, d. Tim Fywell (U.K., 2000).
[6] The film can be viewed by appointment on a flatbed in its original format (eight reels of 35 mm. nitrate print).

adaptations are essentially translations of translations, their notorious unreliability militates against using them as the basis for interpretations.[7]

The films I have selected can all be purchased new on DVD via the Internet, although currently the Renoir and Fywell versions are available only in PAL format. Aditionally, VHS tapes (mostly used) of all of the films can be ordered from Amazon.com or other Internet sites. While these four films are not evenly spread across the one hundred years of sound film production, they do span the last seventy years of the twentieth century. Moreover, taken together, they illustrate the various forces that weigh upon filmmakers seeking to make movies out of novels, from industry imperatives to cultural prejudice. Finally, all four highlight their relationship with the novel by borrowing its title and by setting their tale in mid-nineteenth-century France.

I use Flaubert's novel as the point of reference throughout this study, in the hope that a consideration of the film adaptations of *Madame Bovary* will provide literary specialists with new insights into the novel and a renewed appreciation of Flaubert's genius. However, I wish to emphasize that this investigation into the *Madame Bovary* films does not attempt to evaluate the film adaptations with respect to their "fidelity" to the literary original, an approach that has been seriously questioned in recent years. Rather, the films are judged on their own merits, as works of art in their own right. This study focuses primarily on the ways filmmakers have attempted to reinterpret a nineteenth-century cultural icon to make it conform to their own goals and ideologies. In the case of the French adaptations, it thus adopts the new paradigm for adaptation that Millicent Marcus has proposed:

> I would like to see adaptation as an acute case of an on-going aesthetic program—that of rewriting, re-articulating and re-proposing earlier stories in ways that allow a culture to come to know itself with respect to the past, and to take the measure of its evolution. ("Umbilical Scenes" xix)

Even for the films made outside of France, adopting an approach that regards film adaptations as culturally inflected re-writings of earlier

---

[7] By their very nature, subtitles are incomplete because frames change too quickly for entire dialogues to be recorded.

narratives can be fruitful. In following such a model, this study will investigate, not why *Madame Bovary* has withstood the test of time, but rather why it has held particular appeal for twentieth century directors and their audiences. My analysis also gives primacy to the notion of intertextuality, broadly defined. It has often been argued that cinema, the so-called Seventh Art, is the meeting place for painting, music, poetry, architecture, sculpture, and dance. In a similar way, each adaptation incorporates texts from a wide variety of disciplines, and, as Christopher Orr has asserted, to reduce the study of film adaptations to a binary film-and-book comparison is to neglect the numerous other intertexts that can be identified in each film and thus to impoverish the film and to misrepresent the work of the filmmaker (72). After all, films refer, not only to literature and the other arts, but also to other films, and, as we shall see, interfilmic allusions are a distinctive feature of most of the *Madame Bovary* adaptations.

My study begins (Chapter One) with general comments about the nature of film adaptation and the biases underlying evaluations beased on the criterion of fidelity to the source text. To enable the literary specialist to appreciate the often specious nature of such evaluations, a summary treatment of the fundamental differences between the literary and the visual media is presented here. Those characteristics of *Madame Bovary* that have made it seem so well-suited to screen adaptation are discussed alongside others that have proven challenging for filmmakers. The role played by technology, censorship, industrial imperatives and ideology is briefly discussed, particularly as they relate to some of the lesser-known adaptations of *Madame Bovary* (among others, the Portuguese production *Vale Abraão* [*Abraham's Valley*] and the Bollywood adaptation, *Maya Memsaab*). In Chapters Two through Five, I examine the four chosen adaptations in chronological order, devoting one chapter to each film. Chapter Two outlines the many factors that shaped Jean Renoir's adaptation, from technology and economic constraints to socio-political bias and the influence of painterly technique. This chapter argues that the most defining characteristic of Renoir's adaptation is less its resemblance to a theatrical production, as many scholars have asserted, than its numerous allusions to the art of Jean Renoir's father, the Impressionist painter Pierre-Auguste Renoir. In Chapter Three, the heavy influence of film censorship on Minnelli's Hollywood version is analyzed. Allusions to the scandal that erupted when the novel was first serialized in *La Revue de Paris* in 1856 open and close this 1949 film, and Minnelli's use of this structural frame, as well as many other elements of his film, can be explained by the director's desire to conform to the dictates of the Motion Picture Production Code, thereby avoiding censorship. Chapter Four returns us to France and the celebrated film director Claude Chabrol, whose adaptation typifies the tradition of the heritage film. The results of the director's commitment to historical authenticity and his determination to film the novel (as opposed to making a film *inspired* by the novel) are discussed in this chapter. Chabrol's extensive recourse to the technique of voiceover is analyzed in particular detail. Chapter Five considers Tim Fywell's *Masterpiece Theatre* adaptation, emphasizing the influence of two contexts, public broadcasting on the one hand, and the television medium on the other. A close examination of this adaptation reveals an unexpected sensitivity to wordplay and an effort to capture the famed Flaubertian irony. Chapter Six responds to Dudley Andrew's call for a sociology of adaptation by revisiting the various influences that shape films, and by investigating the *raison d'être* of the cinematic adaptation in general and the *Madame Bovary* adaptation in particular. In an effort to understand what Flaubert's novel represents for the twentieth and twenty-first centuries, Chapter Six also examines the *Madame Bovary* documentary made by Films for the Humanities and then, using insights gleaned from this documentary, provides an overview of four films that have sometimes been regarded as the novel's offspring, although they are not adaptations *per se*. Among these, Woody Allen's *The Purple Rose of Cairo*, which engages with the novel on a more profound level than do the other three, is reserved for detailed treatment. A brief Conclusion is followed by a synopsis of the novel (Appendix A), a filmography (Appendix B), and a glossary of film terms (Appendix C).

A study such as this one is made possible by modern technology. In 1969, Robert Richardson wrote, "One experiences a film under fixed and rigid conditions. One cannot, as with a novel, slow down, speed up, or lay it aside" (72). Richardson's comment, valid in its day, no longer describes the way films are consumed, thanks to the advent of new viewing formats, specifically, the videotape and, more recently, the DVD. Films can now be viewed much as novels are read, with sequences played and replayed, frames frozen, action slowed or accelerated. Such technical advances have refashioned the way viewers experience visual culture, allowing them to be active participants in the communicative process and not the passive consumers that Lester Asheim wrote about in 1951. In addition, films on DVD are frequently accompanied by audio commentaries and outtakes, paratexts that provide information about the production process and deepen the spectators' understanding of the conditions that obtained during the filming and thus of the film itself.

This is a hybrid study, and as a hybrid, it was written with two groups of readers in mind. The first group is made up of literary scholars who have a casual interest in film. To accommodate this group, few assumptions, even about basic film literacy, have been made. The second group of people to whom this investigation is addressed consists of film scholars who seek a better understanding of the complexities of adaptation and who happen also to have high regard for Flaubert's achievement in *Madame Bovary*, whether or not they have ever taught the novel or have even read it recently. The synopsis of the novel in Appendix A was added for the benefit of this group. I would of course be delighted if the book attracted the attention of the general reader as well, the admirer of Renoir or Chabrol, for example, and it will not be necessary, as one of my non-academic friends facetiously suggested, to produce a faculty ID in order to purchase the book! That said, readers familiar with Flaubert's novel will be more likely to find this study rewarding than those who have never read *Madame Bovary*.

The pedagogical applications of this study are obvious. Since, in today's visually-oriented culture, students respond with enthusiasm when literature and culture are taught through film, this book can serve as a guide for professors of such courses.[8] It is also my hope that these pages will encourage other scholars to further pursue the ways in which the film and literary media enter into dialogue with each other, a subject on which there is still much to be said. However, readers of this study, whatever their perspective, are reminded that this examination has two principal goals: 1) to shed light on the many factors that have influenced the adaptation of *Madame Bovary* to the

---

[8] For an early exploration of the way the *Bovary* films can be used to teach the novel, see my "Teaching *Madame Bovary* Through Film." While my current approach has evolved since that article was written, many of the pedagogical strategies remain the same.

screen and in so doing to sketch a history of the novel's popular reception at certain pivotal points in the twentieth century; and 2) to provide stimulating analyses of four of the most easily available adaptations. If in the process, it succeeds in convincing film experts of the inimitable beauty of Flaubert's prose while simultaneously persuading literary specialists that the film adaptations are instructive and eminently worthy objects of analysis, it will have more than achieved its purpose.

1

The Theory and Practice of Film Adaptation

Before analyzing the reasons for *Madame Bovary*'s popularity with film directors and dealing with the *practice* of adaptation as it applies to this novel, I would like to make some general comments about film adaptation and the theory driving the field that has come to be known as "adaptation studies."

No hard and fast rules govern the way in which novels are made into films, and this is perhaps as it should be. As Delphine Jayot has noted, novels escape their authors' control as soon as they are published and read, and indeed, their very survival depends upon their being read and reread, interpreted and re-interpreted (Jayot, 3). Film adaptations are part of this process. Short of the need to require rights to adapt a work that is still under copyright (which is not the case with *Madame Bovary*), there are no legalities at all involved in the process of screening novels (Brady 4). It follows that there are many different modes of adaptation, and the relationship between literary text and film is anything but stable. The film credits often offer a clue as to this relationship. Films that are merely "inspired by" or "suggested by" novels often invent their own titles, and their overlap with the source text may be minimal. Such is the case with *Unholy Love*, Albert Ray's 1932 adaptation of *Madame Bovary*, which is set in Rye, New York, during the flapper era. Notwithstanding the choice of a town which, by its name, recalls Ry, the Norman village that claims to have been the model for Yonville-L'Abbaye, this film parades its independence from the novel in countless ways, as we shall see later. At the opposite extreme is Chabrol's *Madame Bovary* (1991), a heritage film that bears witness to an almost slavish faithfulness to the novel. So extensive is the overlap between novel and film that the credits do not even use the word *adapté* (adapted) but instead present the film as "*Madame Bovary* de Gustave Flaubert." Between these two poles one finds films that are truly "adapted" from novels in that they reproduce their basic plots and main characters while taking certain liberties demanded by good cinematic practice. Spectators who have read the novels on which these films are based will have no difficulty recognizing them, but they may regret—rightly or wrongly—certain excisions that have been made in the transfer from page to screen.

A number of critics have attempted to classify film adaptations according to their degree of overlap with the source text. Geoffrey Wagner, for example, suggests three possible categories, ranging from the most overlap to the least: transposition, commentary, and analogy (222-27). As useful as such categories may be, they encourage scholars to think in binary terms when dealing with film adaptations, and to judge the film solely by its relationship with the book. Indeed, for decades, discussion of film adaptations turned almost exclusively on the issue of fidelity. Scholarly essays, structured by the comparison of film to novel, shuttled back and forth between the two. Their interest centered on the way a particular screen adaptation "reproduced" a particular novel, and the films were judged according to whether or not they were "faithful" to the fictional narratives that inspired them. This evaluation turned out to be more complicated than it seemed at first blush, for it was generally acknowledged that films could be faithful to the "spirit" of a literary text without being faithful to the "letter." Just exactly what the "spirit" of a text was, nobody knew for sure (Christopher Orr 2). In fact, the inability to define this elusive concept eventually gave way to the realization that "spirit" was clearly a matter of personal interpretation. The business of adapting literary fiction to the screen was seen in a new light; what were filmmakers if not interpreters? Moreover, since it had long been acknowledged that the literary text was open, subject to multiple, equally valid readings, it stood to reason that film adaptations would differ from each other. Such a conclusion followed naturally from the assessment that, as Neil Sinyard put it, "adapting a literary text to the screen is essentially an act of literary criticism" (x).

In recognizing the subjectivity of what was once considered simply the pictorialization of the literary work, critics delivered the first blow to the fidelity argument. The second attack, more damaging, came when the technical complexities of the transfer were considered.

Could one semiotic system *really* be substituted for another? Or, to put the question another way, could the "stuff" of novels (words) be effectively "translated" to the "stuff" of cinema (images and sounds as well as words)? Those critics, film theorists and filmmakers who believed they *could* tended to place a high value on fidelity. They were essentialists, in the sense that they believed that works of literature had an "essence" that could be extracted—indeed *had to be extracted*—and transferred to the screen in order for the film adaptation to be "worthy." Expressed in narratological terms, those in the "fidelity" camp believed that *story* and *discourse* were separable, i.e., that it was possible to tell the *same story* in two different media. Chabrol, following his mentor René Clair, was guided by this belief. He was in good company. Paul Ricoeur, Roland Barthes, and A.J. Greimas, to name only the French contingent, were convinced, in the words of Millicent Marcus, that there was a "universal, nonspecific code of narrativity which [transcended] its embodiment in any one particular signifying system" (*Filmmaking* 14). In the opposite camp, one could find Jean Mitry and Gérard Genette, critics who believed the identical story *could not* be transferred from one medium to another. Filmmakers and critics who subscribed to this opinion saw the literary text only as raw material to be refashioned, or, as André Gardies puts it, "une sorte de banque de données" [a kind of database] (5). The scales are tipping increasingly in favor of this perspective.

In recent years, discourse about film adaptations, "the most narrow and provincial area of film theory," in the words of Dudley Andrew ("Adaptation" 452), has undergone an important shift. Fidelity to the source text is no longer viewed as the ultimate measure of value, recent theorists having come increasingly to question the importance of a notion that implicitly relegates the film to an inferior position with regard to the literary text that inspired it. Millicent Marcus defines *fidelity criticism* as "the tedious and predictable listing of the film's sins against its literary source," ("Umbilical Scenes" xix) and Robert Stam points to the "profoundly moralistic" language of traditional adaptation criticism, "awash in terms such as *infidelity, betrayal, deformation, violation, vulgarization* and *desecration*, each accusation carrying its specific charge of outraged negativity" ("Beyond Fidelity" 54). The reasons for such emotionally charged language, or what Marcus terms "the fidelity critic's savagery" ("Umbilical Scenes" xix), are not difficult to fathom. The bias against film adaptations has a long history, and as Joy Boyum argues, it stems largely from the widespread view that literature is a higher art form, addressed to an elite, whereas cinema is entertainment, intended for the masses (8). Robert Stam identifies three other prejudices that are implicit in the discourse of fidelity:

> *seniority*, the assumption that older arts are necessarily better arts; *iconophobia*, the culturally rooted prejudice (traceable to the Judaic-Muslim-Protestant prohibitions on "graven images" and to the Platonic and Neoplatonic depreciation of the world of phenomenal appearance) that visual arts are necessarily inferior to the verbal arts; and *logophilia*, the converse valorization, characteristic of the "religions of the book," of the "sacred word" of holy texts. ("Beyond Fidelity" 58)

Thanks to these analyses of the prejudice of traditional adaptation criticism, we now recognize both what Horton and Magretta term "the perverse backwardness of the adaptation-as-betrayal approach" (1) and its unhistorical nature (Mayne 101). And yet where do we go from here? Millicent Marcus proposes an alternative to the dualistic manner in which scholars have traditionally treated the topic. In her view, the relationship might be better characterized as triangular, with screenwriting and its four distinct phases (subject, story line, treatment, and screenplay) as intermediate stage (*Filmmaking* 23). This enlightening perspective has the advantage of shifting the attention to the many factors that shape the film adaptation. In a similar vein, we might consider Robert Stam's notion of "transtextuality," borrowed from Genette. Stam, seeing artistic texts (specifically films, for present purposes) as creative enterprises that engage in a "veritable dance of relations" (*François Truffaut and Friends* xiii) among various sorts of texts, likewise eschews binary studies in favor of a more holistic approach to film adaptations and the elements that mold them. It is to these elements that we now turn, using *Madame Bovary* as our principal exemplar and reflecting once again on the question posed in the Introduction: what explains this novel's popularity with filmmakers? It is one thing to comprehend why this novel should have become a cultural icon, quite another to appreciate its cinematic appeal. Why have so many directors attempted to make *Madame Bovary*?

Perhaps the most obvious of the many reasons that one might proffer is the highly visual nature of Flaubert's descriptions. Consider the following passage, in which the Norman countryside is evoked:

> La pluie ne tombait plus; le jour commençait à venir, et, sur les branches des pommiers sans feuilles, des oiseaux se tenaient immobiles, hérissant leurs petites plumes au vent froid du matin. La plate campagne s'étalait à perte de vue, et les bouquets d'arbres autour des fermes faisaient, à intervalles éloignées, des taches d'un violet noir sur cette grande surface grise, qui se perdait à l'horizon dans le ton morne du ciel. (69)

> [It was no longer raining; day was dawning and, on the leafless branches of apple trees, birds were sitting motionless, fluffing out their little feathers in the cold morning wind. The flat countryside stretched out as far as the eye could see, and at distant intervals, clumps of trees surrounding farmhouses made stains of deep purple on the large gray surface that blended at the horizon with the dull tones of the sky.]

Flaubert's poetic description, taken from a passage that narrates Charles's pre-dawn journey to les Bertaux where he has been summoned to set a broken leg, captures the quiet beauty of the countryside as seen from a moving conveyance. (Whether Charles is on his mare or in a carriage behind it, we do not know.) Simultaneously attentive to detail (the fluffed out feathers of the birds) and to the sweep of the landscape, the description virtually begs for transfer to the screen, where through zoom-ins and panoramic long shots the moving camera can provide a visual equivalent to Flaubert's prose.

In addition to appealing repeatedly to the reader's sight, Flaubert demonstrates a marked preference for *showing* rather than *telling*, a phenomenon that has been termed the novel's "concretized form."[1] Flaubert does not *tell* the reader that Charles is simple-minded; it is through the character's actions and words that his lack of intelligence becomes apparent. Together with the impersonal narration (often compared to the camera's alleged neutrality) and the proto-cinematic use of such techniques as cross-cutting (a technique that

---

[1] See Spiegel, who defines concretized form as "a way of transcribing the narrative, not as a story that is told, but as an action that is portrayed and presented, that seems to reveal itself to the reader apart from the overt mediations of the author." 6.

director and film theorist Sergei Eisenstein, among others, has recognized in Flaubert's novel [12]), this preference for showing was believed to make *Madame Bovary* an ideal text for screen adaptation.

Recent analyses have uncovered even more features of Flaubert's prose that anticipate cinema. In his highly illuminating book on film and the novel (*Literature* 144-90), Robert Stam points to the precision with which Flaubert records the characters' gestures and attitudes, the novel's meticulous notation of sounds, a film-like manipulation of distance, the ability to render movement in a way that evokes the tracking shot, the "Impressionist approach to light" (*Literature* 157). It is no surprise, then, that filmmakers from Albert Ray to Carlos Schlieper, tantalized by this archetypically proto-cinematic novel, have applied themselves to the sacred task of "making" *Madame Bovary*. And yet they have often found their efforts unrewarded. Decoding the novel above all as the tale of a delusional woman who brings ruin upon herself and her family through her acquisitiveness and her doomed search for lasting passion, they have been stymied in their attempts to represent some of the novel's more subtle allusions and meanings. In order to understand why the results of their efforts have been so uneven, it is useful to review elements of the art of adaptation, specifically as they apply to Flaubert's masterpiece.

I want to begin by making some observations about basic differences between the literary and visual media, and I beg the indulgence of those readers who are students of cinema. However well-known these differences may be to film specialists, they have frequently been either misunderstood or underestimated in criticism of film adaptations.[2] I wish to emphasize that, in discussing the differences between the two media and in focusing on the challenges faced by filmmakers who seek to adapt *Madame Bovary* to the screen, I am not adopting a hierarchical stance that privileges the literary work. Rather, because we are dealing with an operation that begins with a novel and ends with a film, my goal here is simply to explain some of the complexities involved in this transfer. Obviously, there are things that films can do *better* than novels. Seymour Chatman was one of the first critics to acknowledge this fact (note the title of his

---

[2] This misunderstanding results in what Robert Stam refers to as "the myth of facility." (See Stam and Raenga 7.)

1980 article, "What Films Can Do that Novels Can't and Vice Versa"), and today, such well-known critics as Robert Stam and Linda Hutcheon make a point of overturning the usual clichés that emphasize the filmmaker's handicaps. Hutcheon categorically rejects what she terms "the negative discourse of loss" (37) that characterizes discussion of film adaptation, and to illustrate her point, she broadens the topic to include adaptation in more general terms (e.g. the transformation of a novel into a radio play or a stage production, a film into a novel, an opera, etc.). Pointing out that the emphasis on "loss" from print to performance is wrong-headed, Hutcheon insists that each genre has its own means of expression, its own plusses and minuses. Although this scarcely debatable assertion bears keeping in mind, it nevertheless seems helpful to examine those elements of the literary text that require the most ingenuity on the part of those would adapt novels to the screen.

It has often been pointed out that novels, by their very nature, are more vague and "indeterminate" than films. George Bluestone encapsulates this distinction as follows:

> Where the moving picture comes to us directly through perception, language must be filtered through the screen of conceptual apprehension. And the conceptual process, though allied to and often taking its point of departure from the percept, represents a different mode of experience, a different way of apprehending the universe. (20)

For Bluestone, the distinction, then, boils down to an opposition in the way the two media are consumed: perception versus conception. Although modern film theorists would perhaps be less categorical, there remains some truth to the distinction. The characteristics of the written word enable readers of *Madame Bovary* to create in their mind's eye their own Norman countryside, their own characters. However, when they see a film adaptation of the novel, they are forced to accept someone else's rendering of the setting and the characters; forced, for example, to see Lila Lee or Jennifer Jones, Isabelle Huppert or Frances O'Connor in the title role. While one may legitimately question the wisdom of a director who casts, say, a 42-year-old actress as 18-year-old Emma, judging a film adaptation according to whether or not the principal actors conform to one's expectations is a far more questionable practice. As Seymour Chatman observes, a novelist can tell us that a character is "pretty," and it is up to the reader to interpret the adjective (131). A film director, on the other hand, has no choice but to choose an actress who conforms to some recognized canon of female attractiveness. The choice rarely satisfies everyone, since, as Chatman argues, "pretty" is not merely a descriptive adjective but an evaluative one, and "one person's 'pretty' may be another person's 'beautiful' and still a third person's 'plain'" (131).

The film medium's need—or ability, depending upon one's perspective—to make concrete what is left abstract in a novel is known as "concretization" and it is one of the filmmaker's most difficult tasks. Notwithstanding the much-lauded photographic accuracy of *Madame Bovary*'s descriptions, there are numerous blanks that must be filled in by the film director, the episode of the clubfoot operation being a case in point. Here, Flaubert is uncharacteristically parsimonious with details (Donaldson-Evans, "A Medium of Exchange" 23). Where precisely does the surgery take place in this pre-Pasteurian era? How is the health officer attired? Who is present in the room as the operation is being performed? Is anything administered to dull the pain? Indeed, how much pain does the patient feel? These details—and many others—must be supplied by the filmmaker, based upon his interpretation of the text.

An equally daunting process that awaits the filmmaker who would transpose a novel to the screen is editing. In trimming a full-length novel so that it will fit what has been termed the "Procrustean bed of film length" (Fred Marcus xvi), episodes and characters not deemed essential to an understanding of the central plot are frequently eliminated. Where *Madame Bovary* is concerned, this has meant the deletion of the novel's entire first chapter, and in most adaptations, most of the last three chapters as well. Some filmmakers (e.g. Schlieper, Minnelli) have substituted structural frames of their own, but Emma's story is no longer enclosed in that of Charles, and the incurable mediocrity of the character who will become Emma's husband must be established in other ways. Charles's timidity, represented by Flaubert as the inability even to pronounce his own name properly when he is under stress, must likewise be represented elsewhere. Thanks to the textual redundancy, both of these traits are easily established; lost, however, is the classroom metaphor and the poignant vulnerability of the bumbling, mumbling schoolboy. Lost, too, are the metaphorical implications of the structural enclosure. Just as the novel's title denies the protagonist an identity of her own (something that has been observed by numerous literary critics), so also does its structure imprison her in a male perspective. When the reader first sees Emma, it is through Charles's eyes, a point of view that some, but not all, filmmakers have retained.

Another important challenge facing the filmmaker who decides to adapt literary works to the screen is the externalization of the characters' thoughts. Accessing the subjectivity of *Madame Bovary*'s characters is a particularly vexing problem not only because of the protagonist's active and fertile imagination, but also because the main characters—with the exception of Homais, who is literally defined by his discourse—are not in the habit of articulating most of their thoughts. Flaubert's readers are given access to their mental landscapes, and for this reason, transposition to the visual medium requires creative solutions. Some directors (e.g. Renoir, Cardinal) have opted for an expansion of dialogue, an imperfect solution at best, because the failure of communication at all levels is one of the novel's tropes. (Not only does Emma lack a reliable confidant, but her inability to put into words what she is feeling is frequently evoked.) Other directors (Minnelli, Chabrol, Fywell) have used various forms of voiceover, some more successful than others. Notwithstanding George Bluestone's contention that "[the] microdrama of the human countenance permits the reading of the greatest conflicts in the merest flicker of an eye" (27), close-ups of the face can reveal only emotion, and they are sorely lacking when the revelation of specific thoughts is required. Of course, as Morris Beja has rightly pointed out, a character's thoughts may be expressed as external actions, although he allows that "ideas [the realm of thought] are more economically treated in written literature than in film" (58). Even Linda Hutcheon, who attempts to debunk the "cliché" according to which "interiority is the terrain of the telling mode," is forced to concede that "elaborate interior monologues and analyses of inner states are difficult to represent visually in performance" (58).

Flaubert's abundant use of free indirect discourse, in which the narrator's voice mingles with that of the character's, often to ironic effect, also presents a problem for the filmmaker. Whereas the shifting narrative viewpoint created by Flaubert's use of this narrative style can be easily transferred to the screen, the camera naturally embracing the perspective of different characters, the *simultaneous* representation of two viewpoints and the ambiguity and irony that often result are difficult to convey in film, where differing perspectives must be represented sequentially.[3]

Related to the difficulty of representing thought is what critic Karl Kroeber regards as cinema's inability to use a technique known as "side-shadowing," a strategy common to literary fiction and especially prevalent in *Madame Bovary*. While, in Kroeber's view, film "cannot display what is never visible" (3), written narrative can stimulate readers to imagine things that never happened or that might have happened differently. Through his use of free indirect discourse, Flaubert engages in side-shadowing, getting us to imagine what Emma's life might have been like if Charles had been more intuitive, if Emma had married into the aristocracy, if Rodolphe had kept his promise to run away with her. In giving readers awareness of Emma's private fantasies (which, as Kroeber points out, are nothing more than "commodified clichés" [101]), Flaubert allows us simultaneously to enter into her life in a very subjective way and to judge her dispassionately, thus creating "ethical uncertainties [...] ever-present in the novel" (102). From Kroeber's perspective, this kind of "make-believe," enabled by the power of the written word, is inaccessible to the movie-goer.

A fourth quandary that besets filmmakers who turn novels into films is the representation of the past. It has sometimes been said that whereas novels can make use of all the tenses, film time is an eternal present, with spectators experiencing narrative events simultaneously with the characters. Obviously, flashbacks and flashforwards can be used to evoke the past and future respectively, but how does a filmmaker represent the tedium of habitual action as Flaubert does so brilliantly with his use of the imperfect tense? How does one capture on screen the boredom so poignantly and masterfully evoked by the sentence that begins, "Mais c'était surtout aux heures des repas qu'elle n'en pouvait plus" [But it was especially at mealtimes that she found her life unbearable] (137)? The novel's sentence evokes the mind-numbing monotony of oft-repeated dinner-table scenes; because the filmmaker will not have the luxury of showing Emma and Charles at table on numerous occasions, another means has to be found to

---

[3] The sole exception to this rule might be the presentation of different viewpoints through the use of a voiceover narration that mocks the picture on screen.

represent the repetitive nature of the episode, to give "à la visualisation d'un événement singulier une valeur itérative" [an iterative value to an event shown only once] (Gardies 90). The montage sequence (so famously used by Orson Welles in *Citizen Kane*) is one solution; dialogue is another. In either case, the transposition requires creative adjustments.[4]

The representation of irony also challenges the filmmaker, although certain types of irony (e.g. dramatic irony or irony of fate; see Bluestone 152) are a by-product of the narrative itself and are more easily represented than others. However, like other aspects of narrative tone, irony is often conveyed by language, and when this is the case, filmmakers have a notoriously difficult time representing it on screen, "not in dialogue, obviously, but when used in performance mode" (Hutcheon, 71). Extra-diegetic music that clashes with events represented on the image track can sometimes express ironic intent; shot juxtaposition can be used to the same end. Yet because, like parody, irony can be fully appreciated only if the reader/spectator is sufficiently sophisticated to recognize it for what it is, and because Flaubertian irony is often subtle, this aspect of *Madame Bovary* represents a hurdle to filmmakers, one that has been successfully overcome by few. Indeed, the very act of transferring the text to the screen would seem to doom to failure any attempt to depict what is perhaps the principal irony of *Madame Bovary*, specifically, that it poses as a realist novel even as it mocks the very idea that literary fiction (and not merely romantic fiction) can "reproduce" reality.

In addition to the generic issues facing any director who seeks to adapt a classic of world literature to the screen, a number of problems are truly specific to *Madame Bovary*. Flaubert's preoccupation with language is a case in point. How does one transpose into the visual medium a novel about words, or, more to the point, a novel that marked a turning point in literary history precisely because of its use of language? A second problem is what some have deemed to be Flaubert's almost visceral misanthropy. How does the film director keep spectators from identifying with any of the characters and yet maintain their interest in his film? These are just

---

[4] Robert Stam calls into question the often-evoked "inability" of the cinema to represent past time (Stam and Raeng 20-22) but does not discuss the particular problems of evoking *repeated* past action. Similarly, Linda Hutcheon does not address this situation in her otherwise stimulating discussion of the "temporal truism" (64).

two of the many unanticipated difficulties with which directors have had to contend in their attempts to adapt Flaubert's novel to the screen. What they have found less daunting is the portrayal of some of the novel's better-known themes: the dangers of excessive consumerism, the stifling lives of nineteenth-century women, the pettiness and materialism of the provincial bourgeoisie, the rebellious spirit—some might say the androgyny—of a woman trapped in a marriage to a well-meaning dullard, and the tragedy of lives governed by unreasonable expectations. It seems fair to say that, whatever their shortcomings, most adaptations of the novel have succeeded in bringing into sharp relief the drama at the heart of *bovarysme*.[5]

The basic differences between the literary and visual media having been outlined, let us turn to the other factors that shape the film adaptation, factors particularly relevant to the *Madame Bovary* films. The most obvious of these concerns technique and technology. Early talkies, shot in black and white using stationary cameras, were heavily influenced by theater. Actors were frequently drawn from the theatrical world, and they brought to the cinema an oratorical style perfected on the stage. Dialogues were shot frontally, and actors delivered their lines, not to their interlocutors, but to the camera. Good background projection being largely unavailable in Europe in the early nineteen-thirties, exterior dialogues were shot outside, and the poor quality of the microphones during this period, together with the noisy whirring of the cameras, resulted in an often muddy soundtrack. Yet post-synchronization techniques, although technically possible since 1929, were not often used in the early thirties.[6] In addition to the primitive nature of sound recording, shot duration tended to be long, slowing the rhythm of even the most action-packed films. As we will see, Jean Renoir's adaptation of *Madame Bovary* (1934-5) provides a good illustration of such early technology and film style. Unsurprisingly, films shot during this period have a different "feel" than those shot at the cusp of the twenty-first century. The invention of technicolor, more sophisticated lighting techniques, better sound equipment, computer-assisted editing and other advances in film technique and technology have resulted in films deemed by the public

---

[5] For reasons beyond his control, Renoir's adaptation, in its truncated version, is an exception to this rule.

[6] Many inventions, some more successful than others, were used to reduce camera noise in the thirties. For a detailed history of film technology, see Salt.

to be more "realistic," although this term itself is fraught with problems.

A second factor that shapes a film adaptation is economic. Filmmaking is, to a much larger extent than the book trade, an industry, and as an industry, it has a strong profit motive: it must recoup the considerable expenses of production and ensure a return on the investment of its sponsors. Although publishers must take economic factors into consideration, such factors do not impinge upon the work of authors to the same extent that producers' financial constraints impinge upon the work of filmmakers. Regardless of their budget and notwithstanding their primary goal, the creation of a work of art, film directors must be attentive to this industrial imperative. The need to make a film profitable has two major effects on filming. In the first place, it dictates what one can afford to show on screen and what must be edited out. This is true whether one is dealing with made-for-TV movies or big screen productions. Writer and director Keith Waterhouse wittily summarizes the situation as follows:

> In a novel I can declare war on Russia if I like, and all it costs is the print and paper required to describe the campaign. On TV I would either have to equip, clothe, accommodate, pay and, above all, feed my armies [...] or I have to have a character peering out of a window through a pair of binoculars and crying, "The first, second, third and fourth divisions of the Russians are coming, the first, second, third and fourth divisions of the Russians are coming!" (13)

Obviously, if the filmmaker chooses the second cinematic option proposed by Waterman, he saves money, but something is "lost in translation," so to speak. In the case of the *Madame Bovary* adaptations, a film with low production values will not include scenes from the stage production of the opera *Lucie de Lammermoor* which figures in an important scene in the novel, and the director will have to find a way to evoke the Agricultural Fair without bringing in all the farm animals described by Flaubert. Other *tableaux* that would have to be scaled down or cut altogether would be the wedding and the Vaubyessard ball. Clearly, such ellipses would have a profound effect on the final product.

The second way in which economic concerns impinge upon the film adaptation involves the "adjustment" of the literary source to its new audience, or what some have uncharitably—and often inaccurately, given the increasing sophistication of cinema audiences (see Griffith 33)—termed the "dumbing down" of the narrative. In order to be profitable, even low-budget art films must strive to attract as wide an audience as possible. The shaping power of the mass audience is immense. In practical terms, this means that there have to be some sympathetic characters for audiences to attach themselves to; that dialogues sometimes need to be adjusted for ease of comprehension (an operation that has as much to do with the way films are consumed as with the consumers themselves); that while historical specificity can be maintained (i.e. costumes and setting can be selected to evoke the mid-nineteenth century, however alienating this sometimes is for twentieth and twenty-first century spectators), certain esoteric details that may be misunderstood by modern audiences need to be sacrificed. (Much of Homais's discourse, anchored as it is in the anticlerical, positivistic rhetoric of the age, falls into this category.) Anachronisms are sometimes introduced deliberately so as not to put off modern spectators. Fywell, for example, gives us an Emma with clean-shaven armpits; Minnelli provides Charles with a sterilizing bath for his surgical instruments.

A third factor, not unrelated to the second, is that of censorship. In the discussion of a novel written during the heavily censorious Second Empire, a novel whose author was, in fact, brought to trial for alleged offenses to public morality and religion, this is an especially relevant concern. There will be—and there *are*—substantial differences between an adaptation such as that of Vincente Minnelli, produced in the late nineteen-forties, a period of strict enforcement of the Motion Picture Production Code and that of a late twentieth-century production, subject only to a rating system that limits viewer access to the film, not film production itself.[7] Like Flaubert, forced to resort to any manner of subterfuge in order to represent the erotic dimension of his tale, film directors working during a period of strict censorship were obliged to treat sexuality with extreme discretion and to camouflage any suggestion that immoral conduct could actually be the source of pleasure. According to the terms of the Code, films had to uphold high standards of morality. This meant, among other things, that marriage had to be presented in a positive light and adultery could

---

[7] It should be noted, however, that the current rating system does have an impact on gross receipts, since it can limit a film's potential audience. The secretive nature of the rating process has given rise to considerable controversy. See A. O. Scott and Catherine Donaldson-Evans.

not be made to look attractive. Fifty years later, after the Sexual Revolution had taken place and the Code had been reduced to an historical footnote, the Anglo-American public had a very different notion of what was permissible on screen: the camera no longer needed to cut to the treetops when Emma falls into Rodolphe's arms during their first woodland excursion, and Emma and Léon could be shown in bed together.

Censorship reflects but does not fully encompass prevailing ideologies. If *Madame Bovary* has been adapted to the screens, large and small, at least eighteen times and in at least eleven countries (Argentina, Bulgaria, England, France, Germany, India, Italy, Poland, Portugal, the United States and the former USSR), the reasons have to transcend the obvious, i.e. the perceived ease with which the transfer could be made, and the obvious commercial motivation to take advantage of a ready-made market for a classic of world literature. This is where ideology comes in. What purpose is served by adapting this particular novel to the screen in any given year and location? In the case of *Madame Bovary*, the answer is as complex as the novel itself.

Flaubert's eternally dissatisfied heroine, as it happens, is a chameleon. Consider Sheila, the heroine of Albert Ray's *Unholy Love* (1932). Played by Lila Lee, this incarnation of Flaubert's protagonist is the daughter of a gardener who secretly marries her father's physician, and, shunned by the social milieu into which she has married and left to her own devices by her busy husband, turns to a local cad for consolation. When he abandons her, she commits suicide by driving her convertible off a bridge. While it is true that the film contains ample social commentary about the dangers of "marrying up," little sympathy is spared for the conniving, spoiled, and immoral heroine, the archetypal blond bombshell of the 1930s. Instead, the film's compassion goes to Dr. Jerome Preston Gregory, "Jerry," the doctor who "married down." Filmed in the wake of the 1929 stock market crash, this film is clearly the product of an era marked by a sense of economic vulnerability, here expressed in a moralistic attitude towards crossing sacrosanct class lines in marriage. The title of this film bears eloquent witness to the moral point of view it adopts.

Die Nackte Bovary (literally, *The Naked Bovary*, but mistranslated into French as *Les Folles Nuits de la Bovary* [*The Wild Nights of the Bovary Woman*], *nackte* ["naked"] presumably having been taken for *Nächte* ["night"]) is Hans Schott-Schöbinger's erotic adaptation of 1969. In this German-Italian collaboration, Emma (played by a heavily made-up Edwige Fenech) is represented as a loose woman almost from the start, and the cloth merchant, who has delusions of his own, becomes the arch-villain. The names given to the unscrupulous salesman, Adolphe, and to the debt collector, Lumière, suggest that an allegorical impulse is driving this soft-pornographic production. Although Emma gives in to Adolphe's sexual demands, the usurer does not succeed in destroying her any more than that other Adolphe had succeeded in destroying France during World War II, despite Vichy and the Nazi Occupation. On the point of committing suicide by leaping from a bridge, the adulteress has a change of heart and returns to her husband. What motivated this film, released just as Europe was preparing to celebrate the twenty-fifth anniversary of the fall of the Third Reich? Certainly, the very gesture of turning a masterpiece of French literature into a quasi-pornographic film seems hostile. Was Schott-Schöbinger's compliant heroine a metaphor for France herself, seen through the eyes of those to whom she had submitted? In this case, his film appears as a sly rebuke of the French film industry (whence "Lumière") that had been profiting mightily from an *ex-post-facto* glorification of the Resistance. Whatever the case, it may not be coincidental that this adaptation appeared the same year as Ophuls's *Le Chagrin et la pitié*, one of the first films to dare to treat the subject of the French collaboration with the Nazis. To dismiss Schott-Schöbinger's film out of hand because of its lack of esthetic merit, as some critics have done, is to ignore the numerous hints of a political dimension.[8]

The exotic Bollywood adaptation by Ketan Mehta, *Maya Memsaab* (1992), with its musical interludes, is informed by Hindu philosophy. Set in modern India, this version is framed by an investigation into the death of Emma's Indian avatar, Maya Memsaab. As the opening credits roll, two detectives question Charu, Maya's husband, the film's hermeneutic stance being thus foregrounded. The investigation will punctuate the narrative as successive witnesses are summoned, in a technique which, as Stam points out, is reminiscent of

---

[8] The critics' disdain for this film is typified by the comment made by Klaus-Peter Walter, who deems it unworthy of examination because it takes Flaubert's novel "uniquement comme prétexte pour débiter des séquences des copulations" [purely as a pretext for showing scenes of copulation] (93).

Citizen Kane (*Literature* 183). Presented in flashbacks through the testimonies of the male characters, Maya, played by the exquisite Deepa Sahi, becomes the very personification of the illusion and deception usually associated with Western values. Indeed, the concepts of "illusion" and "deception" are imbedded in the protagonist's name, for in classical Hindi, *maya* has both meanings. Furthermore, *Memsaab* (Mrs.), as a form of address, evokes Western women, having come into use in India during the colonial period as a means of showing respect for European females.[9] Maya's appearance changes as she undergoes a metamorphosis, from the sweet if emotionally unbalanced young woman who falls in love with Charu, her father's physician, to the demanding, dissatisfied wife who vandalizes her own home and stages her bogus murder to test the depths of her husband's love for her. When finally she begins to turn to extra-marital affairs to satisfy her sexual craving, the modest saris in which she is draped at the outset of the film are replaced by such telling items of Western dress as leather pants and tight skirts with deep, revealing slits. Although the pants may evoke androgyny, it is above all to the corrupting influence of the West that the sartorial transformation seems to allude. The British, who "left this memsaab behind" when India won her independence from colonial rule, are particularly targeted. As for Maya herself, she becomes progressively *dis*-illusioned, like Emma Bovary, and she comes to understand a fundamental principal of Hinduism which is inscribed in her name as well, since it is known as "maya": *all* is illusion. Her understanding derives not only from her experiences but from her reading, and it is not by chance that a copy of Flaubert's novel features prominently as a prop in a scene that is shot in the protagonist's bedroom.

National ideology also structures Manoel de Oliveira's *Vale Abraão* (*Abraham's Valley*), set in twentieth-century Portugal and based on a novel that was to be the Portuguese *Bovary* and that the director himself had commissioned author Agustina Bessa Luis to write. Oliveira cleverly situates his heroine in Emma Bovary's lineage, but signals her difference from her fictional elder by removing an "m" from her name, thus also bringing it into conformity with the Portuguese spelling. Indeed, this Ema is a twentieth-century

---

[9]Additionally, the Hindi word "mem" means "Western woman." I owe this information to a friend, Ahmad Bilal.

Portuguese offspring of Flaubert's heroine, living in Abraham's Valley, a land of Biblical resonances, where her rebellion against the combined forces of patriarchy and religion make her a figure for the Portuguese nation, stuck in a time warp and unable to evolve. In order to prevent spectators from identifying too closely with his heroine, Oliveira has used two different actresses to play her. Both of them limp, a physical sign, according to critic Annick Fiolet, of her "difficulté à vivre dans le monde réel" [difficulty living in the real world] (n.pag). While it is true that the basic plot of *Madame Bovary* has been retained—*Vale Abraão* tells the story of a woman who marries a doctor, becomes bored, takes on lovers, and then dies— Oliveira's film (following Bessa Luis's novel), an adaptation of an adaptation, in effect re-invents the nineteenth-century classic, altering it in numerous important ways in order to make it an appropriate vehicle for his own ideology.

Technology, budget, censorship, national and personal ideologies: to these major variables that shape film adaptations, one could add a host of less important but nonetheless significant influences. French heritage films have their own conventions, for example, and they differ from the conventions usually associated with Hollywood productions, which differ in turn from those of made-for-TV productions. Moreover, individual studios have a "house style." Even the filmmaker's life experiences can—and do—affect the way he brings a novel to the screen.[10]

These, then, are the factors that will be considered in our analyses of the adaptations by Renoir, Minnelli, Chabrol, and Fywell. As we will see, all four of the *Madame Bovary* adaptations under investigation here are marked to a greater or lesser extent by the conditions in which they were filmed and by the ideological biases of their creators.

---

[10] If I use the masculine pronoun when speaking of filmmakers, it is because none of the *Madame Bovary* adaptations has been filmed by a woman. This is not to say that feminine influence has been absent: Oliveira based his film on a novel written by Agustina Bessa Luis, and Tim Fywell used a filmscript written by a woman, Heidi Thomas.

2

Renoir (1934): Framing Emma

Still recognized as one of France's most talented filmmakers, Jean Renoir was born in Paris in 1894, but in fact spent the second half of his life in the USA. He died in Beverly Hills in 1979. Although his career began in the silent era and spanned forty years and two continents, his reputation rests largely on films made in France in the 1930s. Of these, *La Grande Illusion* (1937) and *La Règle du jeu* (1939) [*The Rules of the Game*] are most often cited as his masterpieces. Renoir is also known for his outstanding adaptations of such literary classics as Maupassant's "Une partie de campagne" (1881) [A Country Excursion], adapted in 1936; and Zola's *La Bête humaine* (1890) [*The Beast in Man*], filmed in 1938. These latter accomplishments are surprising because the filmmaker resolved at the outset of his career that he would avoid adapting literary works for the screen. Writing his memoirs in 1974, he describes his dawning realization that his original resolution was misguided and that adaptation was not incompatible with creativity:

> Après tout, ce qui nous intéresse dans une adaptation, ce n'est pas la possibilité de retrouver l'œuvre originale dans l'œuvre filmée, mais la réaction de l'auteur du film devant l'œuvre originale. Cette réaction peut nous entraîner à des résultats qui paraîtront sans rapport avec celle-ci, qu'importe. On n'admire pas un tableau à cause de sa fidélité au modèle, ce qu'on demande au modèle, c'est d'ouvrir la porte à l'imagination de l'artiste. (246)

> [After all, what interests us in an adaptation isn't the possibility of finding the original work in the filmed work, but rather the director's interpretation of the original work. That this interpretation can lead to results that may appear unrelated to the original work is irrelevant. We

don't admire a painting because of its fidelity to the model it depicts;
what we ask the model to do is to open the door to the artist's
imagination.]

The analogy between painting and moviemaking came naturally to the
son of the Impressionist artist Pierre Auguste Renoir. Associating the
art of the painter with that of the director who adapts literary works to
the screen, and the painter's model with the literary work, Renoir lent
the weight of his reputation to an early defense of the "freedom" side
of the "fidelity" debate. Although his use of the term *auteur* betrays
the influence of New Wave theorists who emphasized the autonomy
and creativity of the film director, previously regarded merely as one
member (albeit an important one) of a production team, his insistence
on allying his art with that of his father testifies to his deeply personal
perspective on the art of the filmmaker. One could of course speculate
about the œdipal dimension of this perspective: it is well-known that
Jean Renoir married his father's model, Andrée Heuschling, not long
after his father's death in 1919, and moreover that he decided to direct
films in order to make his young wife a movie star (Alan Williams
136), an ambition he accomplished repeatedly during the silent era,
when Heuschling became known by her stage name, Catherine
Hessling. However, for purposes of the present study, the importance
of Renoir's propensity for associating filmmaking with painting lies in
the way this mindset finds expression on the screen, or, to use Robert
Stam's term, the way in which this "transtextuality" is realized in
Renoir's *Madame Bovary* (*François Truffaut and Friends*, xiii). As
we have noted, film's identity as a composite art that draws on poetry,
sculpture, painting, music, dance, and architecture is well known.
While it would be foolish to deny the strong influence of theater on
Renoir's adaptation of Flaubert's novel, one could easily defend the
thesis that it is above all the art of painting that gives the film its
peculiar unity, that both semantically and syntactically, the paternal
influence: is omnipresent in this adaptation of *Madame Bovary.*
Renoir's populist sympathies:and and his predilection for symbolism
are also revealed in this adaptation, as we shall see.

In order to understand the particular challenges that
accompanied the filming in 1933 of a novel published in 1857, we
need first to examine the historical and socio-political context in
which the film was made. While French filmmakers had enjoyed a
sterling reputation prior to World War I, Hollywood reigned supreme

by the time the war was over, and this domination continued throughout the 1920s and beyond. According to Dudley Andrew, only sixty of the three hundred films projected in France in 1929 were French (*Mists* 9). Furthermore, in 1933, France was still in the throes of an economic depression, even as other countries were emerging from the slough of despond resulting from the stock market crash of 1929. Hitler's rise to power as Chancellor of Germany's Third Reich in 1933 "had thrown a political pall over Europe" (Sesonske 40), and the entire continent was in danger of being submerged by a wave of Fascism. French cinema, which had no integrated studio system on a par with that of Hollywood,[1] was particularly vulnerable to difficult economic and political conditions, because each film had to be built from the ground up, so to speak. In short, the cinematic hegemony of the United States was profoundly threatening to the French film industry, if indeed the word "industry" can even be applied to the loosely organized individual teams producing films in France at the time.

So it was that when the publisher Gaston Gallimard offered to advance the money to adapt Flaubert's novel to the screen and phoned Jean Renoir to ask if he would be willing to direct the production, Renoir accepted with alacrity, convinced that to bring such an important piece of France's literary heritage to the film-going public was, potentially, an effective way of competing against Hollywood. Nor was his enthusiasm tempered by Gallimard's principal condition: the publisher's mistress, the mature actress Valentine Tessier, had to be cast as Emma. Gallimard had in fact originally engaged Roger Martin du Gard to write the script and had made overtures to two directors, Jacques Feyder and Robert Siodmak, prior to contacting Renoir (*Mists* 281). When Feyder declined to direct the stout, forty-two year old Tessier in the role of Flaubert's young protagonist, Martin du Gard dropped out too. Siodmak, likewise, declined Gallimard's offer. Renoir, whose marriage to Andrée Heuschling had by now broken up, appears to have had no similar misgivings about the casting. Indeed, he knew and liked Tessier, well-known for her roles on the stage, and he was so taken by the idea of using theater actors in his film that he rounded out the cast with other celebrated

---

[1] The vertically integrated film company founded by Renoir's friend Pierre Braunberger was an exception to the rule.

actors from the French stage. Both the camera work and the dialogue, which Renoir wrote himself, betray film's early links with theater. The dialogue appears to have been written for maximum dramatic effect, the characters are often shot frontally, as though they're on stage, and the conversations are filmed in long takes, as medium shots that include both participants rather than as shot/reverse shot close-ups. The reasons for Renoir's decision to emphasize the theatrical in this film—a strategy he had not used in his earlier works, and one that most other French filmmakers of his era had already abandoned—were never articulated, although one might surmise that in avoiding close-ups and point-of-view shots, the director felt that he was in conformity with the novel's impersonal narration. It may be, too, that such a format allowed him to take advantage of his actors' theatrical talents while dealing with the problem of Tessier's age by eschewing unforgiving close-ups. However, there were serious economic incentives as well. Gallimard had already engaged a prominent composer, Darius Milhaud, to write the score, and the canonical status of Flaubert's novel was of course an article of faith. With his own increasingly prestigious name added to the list of credits, along with the names of such beloved theatrical celebrities as Valentine Tessier, his brother Pierre Renoir (cast as Charles), and Max Dearly (who played Homais), Renoir believed that a box office success was guaranteed. Unfortunately, he had seriously miscalculated and his film was badly received.

Today the failure of Renoir's *Madame Bovary* is generally attributed to economic factors. The original version ran to three and a half hours. Fearing a commercial disaster, the distributors insisted that it be reduced to less than two hours, a mutilation which—however necessary it may have been in this era of the double feature—all but ruined the film.[2] Furthermore, Gallimard allegedly lost interest in the project when his mistress abandoned him for Renoir's brother, Pierre, and he not only refused to pay for the over-budget film but failed to use his influence to save the film from the butchers in the cutting room (Bertin 104-5). The resulting production pleased few spectators, and critics regarded it merely as a chain of poorly sutured grand scenes, complaining that there had been no attempt to depict the

---

[2] It would be helpful if one could view the footage cut from the original version. Unfortunately, it was destroyed.

humdrum nature of Emma's daily life. Renoir himself admitted that he found the truncated version "boring," whereas in its original form, the film, which had been shown five times at the Billancourt Studios, had been well-received by the public. To further seal the film's doom, two days after its January 4th (1934) release at the Ciné-Opéra, on February 6th, Paris saw the bloodiest riots since the Commune of 1870 as leftists fought against pro-fascists (Bertin 105; Andrew and Ungar 55). On February 8th, a political scandal erupted in France when Serge Alexandre Stavisky, a well-known financier with ties to the radical government then in power, was discovered shot and near death in a mountain chalet near Chamonix.[3] He died the following day. In the wake of this event, an avid press uncovered other scandals, and by the end of the month the Minister of Justice and the Prime Minister (Camille Chautemps) had resigned. All this political turmoil contributed to make a box-office disaster out of a movie that, in Renoir's recollection, was filmed lovingly and joyously "en famille" in Lyons-la-forêt, Rouen, and Ry (Normandy).[4]

Yet it would be disingenuous to place the lion's share of the blame for the failure on the political, economic, and social context of the times. A film adaptation of Victor Hugo's *Les Misérables*, directed by Raymond Bernard and released just one month after *Madame Bovary*, was a stunning success. In fact, the shortened version of Renoir's adaptation was simply too disconnected for its audience to follow, and while it is true, as Sesonske contends, that "our familiarity with the novel bridges the gaps in continuity" (146), one cannot assume, and one could not assume even in 1934, that most of the

---

[3] Andrew and Ungar point out that doubt remains even today as to whether Stavisky had killed himself or had been murdered by the police, who feared that he would reveal compromising activities on the part of government officials (16).

[4] This was Renoir's perspective, not Gallimard's. "Grâce à ma propension à travailler avec des copains, j'ai connu souvent l'extase de l'intimité pendant la réalisation d'un film. Pendant le tournage de *Madame Bovary* en 1933, notre vie dans la petite ville normande de Lyons-la-Forêt nous avait fait oublier nos préoccupations habituelles. Notre 'famille' comprenait d'ailleurs Pierre, mon frère. Valentine Tessier était comme une sœur pour moi. Tous les soirs, nous nous réunissions autour de Gaston Gallimard, un des commanditaires du film." [Thanks to my propensity for working with friends, I have often known the ecstasy of intimacy while making a film. While we were shooting *Madame Bovary* in 1933, our life in the little Norman village of Lyons-la-Forêt made us forget our usual worries. Furthermore, our 'family' consisted of my brother Pierre. Valentine Tessier was like a sister to me. Every evening, we got together with Gaston Gallimard, one of the film's partners.] *Ma Vie et mes films*, 107.

film's spectators were in fact familiar with the novel. Even if they had read it, their memory of the details would be at best incomplete. To give just one example of the damage wreaked by the cuts, Léon has been on-screen for only about fifteen seconds before he appears in the opera scene. He has been mentioned earlier in conversations, but his only actual appearance takes place in the course of a brief encounter, when a carriage in which Charles and Emma are riding crosses paths with a carriage driven by Léon and Guillaumin. In the absence of any representation of his shyly flirtatious behavior towards Emma, and Emma's reaction to it, spectators who are not intimately familiar with the novel have difficulty understanding Emma's visit to the priest, Father Bournisien, which in the film occurs immediately after the Vaubyessard Ball.

The casting, too, has been almost universally criticized by film critics and scholars alike, and although canons of beauty have certainly changed in the seventy plus years since the film was made, the consistency of complaints about Valentine Tessier, in particular, strongly suggests that this was a factor in the film's poor showing at the box office. Very occasionally, someone leaps to defend Renoir's choice—as if he had freely made it—but the general consensus is that Tessier's performance is mannered and overly melodramatic, and she is deemed too mature for the part of Flaubert's young dreamer.[5]

However acquiescent he appears to have been to industry demands, Renoir must have found it difficult indeed to make a satisfactory adaptation of *Madame Bovary* under the circumstances. It is thus remarkable that, despite the disappointing box office revenue, despite the generally disparaging reviews, despite the fact that it *preceded* Poetic Realism, the movement that provided the world with the best—and best-known—French films from this era, this early adaptation provokes discussion even today. Through a close examination of the film, we will attempt to explain why this is the case and will reveal some of the strategies the filmmaker employed, strategies that make this adaptation not only important in its temporal context but consistent with Renoir's practices throughout his career.

---

[5] Cf. for example Sesonske: "Emma is a tiresome woman, and Valentine Tessier plays her as tiresome—the fault lies not in the characterization but in the character" (151). See also Durgnat: "we may say that Renoir 'miscasts' so that a character refuses all our preconceptions, is given freedom to *achieve* moments of truth" (95).

Shot in black and white, observing a strictly linear format (without flashbacks), Renoir's *Madame Bovary* begins with an intertitle that situates the first scene: "Les Bertaux: Juillet 1839." Renoir, like nearly every director after him, chooses to eliminate the novel's first chapter. As we will see, Renoir's first scene represents an attempt in shorthand to convey not only the essential information provided in the novel's first chapter, but also that of the sixth, which contains a lengthy flashback to Emma's youth. Films, like novels and all other modes of communication, count on redundancy to make them intelligible, and Renoir multiplies the incidents that reveal Charles's mediocrity partly by following Flaubert. For example, as in the novel, Charles is unable to conquer his timidity to ask for Emma's hand in marriage and therefore allows her father to speak in his place; he again displays his awkwardness at the Vaubyessard ball, bungles the clubfoot operation, fails to understand the plot of *Lucie de Lammermoor*, spills an orange drink on a woman's dress at the Opera, and remains oblivious to his wife's suffering until the very end. However, Renoir also displays a certain creativity in his portrayal of Charles, turning the constraints of the cinematic medium into advantages both through his omissions and his additions. For instance, he fails to show Charles setting old Rouault's leg or bleeding Rodolphe's servant, two of his rare displays of medical competence (however rudimentary), and the invitation to the Vaubyessard ball is presented not as a means of thanking Charles for curing the Marquis of his gumboil but rather as a spontaneous gesture motivated by the Marquis' desire to become better acquainted with Charles's pretty wife.[6] Furthermore, he invents dialogue—and this right from the

---

[6] It is true that in the novel, the Marquis also decides to invite the couple after meeting Emma and discovering "qu'elle avait une jolie taille et qu'elle ne saluait point en paysanne" [that she had a lovely figure and didn't have a peasant's manners] (113); however, he has already had reason to be grateful to Bovary not only for the successful medical treatment (Charles has cured his gumboil "par miracle" [miraculously]), but also for giving him cuttings of some healthy cherry trees. The spectator of the film, noting Renoir's emphasis, returns to the novel and discovers that there is in fact a clear progression in these three events, marked by the Marquis' escalating reactions to them. While he sends an employee to pay the bill after the medical procedure, he goes in person to thank Bovary for the cuttings, and it only after catching sight of Emma and noting her noble bearing that he extends the invitation. In writing of the BBC adaptation of George Eliot's *Middlemarch*, Ian MacKillop and Alison Platt assert that it "bring[s] to life some of the beauties that may have been sleeping in the novel" (88), that a good adaptation can "*restore* a

earliest scenes of the film—that suggests an ironic perspective on Charles's social role and exposes the contrast between this role and the romanticized expectations that Emma has of him. One such dialogue occurs just after a scene in which Emma has claimed that it is more elegant for a doctor to make his rounds on horseback than in a carriage. Renoir cuts to a high-angle long shot of a man riding a horse across the town square. "Eh bonjour, mon cher!" [Well, hello, my friend!], cries a bearded fellow standing in the square, and then, in a humorous aside, "Esculape à cheval...quel beau spectacle!" [Aesclepius on horseback...what a fine sight!] The rider comes into focus: it is of course Charles. "Bonjour, Homais," he replies. Through Homais's allusion to the Roman god of medicine, Renoir may have intended merely to evoke the pharmacist's self-interested flattery and his pretension, but the hyperbolic epithet is so clearly ridiculous that it also has the effect of underscoring the humble nature of the provincial health officer's profession. What a fine sight indeed, this round-faced, second-rate doctor plodding through the town square on his nag, projecting an image that is diametrically opposed to Emma's initial notion of Charles as glamorous, chivalrous, and elegant.[7] But Charles's decidedly unheroic demeanor is not limited to the professional sphere. In the film's very next scene, his submission to his mother's will is represented, again through dialogue: "Charles m'a épousée parce qu'il m'aimait," [Charles married me because he loved me] says Héloïse to Madame Bovary senior during the course of an argument; "Il vous a épousée parce que je le lui ai dit," [He married you because I told him to] replies his mother. Charles's lack of independence will also be reinforced by his helpless appeals to his mother. The childishness of his repeated cry ("Maman! Maman!") is underscored for the spectator in another scene invented by Renoir when Berthe utters the same words as she hangs on Emma's dress while Félicité attempts to hem it.

If Charles's inexperience and lack of imagination are suggested by the dialogue, his virility is called into question in the tracking shot that follows the very first scene between Emma and Lheureux. Charles has bought a carriage for Emma and he follows her when she

---

work, as a painting can by restored by cleaning" (88). At least where my own reading is concerned, I find myself in the presence here of a similar "restoration" of the novel by the film.
[7] Sesonske points this out as well. (See p 147)

runs excitedly to it and climbs aboard. Emma holds the reins as she and Charles ride through the countryside in their new conveyance, past the church and a herd of silent cows. Women driving carriages were hardly the norm in 1857, and even in 1934, when the "horseless carriage" was becoming more common, one did not often see women in the driver's seat. Thus, Renoir's decision to give Emma the reins has clearly symbolic value, pointing to the passivity of a husband who becomes a stereotypical cuckold. (Renoir will use this conceit again in *Une partie de campagne* when he shows Henriette rowing her doltish husband away from the island retreat where she had unexpectedly encountered the man who had initiated her to the joys of physical intimacy some years earlier.) The carriage ride ends with Charles attempting to kiss his wife, a display of affection she does not welcome ("Vous allez me froisser!" [You're going to rumple my dress!]), any more than the novelistic heroine welcomes Charles's affectionate attentions as she is getting ready for the Vaubyessard Ball. (Indeed, Emma's words come straight from the novel.) Moreover, as Rebecca Pauly notes, Renoir's carriage scene is strikingly opposed to the famous ride with Léon, when, as in the novel, the cab becomes a love nest. Charles's questionable virility— or, perhaps more accurately, his inability to satisfy his wife sexually— is further suggested in the film by a significant chronological change: Renoir's Emma betrays Charles with Rodolphe for the first time *after* the clubfoot operation, *before* the disastrous results are known, suggesting that her husband's professional renown is insufficient to inspire fidelity, and thus that her need for other men is motivated by carnal desire.

While later directors use voiceover and interior monologue to expose the interpersonal dynamics that had been revealed largely through free indirect style in Flaubert's novel, Renoir relies throughout on dialogue and symbolism. And among the symbols, animals are among the most important. I would like to illustrate Renoir's technique by analyzing an early farmyard scene, invented by the director, which draws its full significance from its juxtaposition with surrounding scenes. Specifically, this scene features Emma scattering seed for geese, then attempting unsuccessfully to separate a piglet from its mother. The squealing piglet wriggles out of her hands and returns to nurse with the other members of the litter. This apparently gratuitous vignette is inserted between two scenes featuring

Héloïse, Charles's first wife. In the first of these, Madame Bovary
Senior and Héloïse exchange harsh words, and Charles is forced to
mediate. After her mother-in-law's departure, Héloïse forces Charles
to swear on a prayer book that he will not return to the Rouault farm,
Les Bertaux. (A similar promise is extracted from Charles in the
novel.) In the second scene (immediately following the farmyard
scene), we see Héloïse hanging out the wash. Suddenly she clutches
her breast and sinks to the ground, dead from what one presumes to be
a heart attack or massive stroke. "Monsieur Bovary! Monsieur
Bovary!" cries the maid. "Madame ne bouge plus!" [Madame has
collapsed!] Renoir uses a dissolve to join this scene with the next, and
the image of Héloïse's body draped across her laundry basket fades as
her casket comes into focus. Immediately following the funeral scene,
the camera cuts to Les Bertaux, where Charles is once again a visitor.
Alexander Sesonske (147) believes the farmyard scene is a simple
allusion to the way Charles sees Emma, in harmony with nature.
However, this interpretation is difficult to defend, because Charles is
not present in the scene. I would suggest, rather, that thanks to
Renoir's editing, it is imbued with symbolism. The contrast between
the irrepressible movement of the piglets and the stillness of Héloïse's
corpse in death is pointed enough, but when the entire sequence is
taken into account, a thematic continuity becomes apparent. Emma
tries unsuccessfully to separate a nursing piglet from its mother.
Besides causing strife between a *human* mother and her child, Héloïse
attempts to keep Charles away from Emma. Hence the seemingly
gratuitous farmyard scene comes to symbolize the futile nature of
Héloïse's efforts: when Charles *does* return to Les Bertaux, he will
accept a drink from Emma, who tells him proudly that she made the
liqueur herself. The statement, which does not appear in the novel,
establishes a link between Emma and the sow, who nourishes her
piglets with her own milk.

The squealing, rooting piglets of the brief farmyard scene are,
however, of minor symbolic importance in comparison to the horses
and cows, which become a veritable leitmotif in the film. Emma's
original insistence in seeing Charles as her valiant knight is amusingly
illustrated early on, when, after the search for Charles's whip brings
Emma and Charles into embarrassingly intimate contact (as in the
novel), Emma accompanies Charles to the farmhouse door. Just as
they reach the doorway, we hear the neighing of a horse, a patent

symbol for Emma's romanticized image of a chivalrous lover (and an appropriate one, given that the word "chivalrous" is etymologically linked to *cheval*, the French word for "horse"). Emma, expecting Charles to declare his love, is disappointed when he simply bids her adieu. She comes back into the house, runs up the stairs, and throws herself on her bed. Old Rouault, seeing his daughter rush by, offers to accompany Charles to his carriage. Once again, the door frames the characters, but this time, the barnyard noise is different: we hear loud mooing of cows as the two men pass through the door, a rather transparent symbol of the bovine nature of Emma's *chevalier.*

Flaubert's Emma would have liked to live "dans quelque vieux manoir, comme ces châtelaines au long corsage, qui, sous le trèfle des ogives, passaient leurs jours, le coude sur la pierre et le menton dans la main, à regarder venir du fond de la campagne un cavalier à plume blanche qui galope sur un cheval noir" [in some old castle, like those ladies of the manor with their long bodices who spend their days beneath arched trefoils, leaning on the parapet, chin in hand, watching a horseman with a white plume galloping up on a black stallion] (101). Instead, she lives in Charles's humble house, and from her window, between two pots of geraniums, she watches him saddle up his "vieille jument blanche" [his old white mare] (95) each morning and ride away:

> Et alors, sur la grande route qui étendait sans en finir son long ruban de poussière, par les chemins creux où les arbres se courbaient en berceaux, dans les sentiers dont les blés lui montaient jusqu'aux genoux, avec le soleil sur ses épaules et l'air du matin à ses narines, le cœur plein des félicités de la nuit, l'esprit tranquille, la chair contente, il s'en allait ruminant son bonheur, comme ceux qui mâchent encore, après dîner, le goût des truffes qu'ils digèrent. (95-6)

> [And then, along the main road that stretched endlessly before him like a long ribbon of dust, through sunken lanes shaded by overhanging trees, down paths knee-deep in sheaves of wheat, with the sun on his shoulders and the morning air in his nostrils, his heart full of the preceding night's pleasures, his mind tranquil, his body satisfied, he rode away ruminating his happiness, like those who, after dinner, continue to savor the taste of the truffles they've just eaten.]

The delightfully apposite contrast between Emma's dreams and the reality of her life as a provincial housewife is rich with innuendo. In her dreams, the horseman is galloping towards her on a black stallion;

in reality, her husband is riding away from her on an old white mare, his heart, mind and flesh as satisfied as Emma's are dissatisfied. Flaubert's use of the concrete verbs *ruminer* and *mâcher* with abstract nouns (how does one "ruminate happiness" or [literally] "chew taste"?) is of course not gratuitous, and countless scholars have remarked on this scarcely subtle allusion to Charles's bovine nature, inscribed moreover in his patronymic, "Bovary" (*omen, nomen*). But how does one transcode this information in the indexical medium of the Seventh Art? Renoir's approach is two-pronged: he uses cows as a leitmotif and, no doubt under his direction, his brother Charles speaks with a noticeably nasal voice throughout, a voice that recalls the lowing of cattle. While other animals are heard and seen (in addition to the cows, horses, and pigs, we see geese and chickens, and the soundtrack features the chirping of birds and the barking of dogs), it is the cows and horses that are most prominent on both the image track and the soundtrack.

Renoir's film is replete with binary oppositions, and the somewhat heavy-handed symbolism of the horse/cow opposition sends us back to the novel, where a rereading of selected passages renews our appreciation of Flaubert's art. Here, too, it is clear that Emma initially attempts to envision her husband as a horseman. However, it becomes increasingly evident that her expectations are too great, for Charles has limited knowledge of the equestrian sport. Emma is particularly upset "[quand] il ne put, un jour, lui expliquer un terme d'equitation qu'elle avait rencontré dans un roman" [when, one day, he couldn't explain a riding term that she had come across in a novel] (107). Small wonder, then, that she should turn to Rodolphe, a true *chevalier* who proposes that they go riding together.

Renoir's take on Rodolphe's seduction of Emma emphasizes the role played by horses, real and symbolic. Whereas in the novel, Flaubert had juxtaposed in ironic counterpoint the official discourse at the Agricultural Fair and Rodolphe's romantic clichés, the filmmaker's camera moves back and forth between Homais attempting to persuade Charles to proceed with the surgical correction of Hippolyte's clubfoot and Rodolphe trying to persuade Emma that "la morale du monde" [society's morality] is irrelevant. Just as Homais exploits Hippolyte (whose name and condition identify him with the horse) as a vehicle for his personal ambition, Rodolphe will use horses to realize *his* ambition—seducing Emma. By cutting directly from the surgical procedure to a shot of Emma riding through the woods with Rodolphe, Renoir succeeds in linking Homais's metaphorical seduction of Charles with Rodolphe's literal seduction of Emma. The crosscutting technique also sets up a parallel between the operation and the lovemaking, both of which remain off-camera, and both of which bring first pleasure (Hippolyte kisses Charles's hand in gratitude), then pain. If Charles's botched operation on Hippolyte's clubfoot turns into a public display of his surgical incompetence, it also evokes—on a symbolic level—his ignorance of horses.

The symbolism with which Renoir invests animals can be illustrated by an anecdote from the filming. Robert Aron, the production director, recounts that during a reconnaissance tour of the wooded area in which Renoir had decided to situate Emma's first infidelity with Rodolphe, he had seen a rabbit emerge from its warren. Delighted, he decided that this would be the perfect symbol to suggest Nature's collusion with his adulterous heroine. Unfortunately, the rabbit was uncooperative. It took an entire extra day of filming, with all of the attendant expense for the camera crew, the sound crew, and other personnel, before the skittish rabbit decided to venture out of its hole. Back in the studio the following day, Renoir, reviewing the previous day's shoot, decided that the animal added nothing to the scene. The footage obtained with so much difficulty was therefore excised.[8]

Renoir's intense love of nature did not blind him to the symbolic possibilities of other phenomena. Such leitmotifs as the dusty ribbon of road unwinding behind a carriage as the rhythmic trotting of a horse can be heard on the soundtrack, or the profile of Hivert's "Hirondelle" moving *right to left* across the screen on the horizon punctuate the film. In both cases, these conventional strategies for evoking the passage of time have been slightly altered to suggest nostalgia for the past. In the first instance, which, by the way, makes use of a standard painterly technique, the emphasis is on where the carriage has been rather than where it is going.[9] In the second, Renoir has reversed the convention according to which forward movement is

---

[8] This story, narrated by Robert Aron, was reproduced in *Renoir in France*, ed. Frank Curot.

[9] Delphine Jayot believes that Renoir is giving us Emma's perspective here, as she is seated at the rear of the coach, and that the filmmaker's intention is to convey a sense of monotony (50).

depicted as *left to right* across the screen. Other symbols evoke the inevitability of Emma's destiny. The moving hands of the clock above Rodolphe's fireplace mantle suggests that time is running out for Emma, and thus provides a somber backdrop to Emma's histrionics in her final encounter with her lover; a skull and crossbones on the wall behind Justin and Emma as Emma persuades Justin to give her the key to the laboratory also has a highly transparent prophetic function.

In addition to his predilection for symbolism, Renoir was known for what critic Pierre Leprohon refers to as his "folk realism" (32), expressed in his tendency to include sympathetic portrayals of the lower classes in his films. Indeed, his immense compassion for the working class and his almost Flaubertian disdain for the bourgeoisie are evident in many of his productions, *La Règle du jeu* being perhaps the best known. In *Madame Bovary*, the populist sympathies that were to ally him with *le Front Populaire* [*The Popular Front*] can be gleaned from the numerous scenes that include peasants at work and at play, scenes that are all the more remarkable in view of the draconian cutting that was required in order to bring his film down to the length required by his distributors.[10] One such scene, actually added by Renoir, features a group of peasants around a pool table, their game suspended as they watch the club foot operation. Here, the peasants become spectators within the cinematic space, and their presence has a clearly symbolic value (Donaldson-Evans 21-34). However, in a film that focuses on the dissatisfaction of a provincial *bourgeoise*, what is important is that this seemingly gratuitous inclusion of a scene depicting the lower class is motivated by the director's social conscience and political beliefs. Renoir's *Madame Bovary* tilts noticeably to the left.

Another feature of this adaptation can be located in what Sesonske refers to as the "technique of commentative repetition" (148), i.e. the "doubling" or even "tripling" of similar scenes with variations that seem to function as "commentaries." We have already seen one example of this technique in Renoir's film: Charles's rebuffed attempt at intimacy during the film's first carriage ride versus Léon's successful seduction in the closed cab later in the film. Another such example is Charles's intervention on Héloïse's side in

---

[10] The Popular Front was a coalition of left-wing movements that came into being between the World Wars.

an argument between his first wife and his mother ("Maman, ma femme est malade; il faut la ménager" [Mother, my wife is sick; we mustn't upset her]) versus his later support of his mother when she argues with Emma ("Emma, je t'en supplie: fais pas de drames. Maman est vieille; elle est un peu nerveuse." [Emma, please! Don't make a scene. Mother is old; she's a bit high strung.]). One of the most suggestive of these repetitions is the one that links three scenes, the first at the Vaubyessard ball, the second at the Opera, and the third at the costume ball Emma attends with Léon. The costume ball alludes back to both of the earlier scenes, to the first because it features dancing and to the second because it also includes a stage performance. Whereas Emma had been in the center of the action at the aristocratic ball, and, at the Opera, had watched, entranced, as the drama of *Lucie de Lammermoor* unfolded, she is singularly apathetic and uninvolved at the masked ball. Indeed, she is not in costume, she does not dance, and she does not listen when a female vocalist is called to the stage to perform. It may well be, of course, that a scene cut from the film had shown Emma dancing in her masculine attire, as in the novel ("Elle mit un pantalon [...] [et] sauta toute la nuit, au son furieux des trombones" [She put on a pair of trousers and pranced around all night to the frenzied sound of the trombones] (430)). In the shortened version, however, this ultimately fruitless attempt at escapism is missing, and thanks to the "commentative repetition," one has the impression of a steady decline following the "epiphany" of the Vaubyessard Ball. Like the Emma of the novel's last chapters, "[qui] éprouvait...une courbature incessante et universelle" [who felt...an unremitting and overwhelming weariness] (429-30), the morose heroine of this last scene is fatally overcome by fatigue and indifference.

If Renoir's use of symbolism (often inspired by Nature) and commentative repetition, his predilection for shots that include the working class, and his tendency to film his actors as though they were on stage all mark his adaptation of *Madame Bovary*, the single most important feature of his film is its intergeneric borrowing from painting, the art of Renoir's father. Whether through its use of painterly technique, the lyricism of the nature scenes (Stam, *Literature*, 163), its frequent inclusion of paintings in the mise-en-scène, its use of shots that sometimes evoke nineteenth-century paintings, or, most importantly its tendency to enclose the heroine in claustrophobic "inner frames" within the "natural" frame of the cinematic shot, Renoir's *Madame Bovary* repeatedly and obsessively bears witness to the paternal influence, an influence so pervasive that it becomes the defining characteristic of the film. To appreciate this influence, we must return to the film's beginning.

The intertitle that opens the film ("Les Bertaux: Juillet 1839) gives spectators a temporal and spatial context for the action. An establishing shot follows: the camera tracks slowly to the left, past farm buildings with thatched roofs, past a stand of trees and a low stone wall, past pigs whose squealing is barely audible over the jaunty musical score. The music then stops, replaced by the lowing of a herd of cows grazing in the middle distance. A dissolve connects this bucolic scene to an interior shot of Charles, who is studying framed pictures on the walls of what we suppose is Emma's room. He has his back to the camera, and the spectator glimpses his shining pate through his thinning hair. An off-screen voice tells us what he's looking at ("Voyez mes gravures. Celle-là est Marie Stuart" [Have a look at my engravings. That one represents Mary Stuart]) as the camera pans left to reveal the speaker, Emma, who is facing the camera, framed in a window well. A dialogue follows:

> EMMA. N'est-ce pas qu'elle est belle? Elle me fait rêver. Comme j'aurais aimé vivre dans ce temps-là! La vie était moins étroite, les sentiments plus élevés et les hommes plus chevaleresques.
>
> CHARLES, *d'une voix nasillarde*. Ah oui, vous avez tout à fait raison.
>
> [EMMA. Isn't she beautiful? She sets me to dreaming. How I would have liked to live during those times! Life was less stifling. Sentiments were loftier, men more chivalrous.
>
> CHARLES, *in a nasal voice*. Oh yes, you're absolutely right.]

Emma smiles. Her pause leads spectators to anticipate a change of subject, but their expectations are not fully met, as the ensuing conversation reveals:

> EMMA. Vous allez toujours à cheval pour visiter vos malades?
>
> CHARLES. Ah, oui, c'est plus commode qu'une voiture avec les mauvais chemins.
>
> EMMA. Je comprends. Et puis c'est tellement plus élégant.
>
> [EMMA. Do you always visit your patients on horseback?

CHARLES. Oh, yes, it's more convenient than a carriage, with the bad
roads we have around here.

EMMA. I understand. And besides, it's so much more elegant.]

In just two shots, Renoir has established the setting for the story and
has communicated the essential characteristics of Emma and Charles:
Emma is a dissatisfied dreamer who wishes she lived in another, more
romantic, era; Charles, distinctly bovine, is agreeable ("vous avez tout
a fait raison"), down-to-earth, and contented. The slide from
chevaleresque to *à cheval* in Emma's discourse is clear enough: she
sees Charles as her knight in shining armor, elegant on horseback as
he makes his rounds. For Charles, on the other hand, the horse is
merely practical. Emma imagines the handsomely attired horseman;
Charles thinks only of the muddy, rutted country roads.

Michel Serceau is correct in asserting that this scene, "qui ne
recourt à aucun montage et doit sa valeur de représentation à la
combinaison des attitudes, propos et intonations respectives des deux
personnages, a l'intérêt de transformer le *personnage* en *caractère*"
[in which (Renoir) doesn't resort to montage and which owes its
effectiveness to a combination of the respective attitudes, remarks and
intonation of the two characters, is interesting in its ability to
transform characters into personalities] (118). However, its
importance surpasses the mere revelation of character. By evoking
Mary Stuart in the film's first dialogue—Flaubert waits until Chapter
VI to mention her, in the context of a flashback that includes allusions
to other illustrious women as well—Renoir accomplishes two things.
In the first place, he reveals the influence of Emma's reading, for it
should be noted that besides being an historical personage, Mary
Queen of Scots became a literary character in the work of Walter
Scott, Schiller, and other Romantics. Secondly, Renoir indirectly hints
at Emma's demise: like the rash, passionate, beautiful woman whose
image she has affixed to her wall, Emma Bovary will meet with an
untimely death. We know that Charles is looking at Mary Stuart's
portrait, but soundtrack and image track are not redundant here—i.e.
Emma's words do not inform spectators of what they are seeing on
screen—because, significantly, Charles's form in the foreground
obstructs the spectator's view of the portrait. However, when the
camera pans left to reveal Emma, she too is enclosed in a frame, in her
case, architectural (figure 1). Renoir's mise-en-scène thus links Emma
and Mary Stuart while at the same time separating Emma from

Charles, the right side of the window well in which she stands appearing as a symbol of the wall between them that will never be breached.

Figure 1. Renoir's *Madame Bovary* (1934).

In a provocative essay on Renoir's adaptation, Rebecca Pauly has noted that Renoir repeatedly frames his characters "in doorways or windows, converting them into family portraits, omens of future demise fittingly accompanied by the dissonant lugubrious soundtrack by Darius Milhaud" (134). Certainly, the novel's first scene appears to corroborate this interpretation, despite the absence of the extra-diegetic music. However, I would like to further refine the observation. While it is true that Renoir seems to have an affinity for architectural features that frame his characters—according to Sesonske, forty of the some two hundred shots that are not country exteriors "have a significant portion of the scene shown through some such aperture" (156)—it is Emma who is most often enclosed in this way, and on at least four occasions, such shots are juxtaposed with allusions (from the sound or image track) to art, as in the first dialogue. Another case in point is the first scene between Emma and Lheureux, which takes place immediately after Emma's father has guessed Charles's intentions to ask for his daughter's hand in marriage. The scene in which Rouault throws open the shutters to signal his daughter's acceptance has been eliminated, as have the raucous wedding scene, the arrival at Charles's house, the revealing wedding night, the whole of the couple's life in Tostes, and the arrival in Yonville. It is impossible to know for certain whether these scenes figured in the film's original version, although it certainly seems significant that the shot of the shutter was eliminated, given its importance to our understanding of subsequent events. Was it perhaps because Rouault would have been framed alone in the window that Renoir chose to delete the scene? Certainly, the spectator who has not first read the novel would be confused by the abrupt cut to the scene with Lheureux, in Emma's home, where the cunning cloth merchant is attempting to sell his wares to Charles's young wife. As in the novel, Emma studies the goods and then exercises her willpower by declining to purchase anything. However, the rest of the scene has been substantially altered by Renoir. Whereas in the novel the cloth merchant simply departs, convinced that he will be more successful in tempting the young woman on future visits, in Renoir's film, Charles enters the room while he is still present, discreetly purchases a shawl for her behind her back, and puts it around her shoulders when Lheureux takes his leave. He then notices a painting on Emma's easel—whereas Flaubert's Emma had sketched, this celluloid Emma paints—and compliments her:

> CHARLES. Quelle jolie peinture! Je n'ai jamais vu de tableaux qui me plaisent autant que les tiens.
>
> EMMA, *incapable de résister à la tentation d'insulter son mari.* C'est parce que tu n'en as pas vu beaucoup!
>
> [CHARLES. What a beautiful picture! I've never seen paintings that I like as much as yours.
>
> EMMA, *unable to keep herself from insulting her husband.* That's because you haven't seen many!]

After promising that he will take her to Italy to the museums one day, when he can afford to do so, Charles turns his attention to his wife's attire:

CHARLES. Ah! Que tu es bien habillée. Sincèrement, je ne connais pas
de dames de la haute société qui soient aussi élégantes que toi.

EMMA, *dédaigneuse*. Comment peux-tu savoir? Tu n'es jamais sorti.

[CHARLES. Oh, how well-dressed you are. Honestly, I don't know any
high society women who are as elegant as you are.

EMMA, *disdainful*. How would you know? You've never gone out.]

An analysis of the structure of this dialogue is revealing.
Charles's two compliments, eliciting similarly cynical reactions from
a newly disabused (if still affectionate) Emma, establish an implicit
parallel between the woman and the work of art, the artist and her
painting. In the same scene, Charles tells Emma that he has bought a
carriage for her. As he describes the carriage, he goes to the window,
and the camera pans left to follow him, bringing the painting into
center frame as it does so. Excited, Emma runs to join him at the
window. Hence, what the spectator sees is the painting in the
foreground, with Emma and Charles framed by the window in the
background. The framing device is all the more effective when Emma
leaves the window and runs out to the carriage. Now the spectator sees
her *through* the window, fully framed, with the painting still in the
foreground. The scene is shot in deep focus, making it difficult *not* to
establish a connection between the painting and the figure of Emma.
Hence, inside and outside are doubly connected, first by the fact that
Emma's painting—a landscape—has brought the "out-of-doors" into
the house, and then because Emma herself, fleeing the confines of her
home, leaves that part of the frame that shows the inside of the house
and rejoins the frame on the other side of the window, outside. If in *La
Grande Illusion*, Renoir's lyrical camerawork emphasizes the illusory
nature of borders by connecting spaces, here interior and exterior
spaces are linked, but to different effect. Despite her best efforts to
escape the confinement of her domesticity, Emma remains a prisoner
within the frame of bourgeois existence.[11]

A third episode in which Emma appears to be associated with a
framed portrait occurs at the Vaubyessard Ball. A high angle shot
framed by columns of the Vaubyessard mansion shows the dancers in
motion. The camera zooms in, then cuts to a shot of Emma and

---

[11] Cf. Duszynski (85-86) for an analysis of the way Renoir evokes Emma's
entrapment through his framing in an early episode.

Charles, on the sidelines, watching the dancers. Emma is invited to dance, and we see the Viscount giving her a lesson in the waltz, then guiding her more and more rapidly through the steps, while Charles watches the whirling couples from the background, his body reflected in a mirror along with the figures of the dancers. He then moves away from the mirror and turns to look at the portraits adorning the wall, shifting his gaze from Emma to the portraits of the Viscount's aristocratic ancestors and back again, thereby suggesting a relationship between them. Emma's dance partner notices Charles and his curiosity is aroused:

> LE VICOMTE. Qui donc est ce drôle d'homme? Il a l'air tout seul, comme en pénitence.[12] Vous le connaissez?
>
> EMMA. Moi, non, je ne le connais pas.

> [THE VISCOUNT. Who's that strange man? He looks all alone, as if he were in disgrace. Do you know him?
>
> EMMA. Me? No, I don't.]

It is obvious that Emma's words reveal an embarrassment at being associated with her unsophisticated husband (in an earlier scene, also invented by Renoir, she had criticized his boots, "des bottes de charretier") [a cart-driver's boots]. Rebecca Pauly has remarked upon the symbolic value of Emma's denial, noting that in fact, she does *not* know Charles, at least not in any real sense of that term (135). Her point is well-taken, although one might argue that with a character as uncomplicated as Charles, there is no unplumbed depth, nothing really to know, (Flaubert tells us that after his death, Canivet, the surgeon, "l'ouvrit et ne trouva rien" [opened him up and found nothing] (501). Rather, it is Charles who does not know Emma. What is more significant in this scene, in my opinion, is what we might term the mise-en-abyme of the gaze. The film's spectators look at characters framed by the camera; the characters in the foreground cast oblique glances at a character in the background; and the character in the background gazes at a portrait. In this way, a connection is established between the characters in the foreground (in this case, Emma and the Viscount) and the painting in the background, with

---

[12] The expression is used in parlor games for someone who has broken a rule and has been slapped with a small penalty. Renoir tended to favor the game metaphor and indeed just a few years later was to make a film based upon it (*La Règle du jeu*).

Charles providing the link, as in the other two scenes. Like Mary Stuart, like the family ancestors whose portraits line the walls of the Vaubyessard mansion, Emma Bovary is associated metaphorically with a distant past.

The last scene in which Renoir uses Charles to suggest a relationship between Emma and a framed painting takes place immediately after Emma has returned from Homais's pharmacy where she has ingested arsenic. She climbs the stairs, and, as in the novel, she sits down at her desk and begins writing the explanatory letter ("Qu'on n'accuse personne..." [No one should be blamed]). In the next shot, we are back downstairs, witnessing the return of Charles. He removes his coat, then turns, and his glance falls on a painting of a man and a woman embracing. He calls up to his wife ("Emma! Emma!") and the camera cuts to the top of the stairs. Charles is shown arriving on the landing, then there is a pan to the right that brings Emma into the frame. She is seated at her desk, framed in the doorway, and we see her as Charles does, in a classic point-of-view shot. It is difficult to say with any certainty that Renoir is suggesting that the truth of Emma's betrayals is finally dawning on Charles; what is clear, however, is that once again, Emma has been framed, both through the symbolic portrait on the wall, and by the "natural" frame of the doorway.

In a timeless essay published in 1962, Jean Rousset remarked that in the novel, Emma is often shown dreaming at the window and that in these instances of inertia and boredom, Flaubert's narrative embraces her viewpoint (109-33). Interestingly, Renoir's film contains few point-of-view shots that give us Emma's perspective on her world (in keeping with the "desubjectivization" that Robert Stam sees as typical of Renoir's work [*Literature* 164]), and we learn of her emotions only through dialogue, facial expressions, and action. The vast majority of the shots *contain* her, and the framing devices used by Renoir diminish the size of the movie frame, multiplying what the critic Jeancolas has termed "l'effet d'étouffement" [the smothering effect] (171). We see Emma framed not only by windows and doors, but by the curtains of her bed, the sides of her carriage, the trees of the forest, and the theater box at the Rouen opera. Even the carriage scene with Leon is altered so that we can see Emma framed by the small carriage window. Whereas in the novel it is only an ungloved hand that emerges from the window, and the emphasis is on the torn bits of paper that are scattered to the wind "et s'abattirent plus loin, comme des papillons blancs, sur un champ de trèfles rouges tout en fleur" [and landed farther away, like white butterflies, in a field of red clover in full bloom] (373), the film shows us Emma in close-up, tearing the letter she had written to Leon.

The dialogue, too, reinforces the idea of a framed Emma, as for example when Homais, trying to persuade Charles to perform the operation on Hippolyte's clubfoot, promises him that his renown would be increased, "ce qui augmenterait vos ressources et vous permettrait de placer Madame Bovary dans un cadre plus élevé" [which would increase your income and would allow you to install Madame Bovary in more elegant surroundings (literally, "in a higher frame")]. While it is true that Renoir often transposes the novel's dialogues to the screen as closely as possible, here he has mischievously changed "célébrité vite acquise à l'opérateur" [a fame quickly acquired by the surgeon] (279) to "notoriété rapide pour l'opérateur" [a rapid notoriety for the surgeon] and has added the comment about Emma. Charles, of course, will fail to place Emma in a "higher frame," but she is framed so often in this adaptation that the spectator has the impression of touring an art gallery. The numerous framed paintings represented in nearly every interior scene, from Emma's room to Rodolphe's, La Vaubyessard to the Rouen hotel and even to Lheureux's shop, only add to this impression, and whatever their mimetic value, they contribute to the notion that in this film's visual grammar, coherence is provided by art. By giving the art of painting such a prominent place in his film, Renoir has cleverly evoked an aesthetic medium that is iconic, an appropriate transposition of words into images. In the novel, the aesthetic medium most often evoked, and the one that gives coherence to Emma's dreams, is literature.

It has often been said that in Flaubert's novel, Emma's story is enclosed in that of Charles, i.e. that Flaubert makes use of a narrative frame, beginning and ending with Charles. As we have seen, Renoir too frames Emma, albeit in a different way. However, the multiple frames within frames that define this adaptation are not the only allusions to the art of painting. The film incorporates several shots that evoke nineteenth-century canvases. The carnival scene provides an example of this phenomenon. In a long-held shot that is typical of Renoir, the camera lingers on raucous young dancers frolicking at the ball, pans right past a solitary woman, unsmiling, who rebuffs the attentions of an obviously drunk party-goer, and then slows as Emma and Léon are brought into the frame. Seated at a café table littered with wine bottles, the disconsolate couple brings to mind the melancholy figures in Degas's *L'Absinthe*. If the composition of the frame differs from that of the painting (the diagonal lines that define the canvas are absent from the film frame), the mood is the same. The head of a sleeping clown (presumably drunk) can be seen at the bottom of the frame, the whole sorry scene completely out of sync with the foot-tapping music featured on the soundtrack. The next shot takes us back to the stage where the crowd has been silenced by the singer's performance. Cut back to the table where, over the off-screen lyrics of a song celebrating springtime, Emma gives voice to her despair: "Alors il n'y a plus d'espoir. [...] plus d'espoir. Je n'ai plus qu'à mourir." [There's no more hope, then...no more hope. I might as well die.] The camera tracks back to show the drunken clown and a couple embracing at the next table. "Nous ne sommes pas du même monde" [We're not from the same milieu], declares Emma haughtily, verbalizing what she had acted out in her relationship with Charles.

It should be noted that while analyses of Renoir's *Madame Bovary* have to date failed to point out the prominent role played by painting, except to mention in passing the "effets de rétressissement du cadre" [effects of the frame-shrinking] (Jeancolas 171), the importance of art in Renoir's other films has not gone unnoticed. In discussing Renoir's film adaptation of Maupassant's short story, "Une partie de campagne," Michel Serceau comments on shots that feature a young woman on a swing, as she is seen—through a window—by two rowers. In Serceau's view—and he is not the first to advance it (see also Leprohon 98)—these shots function as a quotation, evoking Renoir senior's famous painting, "La Balançoire" [The Swing]. The spectator who knows the painting in question likewise sees them as referential. However, Serceau also acknowledges that in this film (and others), "il y a ...un nombre moins facilement repertoriable de plans qui font songer à la peinture sans renvoyer explicitement à tel tableau d'Auguste Renoir...[mais qui sont] toujours, du côté de l'instance auctoriale, des citations" (156) [there are a number of shots, less easy to classify, that are reminiscent of paintings without referring specifically to such and such a painting by Renoir but that nonetheless are meant by the director to be quotations]. Whether or not the spectator notices, remarks Serceau, is irrelevant.

To return to *Madame Bovary*, I would like to suggest that Jean Renoir's evocation of Degas's gloomy canvas was quite deliberate and that, moreover, in a film that has been repeatedly described as one of Renoir's darkest, it reflects the somber mood of the early 1930s when it was made.[13] One might even say that in conveying Emma's depressing experience in such uniformly dark hues, the film is a forerunner of the films of Poetic Realism, films which, in Dudley Andrew's words, communicated an experience of "frustrated desire...oppression...bartered hopes [and] helplessness" (20).[14] But whether or not the relationship is convincing, one thing is clear: Renoir has used painting as a vehicle for his message. The Degas allusion becomes one more filament in a web of allusions to art, be they in the form of framed paintings, architectural frames, or unframed evocations of nineteenth-century art.

Unlike the fleshy young beauties painted in pastels by Renoir's father, Valentine Tessier's Emma evokes, not *joie de vivre*, but a palpable world-weariness.[15] And yet Auguste Renoir's influence is not absent, for the visual poetry of his brushwork is evoked in the final moments of the film. Whereas Flaubert in his unremitting pessimism denies Emma the solace of a peaceful death, Jean Renoir saves her *in extremis* by shooting her close-up and in soft focus on her deathbed in shots that recall the gossamer grace of his father's canvases. This is not to say that he departs radically from the novel's depiction of the protagonist's death: Emma's hideous laughter rings out as the blind man's singing reaches her ears. But her wish to find "le calme du

---

[13] Sesonske too has commented on the "overwhelming darkness" of this film, speculating that the cuts removed some of the lighter moments, because the film is inconsistent with other Renoir films and indeed with his view of life, which he sees as a blend of light and darkness (149).

[14] The term "Poetic Realism" refers to a style of filmmaking that became popular in France in the mid 1930s. Characterized by a realistic focus on the working class and a lyrical style, the films of Poetic Realism are typified by Marcel Carné's *les Enfants du paradis* (*Children of Paradise*). The style was said to have influenced Italian Neo-realism.

[15] Perhaps because of the cuts, we can ascribe her unhappiness only to her disappointments with men; the broader themes of the novel—the revolt against the mediocrity of the provincial bourgeoisie, the nascent feminism of Emma's laments about the limits of a woman's life, etc.—are not represented in the film.

tombeau" [the tranquility of the grave], expressed earlier as she lay smoking a cigarette on a hotel bed next to her lover, Léon, is now repeated as she lies half-conscious on her deathbed with her daughter beside her (figure 2). The impressionistic beauty of the shot recalls

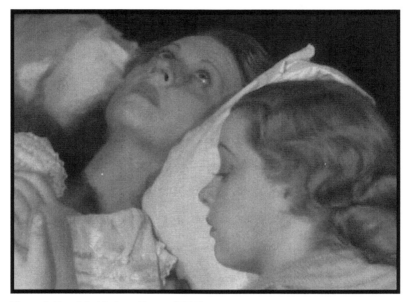

Figure 2. Renoir's *Madame Bovary* (1934).

Auguste Renoir's numerous mother-and-child canvasses, although there is a disturbing irony in the fact that while the paintings are brimming with life, this mother lies on the threshold of death. Mostly, though, the shot stands in sharp opposition to Flaubert's realistic death bed scene, in which Emma's pallid face, wet with perspiration, frightens Berthe. Similarly, in the film's last shot, Emma has fallen back onto the pillow, and the hand of an unseen person enters the frame, gently closing her eyes. Besides recalling a Renoir painting, the soft focus gives Emma an angelic beauty that contrasts sharply with the novelistic Emma's painfully realistic corpse, memorable for the gush of putrid liquids that issues from her sunken mouth. Whatever may have motivated Jean Renoir's shots—a wish to pay homage to his father or, conversely, to compete with him in his own medium (film), a fondness for the actress, a sympathy for the character—the effect is the same: in the end, the filmmaker grants Emma "le calme du tombeau" that she had so ardently desired but did not achieve in her literary incarnation.

In his memoirs, Renoir tells of the early years of his career as a filmmaker, years when, forced to sell his father's canvases in order to finance his films, he watched the progressive stripping of paintings from the walls of his home.[16] Perhaps it was to compensate for what must have seemed to the son like a lack of respect for the father that Renoir gave such a central place to painting in his film. In this respect, *Madame Bovary* does not stand alone, as there are allusions to the painter's art and even to specific paintings not only in *Une partie de campagne* but in numerous other Renoir films as well. But in *Madame Bovary*, as we have seen, Renoir does not limit himself to an occasional evocative shot or a verbal allusion to a school of painting or an artist (as in *La Règle du jeu* and *La Marseillaise*).[17] Rather, the film seems literally "haunted" by images from the Impressionist era, present in the film like ghosts in a dream.[18] A closer analysis would likely find even more direct allusions to the father's canvases, conscious or unconscious. The theme of painting also shapes the film's plot. Renoir establishes Emma's identity as an artist early on, and then gives coherence to his film by framing her throughout until, in the end, she has been transformed into a work of art in her own right. Where Charles has failed to place Emma in a "higher frame," Jean Renoir has succeeded. In this sense, one might say that it was not so much Flaubert who was his model—or even Flaubert's novel—as it was the character of Emma Bovary. And like his father's models, she did indeed succeed in "opening the door" of the artist's imagination.

---

[16] "L'essentiel de ma fortune consistant en tableaux que m'avait légués mon père, mes essais cinématographiques se soldaient par la disparition de ces toiles qui étaient comme une partie de moi-même." [The basis of my fortune was from paintings that my father had left me; my attempts at filmmaking were financed by the selling of those canvases which were like part of me.] *Ma Vie et mes films*, 76-7.

[17] In *La Marseillaise*, the character Javel paints allegories taken from classical mythology; *La Règle du jeu* features a character who studies pre-Colombian art.

[18] I owe this observation to Laurence Porter who points out that such phantasms –also illustrated by the portrait gallery in the Gothic novel, the ugly sculpture on the mantel in Sartre's *No Exit*, etc.—have in the last few decades generated considerable interest among scholars engaged in psychologically-oriented criticism.

3

Minnelli (1949):
Hollywood Rediscovers Emma

It was in Hollywood, California, during an era that was characterized, not by an economic depression and an attendant pessimism but by an ebullient, post-war optimism, that Vincente Minnelli decided to try his hand at adapting Flaubert's "scandalous" novel of 1857. Like Renoir, Minnelli accepted without hesitation when a producer (in this case Pandro Berman) phoned to ask him if he'd be interested in the project. Having experienced a year of inactivity that coincided with a fallow period for MGM, as Hollywood Studios struggled to find their niche in a country that had just been introduced to the marvels of television, Minnelli was eager to get back to work, and he knew Flaubert's novel and liked it (Minnelli 201). He was not the first director to bring Emma to Tinseltown. That distinction, as we have seen, went to Albert Ray who, in 1932, had made *Unholy Love*, a film based loosely on the novel. Nor was Minnelli the first filmmaker after Renoir to adapt the novel to the screen. In the fifteen years that separate Renoir's version from Minnelli's, two other adaptations were released: the first, in 1937, was a German production directed by Gerhard Lamprecht and starring an actress of silent screen fame, Pola Negri; the second, just ten years later, was an Argentine version directed by Carlos Schlieper. However, there is one distinction that belongs to Minnelli alone, that of having brought *Madame Bovary*—or rather, a sanitized version thereof—to the American film-going public in a major Hollywood production that won critical acclaim and achieved a box-office success.[1] Nominated for an Academy Award for best set decoration, Minnelli's adaptation has not however been spared sharp criticism from film scholars familiar with the novel and from literary critics, who decry the considerable liberties the director took with Flaubert's masterpiece. Robert Stam encapsulates the principal objections to the film as follows:

> Minnelli "mines" the novel, as it were, not only for possible production numbers but also for potential melodramatic and spectacular scenes. [...] On every register, Minnelli cultivates an aesthetic of crescendo and excess, in contradiction [...] with a dedramatized "novel about nothing," but effective in terms of mainstream entertainment norms. (*Literature* 173)

Among the episodes "amplified" by Minnelli, the Vaubyessard Ball is the most famous. Indeed, the waltzing scene, filmed with gleeful disregard for the 180-degree rule, is still shown in film classes today, and scholars' continuing discussion of this adaptation testifies abundantly to its importance. Clearly, Minnelli's *Bovary*, filmed by an audacious director who was truly master of his craft, provides an exemplary illustration of 1940s Hollywood style. However, this film was shaped not only by the filmmaker's boldness and his taste for melodrama but also by a certain subservience, perhaps more feigned than real. In order to understand the film's principal characteristics, some familiarity with the director's life and some knowledge of the socio-historical context in which the film was made are essential.

First, the director. Prior to his career in cinema, Vincente Minnelli (1910-1986) had worked at the Chicago department store Marshall Fields as a display artist.[2] He subsequently became involved in theater as a costume designer, working for a time at Radio City Music Hall in New York. Not until 1940 did he move from theater to film, signing on with Metro Goldwyn Mayer at the invitation of producer Arthur Freed. In 1944, he directed Judy Garland in the nostalgic musical *Meet Me in Saint-Louis*, a film that—ostensibly, at least—celebrates family values and traditional morality. During the

---

[1] In his *Directed by Vincente Minnelli*, Stephen Harvey tells us that U.S. returns were estimated to be $2,000,000 by the end of 1949 (the film opened in August), a very respectable box office performance.
[2] Minnelli lied often about his age, and for this reason, scholars disagree about the date of his birth. However, the most authoritative sources (e.g. *A Biographical Dictionary of Film*) list 1910.

filming, he fell in love with his lead actress, and the two were married in 1945. Life with the temperamental, amphetamine-addicted Garland was exceedingly stressful, and the couple separated in 1950, after nearly six turbulent years during which numerous psychiatrists attempted unsuccessfully to "cure" Garland of her crippling anxieties. Minnelli and Garland had one daughter, Liza (born in 1946), and for Minnelli, the parallel between their unhappy situation and that of the fictional Charles and Emma with their young daughter, Berthe, must have been hard to ignore. In his autobiography, he acknowledged that his wife "often made vague references to her fantasy life" and he revealed that although he did not know the content of her fantasies, he had directed his screen-writer, Robert Ardrey, to bring out a conflict between fantasy and reality in Emma's character (202). Minnelli's cinematic version of Flaubert's novel clearly owes much to the domestic strife that he was enduring in 1949. It is also possible that Minnelli, who was rumored to be bi-sexual, found the theme of transgressive love appealing.[3]

Whatever the director's personal reasons for making *Madame Bovary*, the most important influence on this adaptation was the Motion Picture Production Code (MPPC), mentioned earlier. Also known as the Hays Code after Will H. Hays, president of the association that instituted it in 1930, the Motion Picture Producers and Distributors of America, the Code was based upon the belief that motion pictures, powerfully influential, could "affect lives for the better."[4] An unwritten corollary to this belief was that motion pictures could affect lives for the worse, and even a casual glance at the Code reveals that the "for better or for worse" dichotomy was defined in traditional moral terms. Indeed, the Code had initially been drawn up by two Roman Catholics, a Jesuit priest named Daniel Lord and a layman, Martin Quigley, and its most draconian enforcement took place between 1934 and 1954, when the Legion of Decency's Joseph Breen was director of the Production Code Administration. Although the Code was somewhat weakened in 1948 when a Supreme Court

---

[3] See Joe McElhaney, "Vincent Minnelli." This may also explain the attraction of a novel that contains male characters who don't conform to canonical definitions of masculinity. See Mary Orr, *Flaubert: Writing the Masculine*.

[4] *The Motion Picture Production Code of 1930*. Http://www.artsreformation.com/ aoo1/hays-code.html. The Motion Picture Producers and Distributors of America was renamed the Motion Picture Association of America in 1945.

decision requiring that major Hollywood studios terminate their association with movie theaters effectively absolved theaters from adhering to the Code, it remained in force for producers until 1968. At that time, efforts to control movie content were replaced by a rating system that shifted the emphasis to the spectator, limiting young people's access to certain categories of films.

The Production Code was based on three general principles: 1) no film should be produced which would "lower the moral standards of those who see it"; 2) films should limit themselves to showing "correct standards of life"; and 3) neither natural nor human law should be subjected to ridicule. In addition to these general principles, there were specific applications, and of these, the ones most relevant to *Madame Bovary* had to do with sexuality and religion. Among other things, the Code required that films uphold "the sanctity of the institution of marriage and the home"[5] and that adultery "must not be explicitly treated, or justified, or presented attractively" (MPPC, II, 1). Sexually suggestive dancing was not permitted (MPPC VII, 1), and religious faith, its ministers and its ceremonies were to be presented in a respectful manner (MPPC VIII, 1&2). Clearly, a film based upon a tale of adultery would present special challenges, and Minnelli's autobiography reveals in abundant detail the way in which the censors—or fear of them—shaped the film. Once Robert Ardrey had been selected to write the screenplay, Minnelli and producer Pandro Berman set about to find an actress to play Emma. Their first choice, Lana Turner, was rejected by the Breen office because she was perceived as a sex symbol. Breen's representative suggested "an actress with more dignified appeal, like Greer Garson or Jennifer Jones" (Minnelli 202). Berman and Minnelli agreed that the forty-one year-old Garson was wrong for the part; they felt that thirty year-old Jones, properly directed, could succeed in creating a credible Emma, but because she was under contract to her husband, producer David Selznick, MGM had to agree to borrow her and Selznick had to be willing to lend her. A "package deal" was concluded. According to the agreement, MGM would borrow not only Jones, but Louis Jourdan, who would play Rodolphe, and for Léon Dupuis's part, an actor Selznick had brought over from Sweden, Alf Kjellin (rebaptized Christopher Kent by Selznick). Simultaneously, James Mason offered

---

[5] Motion Picture Production Code (Hays Code) of 1930, Article II, preamble.

to play the role of Flaubert in a prologue and an epilogue to the novelistic story proper. Ardrey was assigned to write the extra scenes. Van Heflin, an actor born, like Jennifer Jones, in Oklahoma, was cast as Charles, much to the displeasure of Selznick who thought him too handsome for the part. Minnelli had no similar reservations, knowing Heflin to be a good character actor. The decision to cast as Charles an actor known for his archetypically American good looks, while the two lovers would be played by foreigners, may also have appeased the censors in its association of transgression with the foreign-born (this was after all the era of Communist witch hunts) while at the same time sharpening the opposition between Emma's boredom with the here-and-now and the thrill of her escape into the arms of exotic Others.

Like many of the earlier editions of *Madame Bovary*, which include, as a kind of prologue, a transcript of the famous trial for immorality and irreligion to which the novel, *La Revue de Paris* and its author were subjected in January 1857, Minnelli's adaptation begins with a courtroom scene representing the Madame Bovary trial. In addition, the camera returns to the courtroom after Emma's story has been told. Whatever the primary motivation for accepting James Mason's suggestion that Emma's story be framed with scenes from the trial—certainly, the chance to cast a star as appealing as James Mason was a factor—Minnelli used this device strategically, with a profound understanding of what one might term the censorial spirit. Interestingly, the idea to frame Emma's story, not, as Flaubert had done, with Charles, but rather with allusions to the famous trial during which Flaubert had been accused of "outrage à la morale et à la religion" [offenses against morality and religion] was not altogether original. Carlos Schlieper's Argentine adaptation, released just two years earlier, had used a similar framing device, evoking the trial at the beginning of the film by means of a newspaper headline ("Gustave Flaubert ante la justicia!") [Gustave Flaubert on trial!] and a brief courtroom scene, and returning to the courtroom immediately after Emma kisses the crucifix proffered to her on her deathbed. Although Minnelli does not allude in his autobiography to Schlieper's adaptation, it seems likely that he was familiar with it. However, what in Schlieper were fleeting allusions become in Minnelli's version fully developed scenes—the opening sequence lasts a full five minutes—that constitute a defining structural and narrative device. It is of course true that the courtroom scenes give symmetry to the film and provide the American public with the traditional happy ending they had come to expect of Hollywood films. The adaptation ends, after all, not with Emma's death, but with Flaubert's victory. More importantly, though, by using this frame, Minnelli ensured that the Breen team would not sharpen their scissors on this particular strip of celluloid.

Like Renoir but in a very different manner, Minnelli can thus be said to "frame" Emma. In fact, one might say that there is a triple frame in Minnelli's adaptation, and nowhere more than in this film is Hollywood's predilection for well-defined closure more obvious. The film begins and ends with an intertitle, and if modern cinema theory has it that intertitle cards came into use as a way of compensating for a failure to use more strictly cinematic tools, the practice was still widespread in 1949, when it was not considered a weakness. The opening intertitle reads as follows: "In 1857 there was a scandal in Paris, and a trial before the law. A book had been published." This is complemented, at the film's conclusion, by a slightly longer intertitle, superimposed on the profile of Mason/Flaubert, which announces Flaubert's acquittal. Bracketed in this way, Minnelli's film becomes, not the scandalous story of an adulterous woman, but the more salutary tale of justice served. It is thus not surprising that as the opening intertitle fades, the book, a deluxe edition of *Madame Bovary*, fills the screen. Held aloft by the public prosecutor, who demands "that the publication of this novel be forbidden and that its author, Gustave Flaubert, be found guilty of committing the misdemeanor of an outrage to public morals and established custom," the book is given immediate prominence. Moreover, the fact that it *is* a deluxe edition underscores its status as great literature. Minnelli has time on his side: whereas at the original trial, *Madame Bovary* had not yet been established as a canonical work—indeed, it had not yet been published in volume form—by 1949 few cultured people ignored the existence of Flaubert's classic tale of a deluded woman's inability to accept the humdrum reality of her daily life. Speakers of French may even have known the meaning of the word *bovarysme*, which had made its way into the lexicon as early as 1865. Thus when the public prosecutor, presenting his argument in the most strident terms, refers to Emma as "a disgrace to France and an insult to womanhood... [a] corrupt, loathsome, contemptible creature, [a] woman of insatiable passions, [a] monstrous creation of a degenerate imagination," a sense of the ridiculous must have crept in. The courtroom public, on which the camera focuses periodically, may be convinced—at least initially, before they have heard Flaubert's response—but the people at the movie theater were probably not. During the public prosecutor's impassioned attack, the camera cuts sympathetically to an increasingly discomfited Flaubert who looks to a woman seated behind him for sympathy, only to be greeted by a cold stare. "This is the heroine we are asked to pity, to forgive, why, perhaps even to *love*," concludes the sneering prosecutor. "Gentlemen, nowhere in this entire work does Gustave Flaubert ask us to *blame* Emma Bovary and to find her guilty of her crimes. The State asks you to find Gustave Flaubert guilty of *his*."

The Public Prosecutor's diatribe is pure Minnelli. At the actual trial, the lawyer for the prosecution, Ernest Pinard, had (selectively) summarized the novel, quoting isolated passages to prove that it was dangerous to public morality and insulting to religion. None of the prosecutor's arguments were lost on Minnelli, however, and the film bears witness to the close attention he paid to the accusations.[6] The scenes for which Flaubert was reproached in 1857 have, without exception, been removed or seriously altered by Minnelli. Hence the scene featuring the old Duke de Laverdière, with its allusion to Marie Antoinette, has been edited out. Likewise, the dance with the viscount at the Vaubyessard ball, highly sensualized in the novel and condemned as "obscene" and "perverse" by the prosecutor, is purged of its sexual nature in the film, where the emphasis is on the dizziness experienced by Emma as a result of the whirling and twirling of the dance. The exultant "J'ai un amant!" [I have a lover!] to which Flaubert's prosecutor also objected, is similarly deleted, as we have seen. Ditto for the scene in the carriage with Léon, the scene in which Emma goes to see Bournisien, the priest; and the blind man's song, which, in the novel, serves as an ironic counterpoint to the mumbling of the priest as he administers Extreme Unction. In fact, the blind man is deleted altogether in this version, a deletion that Elizabeth Ladenson attributes to the Code's warning about the treatment of "low, disgusting, and unpleasant" subjects (44). As for the words of the liturgy, rendered only indirectly in the novel, they have been stripped of the sensual allusions one finds in the authorial interventions.

---

[6] For a fascinating analysis of the actual trial and the context of Second Empire censorship in which it occurred, see LaCapra's *Madame Bovary on Trial*.

Flaubert's priest had dipped his thumb into the holy oils and then made the sign of the cross on Emma's eyes,

> qui avaient tant convoité toutes les somptuosités terrestres; puis sur les narines, friandes de brises tièdes et de senteurs amoureuses; puis sur la bouche, qui s'était ouverte pour le mensonge, qui avait gémi d'orgueil et crié dans la luxure; puis sur les mains, qui se délectaient aux contacts suaves, et enfin sur la plante des pieds, si rapides autrefois quand elle courait à l'assouvissement de ses désirs, et qui maintenant ne marcheraient plus. (470)

> [that had coveted earthly luxuries so intensely; then upon the nostrils, that had been so fond of warm breezes and the scents of love; then upon the mouth, that had opened to tell lies, that moaned in pride and cried out in lust; then upon the hands that had taken delight in pleasurable sensations; and finally upon the soles of the feet, so swift when she had hurried to satisfy her desires, and that would now walk no more.]

The magnificent irony of this passage, which uses prayer to evoke the most sensual of pleasures, did not escape the Public Prosecutor, who suspected a blasphemous intention on Flaubert's part. Minnelli, correctly surmising that this scene would attract the wrath of the censors, transposed the indirect style into direct style, using the Catholic Church's Liturgy of the Last Sacrament, with an identical formula for each of the five senses: "Through this holy unction, and through His divine mercy, may the Lord pardon all the sins that you have committed through the sense of sight. Amen."[7] Thanks to the liturgical accuracy of the language and the dignified sobriety of the scene, there is no grist here for the censors' mill.

Having thus responded to all of the objections of the original public prosecutor, and having at the same time directed his cinematic prosecutor to deliver his hyperbolic courtroom speech in a manner that can only be described as shrill and acerbic, Minnelli trains his camera on James Mason who, as Gustave Flaubert, speaks in his own defense. Notwithstanding the director's claim that he and Ardrey "devised the historically accurate courtroom proceedings" (Minnelli 203), those familiar with the actual trial know that Flaubert let his lawyer, M. Sénard, do the talking for him, and that, as Robert Stam observes

---

[7] The Latin is as follows: "Per istam sanctam unctionem et suam piissimam misericordiam, indulgeat tibi Dominus quidquid per (visum, auditum, odoratum, gustum et locutiónem, tactum, gressum deliquisti)."

(*Literature* 166), a large part of Sénard's defense involved establishing the fine character of his client and the respectability of the Flaubert family. His argument also rests on the notion that, in quoting out of context, the Public Prosecutor missed those passages in which religion is exalted, Charles's superiority over Emma is underscored, and Flaubert's discretion in his description of physical intimacies is manifest. "M. Flaubert [...] a fait un livre honnête [et] la pensée de son livre [...], éminemment morale et religieuse, [peut] se traduire par ces mots : l'excitation à la vertu par l'horreur du vice" [Mr. Flaubert has written a good book and the philosophy of his book, eminently moral and religieuse, can be summed up by these words: inciting people to virtue out of horror for vice] ("Réquisitoire" 461). This is Sénard's argument, and one can almost imagine Flaubert squirming in his seat at what appears almost as a suggestion that, far from being banned, this book should be on the required reading list for every young woman!

Of the delicious irony of that courtroom defense, there is no trace in Minnelli's adaptation. The suave, handsome Mason, framed by a window and shot in medium close-up, immediately enlists the sympathy of the film's spectators—if not the courtroom audience—by pointing out that things are never as simple as they seem and that he can neither confirm nor deny the accusations. He does not deny having written the passages the prosecutor has cited (presumably before the concluding arguments with which the film begins); nor does he deny "certain unpleasant facts concerning [the] heroine" which the prosecutor has "summed up...as if he were a schoolboy doing a problem of two and two." This demeaning comparison is followed by a self-promotion: "He has indicted me for the crime of forgiveness. What can I say? Forgiveness is still, as I understand it, among the Christian sentiments." The author that most literary critics know as merciless in his portraits thus becomes the personification of Christian forgiveness! Moreover, the celluloid Flaubert had a clear goal in mind as he wrote *Madame Bovary*, that of showing "the vicious...for the sake of understanding it, so that we may preserve the virtuous." Granted, this argument was tendered by Sénard at the actual trial; however, Minnelli's attribution of such a moralistic intention to the author himself, the same author who insisted that he was writing "un livre sur rien" [a book about nothing] is disingenuous at best.[8] Mason's Flaubert denies the public prosecutor's claim that "Emma Bovary is a monstrous creation of my degenerate imagination" and insists rather that "our world created her" and that "[t]here are thousands of Emma Bovarys who've been saved from her fate, not by virtue, but by lack of determination." Never mind that Mason/Flaubert's statement about "thousands of Emma Bovarys" is a paraphrase, not of any statements made by his lawyer at the trial but rather of a comment made by the historical Flaubert in a letter to Louise Colet in 1853 to the effect that "ma pauvre Bovary, sans doute, souffre et pleure dans vingt villages de France à la fois, à cette heure même" [My poor Madame Bovary is probably suffering and crying in twenty different French villages, at this very moment].[9] The comment provokes chaos in the courtroom and the camera cuts to the crowd who have gotten to their feet and are yelling and gesticulating wildly. A bell is rung to call the courtroom back to order, and at this point the cinematic character played by James Mason becomes the narrator of Emma's story:

> Let me take you back, Gentlemen, not to the passages that the public attorney has read for you; let me take you back to the time when Emma was twenty, and she was still Emma Rouault, and lived on her father's farm, the night when Charles Bovary first met her. See her for the first time as he saw her...

The image of Mason/Flaubert fades from the screen, to be replaced by a medium shot of a man on horseback, arriving at a farm before dawn, a chiaroscuro image accompanied by the clip-clop of the horse's hooves on the rain-slicked cobblestones. Mason's voice, heard now in voiceover, continues, providing the transition between the courtroom frame and the embedded story of Emma Bovary: "Charles Bovary took little notice of the farm. It was rude, substantial, lonely, in a way, miserable. He'd seen hundreds of such farms." Leaving aside the questionable accuracy of the description (in Flaubert the farm is "de bonne apparence" [prosperous-looking] (70), the most important feature of this statement is that it establishes Flaubert/Mason as narrator, more specifically as what Sarah Kozloff (using terms first coined by Gérard Genette) terms "an embedded heterodiegetic

---

[8] For Mario Vargas Llosa's interpretation of Flaubert's statement, see *The Perpetual Orgy*, 40.
[9] Letter to Louise Colet, 14 August 1853. (Flaubert, *Correspondance* II, 392).

narrator," "embedded" because we see the character narrating (at least in the beginning), "heterodiegetic" because he is not a part of the story he is telling (77).

Minnelli makes use of the voiceover technique seven times in the first half of the film, with the lengthiest narrative intervention coming very early, to explain that the source of Emma's misery is her convent education. Following the Vaubyessard ball intervention, there are just two instances of voiceover, once when Emma falls ill after receiving Rodolphe's letter ("Was it sickness? If sickness, was it of the body or of the soul?"), and the other, when Emma dies, to provide the transition back to the courtroom. Renoir, as we saw, had attempted to communicate Emma's thoughts through dialogue, action, and mise-en-scène; there were no flashbacks or voiceovers, and the few intertitles he used were intended to establish time and place. But the novel itself had a prolonged flashback to Emma's convent years, and Flaubert's abundant use of free indirect style and shifting viewpoints made transposition to the screen very challenging. Minnelli's solution was not entirely original: there was precedent for revealing inner states of mind and past events by means of voiceover in cinematic adaptations, but the most notable example, set by Robert Bresson in his adaptation of Bernanos's *Journal d'un curé de campagne*, had featured a first-person narration. Third-person voiceovers were—and remain—more rare. The voiceover technique, as Kozloff tells us, is in a sense the superimposition of the oldest form of narration, oral story-telling, over the newest, that of the cinema. However, because of what Kozloff terms "film scholarship's image bias" (26), there is an unfortunate prejudice against the technique among modern film theorists. Such a prejudice may not have existed in the 1940s, a decade during which many genres (the film noir, semi-documentaries, war films and adaptations of literary works) adopted the technique (Kozloff 37). What is important for us, however, is to understand how the technique widens the distance between film and novel. Quite aside from the conflation of author and narrator, which as Robert Stam notes is in itself problematical (*Literature* 167), Flaubert had taken great pains to remove any hint of a guiding authorial presence from his text. In fact, the impersonal narration that was a hallmark of his style caused considerable displeasure to his contemporaries (Henry James most of all) who regretted that he offered no moral compass to guide his readers. Today, this characteristic, praised by critics, is referred to as the "indeterminacy" of the Flaubertian text. Consider, then, the effect of Minnelli's decision to use Flaubert as narrator of Emma's story. Not only is the author not *absent* from his film, he *tells* the spectator what to think of his heroine and her struggles, much like a Stendhalian narrator, in fact.[10] In the courtroom prologue, he had suggested that Emma's problems were the fault of "our world" and in particular, of her convent education. The fact that Mason's Flaubert concerns himself with the etiology of what he terms Emma's "sickness" supports Cheryl Krueger's claim that he "more often resembles a psychiatrist delivering a case history than an author defending his book" (165). The embedded story becomes the illustration of his thesis.

The first sequence furnishes evidence that Kozloff is correct when she contends that voiceover often serves as a vehicle for irony (110). Having attended to Old Rouault's broken leg, Charles descends the stairs to find Emma at the stove preparing an omelet for him. She is wearing an elegant white gown with a fitted bodice and a layered, flouncy skirt, a costume more reminiscent of the attire that Scarlet O'Hara wore in the 1939 production of *Gone With the Wind* than of something one might have expected to see on a Norman farm girl, and indeed, it is not by chance that Walter Plunkett designed the costumes for both, creating for Emma a wardrobe that is extravagant and not a little incongruous (figure 3).[11] Eager to please the young doctor, Emma has spared no effort, and Charles's reaction testifies at once to her success and to his clumsiness: "Mademoiselle, I've come into many a farmhouse kitchen at dawn; I've smelled sour milk, children's vomit...but I've never smelled perfume before." Despite his lack of finesse, Emma is smitten and when he leaves, she leans against the door, smiling dreamily, then rushes up the stairs to her room where she gazes happily out her window. It is over these images of the beautifully radiant Jennifer Jones that we hear Mason's voice:

> Here gentlemen, is the monster; here is the corrupt and loathsome
> creature. Here is the disgrace to France and the insult to womanhood,

---

[10] Stam (*Literature* 167) is reminded of Balzac, but the balzacian narrator is more likely to make generalizations about his characters' conduct, whereas Stendhal's narrators, more personal, seem to me to be closer to the Flaubert/Mason narrator created by Minnelli.

[11] There is incongruity in the dress described by Flaubert as well, for although it is made of coarse wool, it has three flounces, evoking Emma's pretension.

Emma Rouault, the flower beyond the dung hill. How had she grown here, the kitchen drudge who dreamed of love and beauty? What are dreams made of? Where do they come from?

The Prosecutor's epithets, repeated by Mason's Flaubert in voiceover, are now imbued with the irony that results when there is a discrepancy between the image track and the soundtrack. The rhetorical questions

Figure 3. Minnelli's *Madame Bovary* (1949).

are answered by the camera, which pans right to reveal the walls of Emma's room, covered with pictures cut out from fashion magazines, engravings torn from sentimental novels. "The kitchen drudge who dreamed of love and beauty"—a description that would be more befitting of Cinderella than Emma Bovary—has read too much fiction. But this is only one of the reasons for Emma's delusions. The voiceover continues, informing spectators that Emma had spent several years in a convent, where "the discipline, the dreadful conformity, the eternal uniform when a girl's young body is budding" had the opposite of the intended effect, driving Emma "to dream...to live within herself." In this flashback, the camera moves from shots of Emma at the piano, practicing scales, to the old seamstress, secretly lending romantic novels to the schoolgirls, finally, to a shot of Emma reading Mérimée's "Carmen"—a patent allusion to the Femme Fatale. We are told that Emma had learned to believe in "happiness, passion, high romance." Then, the convent scene fades and is replaced by a farm scene in which Emma is tilling the garden and tossing potatoes into a basket. The voiceover explains:

> Emma returned to the farm. Had she been a normal girl, her dream might likewise have ended. But in Emma there was a terrifying capacity for pursuing the impossible. The dream did not end.

The camera cuts back to Emma's room and again pans the wall, as the voiceover continues:

> Here, in these books, in these pictures, we had taught her that the strange was beautiful and the familiar contemptible, we had taught her to find glamour, excitement, in the faraway and only boredom in the here and now. We had taught her—what?—to believe in Cinderella, and now, here this morning, Charles Bovary. Emma Bovary, you cannot know, he is not Prince Charming, he is only a man.

Here, the narrator addresses Emma directly, as if he were occupying the same diegetic space she is. The tone is sympathetic, almost contrite: we in our society, we who send nubile adolescent girls to convent schools and publish books and magazines that nourish their illusions—we alone are responsible for the fate of this gullible young woman who is unable to distinguish between dreams and reality. Jennifer Jones's Emma, with her wide eyes, her naiveté, and her breathless eagerness to impress Charles, inspires interest and sympathy, sentiments intensified during the wedding scene when the beautiful young bride in her immaculate wedding dress falls victim to the aggressive, vulgar behavior of some drunken guests. The voiceover returns to help us to interpret this scene, then again after the wedding night, over an image of Emma standing, disconsolate, at a curtained window, to ask "Could it have been otherwise? She had wept no doubt in the early morning hours. Was Emma the first bride to weep while the bridegroom slept?" Emma wakes Charles to tell him that she is "going to make [him] the most beautiful home in Yonville, this side of Rouen, this side of Paris," and the narrator interjects, "New dreams for old: could this morning have been otherwise?"

It is at this point in the film that Emma's character begins to change. Presented until now as a passive victim of her upbringing, she becomes more active, more vocal, flirting with Léon, spending money frivolously and without her husband's knowledge, bursting into tears at the slightest provocation, making demands. Whereas Flaubert's Emma simply discovers one day that she is pregnant, the cinematic Emma *decides* to have a baby:

> Charles, I want a child. I want a boy, Charles. A boy grows to be a man. A man can be free. If he doesn't like his life, he can change it. If there's anything beautiful, if there's anything grand anywhere out in the world, he can find it.

As the camera pans right across the walls of the attic, covered with the images that had adorned Emma's bedroom at Les Bertaux, the narration, now terser, continues: "New dreams for old." The scene fades, to be replaced by a shot of Emma in bed. She has just given birth, and over an image of the doctor slapping the baby's bottom, we hear, "The dark hours of a woman's life when old dreams perish and new dreams are born." We recognize Charles who, taking the baby to his wife, declares, "Emma, it's a girl." And again Flaubert/Mason intones, "The dark hours, when new dreams perish."

The pattern has been set. From this point on, Emma's life will be defined by a series of dreams and their inevitable disappointments. Her background having been established, there is no longer any need for the sympathetic narrator. The effect of this waning of the narrative voiceover is powerful. Emma, no longer mediated, can be judged solely on the basis of her words and actions,[12] and while it is true, as Judith Mayne astutely observes, that "Flaubert's [...] function as narrator is effectively dispersed, displaced onto other characters in the film" (110), Emma's behavior speaks more loudly than any of the uncharitable remarks that are made about her by the other characters. Coquettish, spoiled, capricious, demanding, neurotic, she gradually loses the spectator's unadulterated sympathy.[13] Minnelli's genius—to have secured the spectator's esteem for the author and his work while

---

[12] See Stern (64) for a complementary interpretation of this fading of the voiceover narration.

[13] Elizabeth Ladenson goes so far as to see a certain "masculinity" in Jones's Emma, evoking Baudelaire's comments on the androgynous nature of Flaubert's character. Ladenson points out that "attributes traditionally viewed as feminine (e.g. manipulativeness, seductiveness, and vanity), when pushed to a certain point become figured as a masculine will to dominate." (40)

simultaneously provoking a disdainful pity for his heroine—was a powerful weapon against the Code.[14] In the film's final voiceover, Flaubert/Mason maintains that "there is truth in [Emma's] story, and ... a morality that has no room for truth is no morality at all." The white-on-black intertitle that follows this narrative intervention proclaims over an image of James Mason that "Gustave Flaubert's acquittal, almost a century ago, was a triumphant moment in the history of the free mind. His masterpiece, *Madame Bovary*, became a part of our heritage to live—like truth itself—forever" (figure 4).

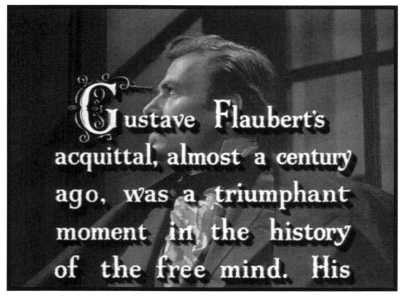

Figure 4. Minnelli's *Madame Bovary* (1949).

Minnelli thus cleverly shamed the censors into giving the film their stamp of approval, for who would want to be associated with the losing prosecution team? Who, in the name of a loosely defined "morality," would want to suppress the truth?

---

[14] Robert Stam recognizes this discrepancy between the way Mason's Flaubert "defends" Emma from her accusers and the way she is represented in the film which "renders a rather ambivalent, and often harsh, judgment on the heroine," but he regards it as paradoxical (*Literature* 167).

But the framing device by itself would not have been enough to win official approval to release the film. According to Minnelli, the censors objected to nearly every scene with sexual content. Even the scene in which Emma licks the inside of her glass to get the last drop of liqueur from it was forbidden as too sensual. Indeed, one can detect the censors' influence throughout the film, both in the descriptive details and the dialogue, the characterizations and certain plot excisions. While it would be useful to both film historians and cultural historians to know whether the alterations resulted from self-censorship or from actual requests on the part of the censors, the end result, for better or for worse, was that many overly explicit sensual details were sacrificed on the altar of late-1940s standards of propriety. In the scene of Emma's first adultery, we see Emma and Rodolphe riding through the woods, two small figures against the grandeur of the landscape. With a great swell of waltz music—the same music that Emma had danced to at the Vaubyessard Ball—the scene dissolves and treetops come into focus. The camera slowly tilts downward, first bringing two tethered horses into frame as they wait patiently for their riders, and then, continuing its downward journey, stopping at the ground, where a lady's hat and a riding crop lie abandoned. The extra-diegetic music leaves little doubt as to what has occurred, but what is most striking about this scene—aside from its conventional occulting of the erotic—is its intertextual allusion to Renoir. In Renoir's adaptation, the camera had tilted *upwards* in this scene, panning right through the trees in a low-angle shot. Flaubert's Emma, returning home after this first fall, escapes quickly to her bedroom where she sits down before the mirror, finding herself transfigured. She repeats to herself, "J'ai un amant! un amant!" [I have a lover! a lover!] and is entranced by the idea of her new identity as someone's mistress. Her thoughts are rendered in free indirect style:

> Elle allait donc posséder enfin ces joies de l'amour, cette fièvre du bonheur dont elle avait désespéré. Elle entrait dans quelque chose de merveilleux où tout serait passion, extase, délire [...] (266).

> [She was finally going to possess those joys of love, that delirium of happiness that she had despaired of ever knowing. She was entering a marvelous realm where everything would be passion, ecstasy, rapture.]

In the context of Emma's eventual fate, such statements are imbued with a strong irony typical of Flaubert. In the transposition to the screen, however, Emma's illusion that marital infidelity could bring happiness has to remain implicit. Quite apart from the difficulty of rendering thought on screen, such a positive representation of adultery would never have escaped the censors' scissors. Eliminating even Emma's ecstatic "I have a lover! a lover!", Minnelli must be content to simply have her look at herself dreamily in the mirror, and this is what he does. Nor does he show Emma in bed, with Charles or with either of her lovers. The scene at Rouen Cathedral, which in Flaubert functions as "un boudoir gigantesque" [a gigantic boudoir] (366) is elided (insulting to religion), as is the carriage ride with Léon (too suggestive). Rather, Minnelli's Emma finally falls into Léon's arms in a squalid Rouen hotel room, and even she begins to realize her degradation: "A horrid little rendezvous in a horrid little hotel. Is this what you think I am?" Her lucidity may be fleeting, but the spectators seize the message. This is just one of several scarcely subtle allusions to prostitution that must have been designed to appease the censors who would have approved of the association of adultery and venal love. It is hardly by chance that the room Léon eventually finds for their weekly trysts is decorated in the style of a bordello (Léon apologizes for having been reduced to renting a room that is "hardly in the best of taste," but Emma, confirming the view that Minnelli feels compelled to give of her, retorts, "I love it!"). However, perhaps the film's most overt allusion to prostitution occurs when Lheureux takes it upon himself to scold Emma:

> I've tolerated your conduct for too long. The things I have witnessed—the cheating, the lying, the insatiable greed; what iniquities, what sordid passions; your child and your husband deceived, all morals abandoned, every loyalty foresworn while you indulged yourself with any man that came your way...

Sick with anguish, Emma hardly notices Lheureux's hyperbole. She begins to protest feebly, only to be slapped with the cruelest insult of all: "I am in the business of making money, Madame Bovary, a recognized, honorable profession which I am confident bears public comparison with yours." Lheureux's patent allusion to Emma's venality is Minnelli's invention. Indeed, Flaubert's Emma is prodigally generous with her lovers, never asks them for money until she is ruined, and reacts with indignation to the scurrilous bargain that Guillaumin tries to strike with her ("Je suis à plaindre mais pas à vendre!" [I am to be pitied, but I'm not for sale!] (445), a sentence that Minnelli must suppress for the sake of consistency. It is true that Flaubert evokes the specter of prostitution when Emma goes in search of Rodolphe's help ("Elle partit donc vers la Huchette, sans s'apercevoir qu'elle courait s'offrir à ce qui l'avait tantôt si fort exaspérée, ni se douter le moins du monde de cette prostitution" [So she set off towards La Huchette, without even realizing that she was now eager to strike the same bargain that had so exasperated her just a little while earlier, and completely unconscious of her prostitution] (451). However, in Minnelli, the theme attains the status of a leitmotif. The discerning spectator, of course, may question the validity of criticism that comes from a character as unsavory as the usually unctuous "scoundrel" Lheureux, but his moralistic diatribe, on top of the other allusions to Emma's identity as a woman of easy virtue ("I find it fascinating! Who would have guessed it? Our own Madame Bovary!" gushes Minnelli's lascivious Guillaumin), clearly sufficed to satisfy the censors that the "immorality" of Emma's actions was being adequately represented. In tandem with the allusions to prostitution, Minnelli's version emphasizes Emma's capriciousness, her extreme narcissism, and her manipulative nature. It is she, more than Homais, who works to persuade a reluctant Charles to perform the clubfoot operation, and when he scoffs at the idea, she gives him a withering look and asks, "Do you want me to love you or don't you?" The ultimatum is worthy of a petulant child, and in fact, Jennifer Jones's Emma is just that.

To complement the demonization of Emma, Minnelli's adaptation exonerates nearly every character who, in the novel, shares responsibility for her fate, with the possible exception of Lheureux. Flaubert's irremediably mediocre Charles, clueless about the role he is inadvertently playing in his wife's misery, is hardly recognizable in Van Heflin's portrayal. Like Renoir, Minnelli eliminates the whole of the first chapter which, in the novel, establishes Charles's lack of intelligence. Minnelli's Charles may have only a modest reputation as a country doctor, but he is fully aware of his limitations.[15] When he

---

[15] Because the French two-tiered system of medical education had no American equivalent, Minnelli has rendered "health officer" as "country doctor." Fywell will do the same. Today we would probably use the term "paramedic."

proposes to Emma (and he does so directly, for this Charles, less timid than his novelistic counterpart, does not need an intermediary), he tells her that he is "not a very good doctor" and will be "lucky [to] make a living." He insists that he is "easy to get along with and [will] be a good husband," but acknowledges that he is "not very exciting." Furthermore, Charles's lucidity extends to Emma's unhappiness, and although he doesn't fully comprehend its source, he has no illusions about her state of mind. Shortly after the Vaubyessard Ball, when a disconsolate Emma expresses her boredom with the tedious regularity of small town life, Charles says, "I wish I were clever. If I were clever, perhaps I could understand you. If I could understand you, perhaps I could help you. I love you so much, Emma." Flaubert's Emma, who would have fallen into her husband's arms if he had shown this degree of sensitivity, "si son regard, une seule fois, fût venu à la rencontre de sa pensée" [if his eyes, just once, had read her thoughts] (106), would have perhaps even respected Van Heflin's Charles who, notwithstanding his sympathy for his wife, is competent enough as a medical professional to sense that for a country doctor to attempt to correct a clubfoot in this pre-pasteurian era "would be butchery" (something that Flaubert's Charles should have known as well, for in France health officers were forbidden from performing such surgery). Although he initially agrees under duress to perform the operation, he cannot go through with it, in a scene which is the single most important departure from the novel. When Hippolyte, strapped to the gurney, reaches for his hand and says, echoing Homais's promises, "I can dance with the girls," Charles throws down his scalpel and unbuckles the patient. He lucidly assesses the situation: "I'm a blunderer all right, and I'll not make him or anyone else the victim of my blunders." Here again, incidentally, we have an inversion of a scene from Renoir. In the earlier version, Hippolyte kisses Charles's hand after the surgery; in Minnelli's, it is when Hippolyte touches Charles's hand that the health officer realizes he *cannot* in good conscience perform the operation.

Minnelli decided against the operation because he felt that "this sequence [the failed operation, the gangrene, and the amputation] would be too gory to be shown" (Minnelli 206). Intimidated once again by the Code, which forbade the showing of what it termed "repellent subjects," a list of which included surgical operations (MPPC, XII), Minnelli reasoned that the "ensuing shame and sense of failure Emma felt could still be shown if Charles, realizing his limitations, refuses to perform the operation at the last moment" (206). Julian Barnes believes that this "adjustment" was dictated by Hollywood's reluctance to "disenchant popcorn-munchers who place their faith in the medical profession" (262). In Barnes's view, Minnelli had to resolve the problem of how to retain the spectators' sympathy for both Charles and Emma, while respecting the laws of causality so important to Hollywood cinema. We pity Charles because he does not deserve the villagers' scorn; we sympathize with Emma, because "everyone can understand how you might be driven to a bit on the side if your husband turns out to be a low-achieving wimp" (Barnes 263).

Although I do not believe that Van Heflin's Charles is a "wimp"—my opinion is closer to that of Robert Stam, who believes he has been subjected to a "patriarchal upgrading" (*Literature* 174)—I do concur with Barnes about the importance of industry imperatives. Whereas Flaubert's narrative strategies keep readers at a distance, Hollywood cannot finance its expensive productions unless it draws spectators into the drama. However, what Barnes and for that matter, Stam, fail to mention is that, under threat of censorship, Minnelli *cannot* diminish Charles to the extent that Flaubert does, for to do so would be to imply that he deserved to be cuckolded.[16] The self-deprecating humor that makes the cinematic Charles so likable, utterly lacking in Flaubert's character, is also motivated by the wish to avoid censorship. "It isn't often that I have the pleasure of murdering such a distinguished patient," Charles tells the Marquis de la Vaubyessard. And, when Léon suggests that he stay an extra night in Rouen to see the final act of *Lucie de Lammermoor*, he protests that he cannot, because "all my patients are waiting for me to get back so that they can die." Nor is he oblivious to his wife's betrayals. When Emma returns home for the last time, after her failed attempt to extract money from Rodolphe and her desperate ingestion of Homais's arsenic, he attempts to show her the auction notice, and then, confronted with her apparent indifference, slaps her across the face. "Come to your senses!" he says sharply. "I'm not going to ask you where you've been; I *know* where you've been. I'm not going to ask you where you were in Rouen; I can guess where you were in Rouen." Charles's growing awareness of Emma's infidelities is also

---

[16] Elizabeth Ladenson makes this point as well (*Dirt for Art's Sake*, 41).

accompanied by a deepening understanding of her illusions. "This is storybook," he had mumbled earlier, when Emma attempted to explain her feelings: "I know you love me; I know you're good to me. Oh I'd rather that you were worthless and dashing and brutal and that you'd strike any man who looked at me." So as not to present Charles in a wholly positive light, Minnelli allows the spectator to see him not only through Emma's eyes but through the critical eyes of other characters as well. The old cleaning woman at the Rouault farm is skeptical about his medical competence, if for the wrong reasons (his youth and his lack of a beard strike her as incongruous for a doctor). Léon's mother laments that Charles is "not brilliant, but then if he were brilliant he'd leave for Paris, and who would stay in Yonville and look after simple people like me?" Homais's expression when Emma tells him that Charles will perform the clubfoot operation betrays lack of confidence in Charles's ability. And Lheureux, finally, tells Emma flatly that her husband "is not a clever man." Charles's words, too, sometimes reveal his lack of intelligence and refinement. In a sentence adapted from the novel, he insists that he would like the opera (*Lucie de Lammermoor*) "if it weren't for the music."[17] However, the only actual weakness that one might attribute to his character is his lack of abstemiousness. Charles overindulges in alcohol on at least four occasions in the film, and at the Vaubyessard ball, he becomes so totally inebriated that he embarrasses his wife, stumbling onto the dance floor and attempting to cut in as she dances with the viscount.[18] It is in the very next scene that we see the couple leaving the château in their carriage, with Emma holding the reins. This scene, too, evokes Renoir, but whereas in Renoir's version, Charles's masculinity seems called into question when he allows his wife to drive the carriage, in Minnelli's film, one assumes that Emma controls the reins because Charles's drunkenness—admittedly, a form of impotence in its own right—renders him incapable of doing so.

---

[17] The sentence from the novel reads as follows: "Il avouait, du reste, ne pas comprendre l'histoire,—à cause de la musique—qui nuisait beaucoup aux paroles" [What's more, he confessed that he didn't understand the story very well because of the music, which really spoiled the words.] (344)

[18] The other occasions on which we see Van Heflin's Charles drinking alcohol are during a reconnoitering trip to Yonville (a scene added by Minnelli), during a dinner table scene with Emma, and after the opera, with Emma and Léon. Flaubert's Charles, the son of a heavy drinker, is criticized by his mother and his first wife for offering a drink to everyone who stops by.

Given that there is no allusion in Flaubert to any alcoholic tendencies on Charles's part, one might wonder why Minnelli felt compelled to make of Charles a "problem drinker." The Code forbade the showing of "the use of liquor in American life, when not required by the plot or for proper characterization" [MPPC I, 4]. Was it because this tale was set in nineteenth-century France that the director decided to add a cultural footnote of his own, further placating the censors by suggesting that the stereotypically French fondness for wine has its risks? Or was it simply an effort to deliver the message that abuse of alcohol leads to ridicule? In either case, Charles's alcoholic tendencies do not entirely remove the sting from Emma's betrayal, but they might have consoled those moralistic spectators who would otherwise have found it impossible to rationalize his victimization. Perhaps the decision was a more practical one: Van Heflin had already earned his credentials as a drunk in *Johnny Eager* (1941). Whatever the case, his drunkenness in the role of Charles is presented as mildly amusing rather than obnoxious, and it does not lessen the spectators' sympathy for him. As Emma's life draws to a close, the camera lovingly focuses on Charles in close-ups that capture the tears glistening in his eyes, and there can be no doubt about which character the spectators are expected to pity.

Emma's lovers, less innocent than Charles, are nevertheless far more engaging in Minnelli's film than they are in the novel. Flaubert's callous Rodolphe is hardly recognizable in Louis Jourdan, the archetypally suave Frenchman in Hollywood movies, whose Rodolphe is also the viscount with whom Emma had danced at the Vaubyessard Ball. Minnelli's decision to conflate the two characters—a decision that earned a sneering indictment from Chabrol—further romanticizes a character who is presented as sensitive and caring.[19] It is, of course, obvious that Rodolphe is a seasoned playboy, and his verbal seduction of Emma is as glib and hackneyed as that of his literary counterpart ("This face that haunts me, drugs me...these hands that were designed for a thousand pleasures, these lips..."). In fact, Minnelli uses a

---

[19] In an interview with François Guérif, Chabrol commented that it was essential for Emma to meet Rodolphe while his servant was being bled, "dans le sordide, avec une saignée, pas dans un bal" [in a sordid way, with a bloodletting, not at a ball]. *Conversations avec Claude Chabrol: un Jardin bien à moi*, 208. Chabrol's disdain for this conflation may also stem from the fact that Flaubert's novel makes it quite clear that Rodolphe is not truly noble.

technique similar to the one used in the novel in order to mock Rodolphe, cutting back and forth between the lover's romantic discourse and the deputy's patriotic platitudes at the agricultural fair. If the evocation of manure, which comes straight from the novel ("fumiers" [manures], 248), is clearly a double-entendre, intending to allude to the insincerity of Rodophe's words, other suggestive phrases from the municipal official's speech almost certainly eluded the censors. An off-screen voice drones on about "the welfare of the seaman" just before Emma and Rodolphe arrive in the empty room next to the stage. How many alert spectators would fail to seize the screenwriter's pun? Similarly, when the deputy continues by evoking "the broad hands of the agriculturalist....sowing his seed, reaping his harvest" at the very moment when Rodolphe begins to seduce Emma, looking at her tenderly, fingering her blouse, Minnelli's metaphoric jab in the ribs is unmistakable. In most of his other appearances, however, Rodolphe's behavior elicits sympathy. During one of Emma's visits to La Huchette, he confesses his love to her in a way that leaves no doubt about his honesty:

> I'm in love. Like a silly schoolboy, I'm falling in love. That this should have happened to me! I'm bewitched...I'm losing my interest in pheasants. [...] I'm losing my senses....me! My house—you know every corner of it as if it were yours. I detest this intrusion. I adore my bachelor privacy...but I adore you more.

As testimony to the sincerity of this declaration of love, Rodolphe empties a drawer full of his old love letters into the fire in Emma's presence. Extra-diegetic music again floods the screen, accompanying this sacrificial act: should we be surprised to recognize once again the waltz music from La Vaubyessard, the same music that overlaid the seduction scene in the woods? As for Rodolphe's cowardly "betrayal" when he refuses to take Emma away with him to Italy as she desires, it is cleverly downplayed, since the emphasis throughout is on Emma and we do not see her lover penning the treasonous letter with its phony tear stains. Rather, in the last conversation they have before the planned departure, Rodolphe tries to reason with Emma. "Your child...This is where dreams leave off, Emma. We couldn't take her with us." Emma's reply is Minnelli's ultimate indictment of her, for she is not only an adulterous wife, but an unnatural mother as well: "I know. How long can I pretend that I have any right to her? I lost her,

Rodolphe; I lost her to Charles; I've even lost her to my servant."
Emma is referring to Berthe's dislike for her, a dislike underscored in
the film's several scenes in which Emma attempts to pick up the
toddler. The child screams each time, and Emma must return her to
her servant, Félicité.

One of the more arresting anecdotes of Minnelli's
autobiography concerns these episodes. In an era when child actors
and actresses were not protected from psychological and physical
abuse as they are today, Jennifer Jones was directed to incur the
child's wrath off-screen by taking away her favorite red shoes. The
strategy was successful until the deathbed scene had to be filmed, a
scene during which the child was to stretch out her arms to her
mother. While in modern times, the problem could have been avoided
by shooting the deathbed scene first, scenes were shot sequentially in
the 1940s, and it took a full day of cajoling—and of course the return
of the red shoes—before Jones was able to overcome the child's
antipathy.   Considerable effort was thus expended in an effort to
portray Emma Bovary as an unworthy mother.

Minnelli's focus on Emma's maternal deficiencies mitigated the
cowardly nature of Rodolphe's behavior. The scene following
Emma's dialogue with Rodolphe—during which, incidentally, the
latter makes no promises—takes place in Lheureux's shop, where an
imperious Emma is ordering the items she will need for the voyage.
When this scene fades, it is replaced by a nocturnal scene that features
Emma and Lheureux waiting for Rodolphe outside Lheureux's shop.
Here, Minnelli has reversed the chronology of two scenes, for in the
adaptation, it is only *after* the carriage passes by at a gallop that
Emma, totally bereft, returns home to find the basket of fruit and the
explanatory note. Significantly, when she runs to the attic and leans
out the window, suddenly beset by a suicidal impulse, it is Charles
who rushes in to save her, whereas in both the novel and in Renoir's
adaptation, Félicité is the one who finds her at the attic window. Van
Heflin's Charles may not win the medal of the Legion of Honor, but
his heroism is visible to everyone but Emma.

As in Flaubert, we do not encounter Rodolphe again until
Emma hurries to La Huchette in a final, desperate effort to get the
money she needs to prevent the seizure and auction of her possessions.
In the novel, Rodolphe tells Emma that she has not changed, that she
is "toujours charmante" [as charming as ever] (452). "Tristes charmes,

mon ami," replies Emma, "puisque vous les avez dédaignés" [My
charms! They can't be worth much, since you rejected them].
Minnelli's Rodolphe, more discriminating, notices that Emma is in
distress despite the time she has taken to make herself up before this
last, futile visit ("You're pale. Those lines around your eyes...I don't
remember them"). Moreover, he's still in love with her. Whereas
Flaubert is at pains to tell us that Rodolphe does not recognize the
sincerity of Emma's protestations of love beneath their banal
expression which he has heard countless times previously, for
Jourdan's Rodolphe, Emma is unique. "Surely other women have
seduced you," teases Emma as she attempts to prostitute herself. "Fair
enough," replies Rodolphe. "I just don't happen to remember you in
terms of other women." This stress on his genuine love for Emma is
diametrically opposed to the emphasis of the novel, which presents
Rodolphe as a hardened Don Juan. When the cinematic Emma asks
Rodolphe why he didn't take her with him to Italy, he replies, "I'm a
fairly courageous man, Emma, but I was afraid of you." Following
Emma's confession that she "asked for too much," Rodolphe declares
grimly: "You asked for something that consumes as it burns, that
destroys everything it touches; I didn't want to be destroyed." The
novelistic Rodolphe had apologized "en termes vagues, faute de
pouvoir inventer mieux" [in vague terms, being unable to come up
with something specific] (452). In replacing indirect speech by direct
speech for the film, Robert Ardrey changes Rodolphe's character. No
longer the impenitent playboy who abandoned Emma with scarcely a
regret when she became too demanding and then, confronted with the
wronged woman, proffered banal and unconvincing reasons for his
cowardly behavior, Jourdan's Rodolphe remains smitten with Charles
Bovary's wife, and his moving explanation for his action has a ring of
authenticity: he realized that he could not satisfy her desires without
becoming her victim. In this scenario, Emma becomes the archetypal
Femme Fatale, a dangerous animal who uses her charms to lure men
into her lair. It is perhaps no coincidence that Minnelli shot *Madame
Bovary* during a decade that saw the birth of a genre in which the Fatal
Woman was a stock character, the *film noir*.[20] Accustomed to the

---

[20] For more on the *film noir*, see *The Film Studies Dictionary*, Steve Blandford, Barry
Keithgrant and Jim Hillier. Interestingly, in the entry for Jennifer Jones in the
Biographical Dictionary of Film, one reads that "it seems odd in hindsight that her

convention, 1949 spectators could have been expected to share Rodolphe's perspective, all the more so because in this scene in particular Jennifer Jones's Emma is manipulative, flirtatious and conniving. Moreover, although Minnelli frames this scene in such a way that the spectator can see all of the luxury of Rodolphe's apartment—the riding crops, the framed portraits, the candelabras, a sculpture, a blazing fire—he abbreviates Emma's diatribe, eliminating references to the numerous trinkets that Rodolphe could pawn in order to come to her aid. Thus, whereas in the novel and in Renoir's adaptation, which follows the novel very closely here, Emma's words tend to underscore the disingenuous nature of Rodolphe's contention that he does not have the means to help her, Minnelli's version places the emphasis rather on Emma's histrionics and does not ask the spectator to question Rodolphe's excuse for denying her request for money.

The hapless young Léon is presented as Emma's victim in Minnelli's adaptation. Sent to Paris by his domineering mother who has become aware of her son's infatuation with the doctor's wife and wishes to remove him from a compromising situation, Léon is too weak to protest. Later, when he becomes involved with Emma and misses work several days in a row so that he might spend time with her, he feigns illness to explain his absence, but his employer is unimpressed. "Dupuis! Tell the woman 'goodbye,'" he barks. A dissolve connects this shot with the next, which shows the corridor outside the hotel room. Léon arrives in full legal garb, hesitating before entering the room and thereby leading the spectator to believe that he has come to end their affair. He does not do so—perhaps out of cowardice?—but he bears other bad news: the property Charles inherited upon his father's death is worthless: "We've had endless conferences, my partners and I. They're very conservative men, of course, but they agree, the estate isn't worth anything." When Léon and Emma leave the furnished room sometime later to "subdue [their] sorrows with wine and music," they come upon Lheureux who tips his hat to greet them and then begins to walk across the square as the camera tracks back to follow him, then tilts down to focus on his legs in a medium close-up. An ominous drumbeat marks each step he

---

dark looks and her real experience as femme fatale and harassed woman never graced a film noir" (379).

takes, an appropriate musical accompaniment for this man who will
become the instrument of Emma's destiny. The scene is followed by
Emma's attempts to negotiate, first with Lheureux, then with
Guillaumin. Having failed in both efforts, she turns to Léon, and it is
in the course of this encounter, when she asks him for fifteen thousand
francs ("a fortune to me, but to you, with all your connections and all
your success...") that he laughs bitterly and confesses the truth about
his aborted legal career:

> I'm still a clerk. I've lied to you. I'm still a stupid little clerk, sitting
> on a high stupid stool that I'll never get off till the day I die. All my
> success...I failed in Yonville. I failed in Paris. Now I can't even
> succeed in pretending that I am what I'm not.

Although Minnelli does not suggest that Emma is responsible for
Léon's failed career, it is obvious that his relationship with her has
been damaging. Hence once again, Emma is positioned, not as victim,
but as victimizer. The boyish Christopher Kent, playful, charming,
with just the hint of a foreign accent, plays a lover who is sincere but
of weak character. The decision to endow him, rather than Charles,
with an authoritarian mother is significant, and even though Madame
Dupuis appears in only one scene, her interaction with her son is
sufficient to define the latter as a helpless momma's boy. Charles, on
the other hand, is independent. Not only has the elder Madame Bovary
been omitted from the film, but his first wife has also been cut;
indeed, he states at the outset that he has no wife. Whereas Renoir's
version, following the novel, had used these women to emphasize
Charles's docility and to underscore the plight of the married woman
in nineteenth-century France (Emma, being the third Madame Bovary
to be presented in the novel, has no identity separate from her
husband), there is no such subtext in Minnelli's version. Whatever
excuses James Mason's Flaubert may have given for Emma's conduct
in the film's early voiceovers, the conduct of the character on screen
leaves the spectator increasingly cold, and this is the way it had to be
in 1949.

The oppressive influence of the censors is thus key to
understanding Minnelli's *Madame Bovary*, something of which many
of the film's critics appear to have been unaware. For example, while
in his book, *The Novel and the Cinema*, Geoffrey Wagner—not
altogether wrongly—refers to this version as a "child's colour-book of

adultery, as seen through 'emancipated' American eyes," he fails to account correctly for the motivation behind the production (252). Hence his criticism of Minnelli's decision to conclude with what he terms "a few gratuitous platitudes from James Mason" (254) betrays his lack of appreciation for Minnelli's constraints. Similarly, while Wagner is certainly correct in emphasizing the shaping power of commercial concerns (particularly with regard to characterization), some of his complaints neglect to take into account certain economic realities. Minnelli's Yonville is "a charming French village," not necessarily because this is what the 1949 American moviegoers wanted to see, but rather because the filming took place on MGM's back lot where it was difficult to produce "a town of excruciating Norman boredom, surrounded by long flat empty fields" (255). The critic Michael A. Williams, for his part, believes that Minnelli "tends to romanticize the story, even sentimentalize it, making Emma a much more sympathetic heroine than seems to be the case in Flaubert's text" ("The Director's Eye" n.pag). Williams contrasts Minnelli's adaptation with Chabrol's, and while there is no doubt that the 1949 version is romanticized, in typical Hollywood fashion, Emma's "sympathetic" nature appears to be in the eye of this particular beholder. Stephen Harvey's assessment is perhaps more accurate. Harvey believes that Minnelli has an "ambivalent take" on Flaubert's heroine, "sympathizing with her needs, deploring her self-absorption" (205), and thus that "her example affirms no neatly packaged moral lesson of the sort the Production Code insisted on." In my opinion, this ambiguity results from a disjunction between the Emma presented in the narratorial voiceover, a pathetic victim of delusions for which society is responsible, and the considerably less likable character played by the flamboyant Jennifer Jones, whose words and actions betray a spiraling plunge into the most abject narcissism. Minnelli has managed to have it both ways: he has tweaked the character of Flaubert's heroine just enough to satisfy the guardians of morality and to please the spectators of his era, with their taste for drama and beauty.

What is truly remarkable is that Minnelli has succeeded in making such a memorable film, even within the considerable constraints imposed upon him. Far from being limited to dialogue, structure and character portrayal, Minnelli's originality encompassed nearly every aspect of the film-making enterprise. His mise-en-scène was particularly notable. Like Renoir, the Hollywood director made abundant use of symbolism, and it has been said that "an ethos central to Minnelli's entire œuvre [is] that no visual detail is ever too trivial to matter" (Harvey 16). While Renoir's version made use of bucolic scenes with grazing cows, Minnelli's adaptation features birds in a symbolic role. Is it by chance that in her first encounter with Lheureux, Emma is attracted to a tapestry with a bird motif? Or that the stunning gown she wears to the Vaubyessard ball has a branch embroidered across the bodice, with a bird perched just where fabric meets skin, as if to take flight? An emblem perhaps of her own volatile nature and her longing to be free, the bird is transformed in the end into a symbol of confinement, as we see a parrot fluttering in a small cage in Guillaumin's apartment. One might even interpret this as a directorial wink, an allusion that only connaisseurs of Flaubert would recognize, although in the absence of proof that Minnelli himself knew Flaubert well, such an interpretation would have to remain speculative.

Another metaphor—one that is present in the novel and in Renoir's adaptation, although Minnelli appears to extend it—is that of the mirror, an unsurprising prop in a narrative that treats of narcissism. When Emma gazes at her reflection in the mirror after her first amorous escapade with Rodolphe, she likes what she sees. The ornate oval looking glass at the Vaubyessard ball, similarly, sends back a flattering image, as she catches a glimpse of herself surrounded by potential suitors. The cracked mirror in the sinister hotel room in Rouen, on the other hand, reflects Emma's moral degradation, just as the mirror in which she inspects her tired features before heading out to seek Rodolphe's financial rescue reveals her physical decline. Other forms of glass, too, seem imbued with a symbolic importance, but whereas in the case of the mirrors, Minnelli had only to adapt a symbol that was already present in the novel, he seems to have taken pleasure in creating a symbol of his own in the case of broken glass, as he had done with the birds. Thus, the allusion in the novel to the breaking of the windows at the Vaubyessard château when the air becomes too stuffy in the ballroom, taken up by Minnelli, is supplemented by two other allusions to broken glass, all in the scene of the Vaubyessard ball. Charles watches as a group of young aristocrats down their champagne in a single swallow and then throw their champagne goblets into the fireplace, the ultimate gesture of profligacy. The servants are ordered to break the windows when Emma complains that she feels faint, another example of the extravagance of the wealthy. But when the inebriated Charles, weaving through the crowd in search of his wife, knocks over a tray of liqueurs, sending the glasses smashing to the floor, he attracts scornful looks. As was the case with the mirrors, broken glass derives its meaning from context. The soundtrack, too, reinforces the themes. For the ball scene, Minnelli had specifically commissioned Miklos Rozsa to write a waltz that would reflect Emma's state of mind and Rozsa produced what Minnelli describes as a "neurotic" waltz (Minnelli 206). Whereas this waltz music returns several times when Emma is delusional, a somber tolling of bells punctuates the entire second half of the film, especially in those scenes when she is forced to confront reality.

Filmed in black and white as were most films of this period, Minnelli's adaptation of *Madame Bovary* nevertheless testifies to the evolution of cinematic technique that had occurred since the release of Renoir's 1934 adaptation.[21] Minnelli shot most of the dialogues using the shot/reverse shot strategy, thus making them livelier than Renoir's "staged" conversations. Film grammar, too, was improved, with most of Minnelli's scenes being separated by dissolves, a vast improvement upon the choppy cuts of Renoir's version. Drama is heightened through a larger number of close-ups, fluidity achieved through frequent use of the zoom. And although it is true that, as in Renoir, Emma is objectified by her constant on-screen presence, a feature that forces the spectator to look *at* her rather than seeing the world through her eyes, we have an extended point-of-view shot in the Vaubyessard ball scene, when the 360 degree swish pan showing the walls of the ballroom gives us some sense of her giddiness as she whirls through the dance steps in the arms of the experienced viscount. Culturally, too, Minnelli's film reflects the sensitivities of its era and its geographical context. Or, to put it another way, Flaubert's narrative is translated, not only into the English language and Hollywood style, but also into American culture. Hence, Homais estimates the temperature of Yonville in degrees Fahrenheit only, whereas in the

---

[21] Although technicolor had existed since the twenties and continued to be perfected through this period, it was expensive and therefore did not become popular until the 1960s when color television forced the movie industry to produce films in color in order to compete. (*The Film Studies Dictionary*).

novel he had first given them in Centigrade and then falsely calculated their equivalence in Fahrenheit, a typically Flaubertian jab in the ribs. Medical science, too, is made to conform to expectations: in the film, the surgical instruments intended for use in the clubfoot surgery are sterilized, a modification that is highly anachronistic, asepsis being unknown in the 1840s when this scene would have taken place. The fact that Guillaumin drinks tea, rather than wine, with his dinner is consistent with the novel's description; on the other hand, Minnelli's mise-en-scène, which shows a glass of wine on the table, was no doubt intended to fulfill American expectations: don't all Frenchmen drink wine with their dinner? As for the collapse of the distinction between Rodolphe and the viscount, while it was certainly motivated by the need for concision, as we have seen, Annie Goldmann believes that it also reflects the American belief in equal opportunity, suggesting as it does that a middle-class woman could actually have drawn more than passing attention from an aristocrat when he was in his own milieu (136). Goldmann believes that Emma's role as queen of the ball is also an American adjustment.[22] A different concern no doubt dictated a change in dialogue when the usurious Lheureux who, in both Flaubert and Renoir, had reassured Emma about his prices by saying "nous ne sommes pas des juifs" [we're not Jews] here merely suggests to Emma that he'll give her a special price for the piece of fabric she's admiring ("For you, Madame Bovary, twelve francs a yard"). His comment is immediately mocked by Léon who declares, "For everybody else, 10! What a scoundrel!" The antisemitic subtext is clear, but the epithet, offensive in this post-World War II culture, is avoided.[23]

When all is said and done, however, the deepest imprint on this film adaptation of Flaubert's novel was made by censorship.[24] Black and white in more ways than one, Minnelli's *Madame Bovary* provides an unmistakably moral viewpoint, clearly reflecting the ideology of its era. Had this movie been filmed in technicolor, a scarlet "A" might have been affixed to Emma's forehead.

---

[22] Robert Stam takes up this same argument in his recent book (*Literature* 173).

[23] See Linda Hutcheon (146-49) for a discussion of the phenomenon of transcultural adaptations.

[24] For more on the vagaries of censorship, both in this film and in the famous trial of 1857, see Elizabeth Ladenson's analysis in *Dirt for Art's Sake*.

4

Chabrol (1991): Keeping the Faith

During the four decades that separated Minnelli's Hollywood production of *Madame Bovary* from French filmmaker Claude Chabrol's sumptuous costume drama of 1991, several directors put their professional skills to the test by filming Flaubert's masterpiece.[1] In France, however, the only adaptation produced during this period was a made-for-TV movie directed by Pierre Cardinal from a screenplay by Georges Neveux. Produced in France by Antenne 2 in 1974 and released on videotape in the United States in 1986 by Films for the Humanities, this low-budget film eliminated nearly all of the novel's grand scenes—the wedding, the Vaubyessard ball, the agricultural fair. Indeed, were it not for its pedagogical value (the simplicity of the dialogues made it accessible to the American student population), it would probably be unavailable in any form today.

With the ascendancy of the heritage film in the 1980s, the time was thus ripe for another attempt to adapt *Madame Bovary* to the big screen. That Claude Chabrol should have been the one to undertake the task seems at once pre-ordained and supremely ironic—pre-ordained because of his love for Flaubert and his penchant for satirizing (he would say "representing") the bourgeoisie, ironic because in the late 50s and early 60s, he had been associated with the *Nouvelle Vague* (New Wave) Cinema, an influential if loosely organized movement that disdained the earlier "tradition de qualité"

---

[1] These included two British mini-series, one in 1964, the other in 1975; a West German/ Italian production directed by Hans Schott-Schöbinger in 1969; a Polish film entitled *Pany Bovary, to ja* (*Madame Bovary, that's me*) and released in 1976; and an Italian made-for-TV movie in 1981.

[tradition of quality] from which the heritage films were clearly descended. Besides rejecting what they referred to as "le cinéma de papa" [your father's cinema], the New Wave theorists were adamant in their claim that film was equal in importance to the other arts in general, and to literature in particular. They had been influenced by Alexandre Astruc's concept of the *caméra-stylo* [the camera-as-pen], and thus they stressed the autonomy of the film director who was seen as an *auteur* [an author] in his own right. Adaptations of literary works were not disdained by the New Wave theorists, provided the screenplays were written by cinema professionals rather than literary types (Bordwell and Thompson 465). Furthermore, adaptations made during this period tended to be of non-canonical literary works, often by contemporary writers, as exemplified by Truffaut's *Jules et Jim*, adapted in 1961 from a 1953 novel by Henri-Pierre Roché (Stam, *François Truffaut and Friends*, 9). Mostly, though, the New Wave filmmakers tended to favor low-budget films of personal inspiration, generally filmed on location. It was with the New Wave that Claude Chabrol's career was launched.

The path he had taken from his youth in the provinces to his identity as an adherent of the New Wave was not without deviations. Born in 1930 into a family of pharmacists, Chabrol had completed a *licence* (roughly, a Bachelor of Arts degree) in literature and had studied law for a year before giving in to parental pressure and briefly undertaking pharmaceutical studies. However, he was not destined to follow in the footsteps of his father and grandfather, and the magnetic pull of literature and film proved too strong for him to resist. After one year, he abandoned the pharmacy program.

Chabrol's discovery of Flaubert's classic novel had actually taken place when he was just thirteen years old, long before his university education refined his understanding of literature. He seems to relish telling interviewers that it coincided with the loss of his virginity to a country girl two years his senior. In fact, he speculates that the two events were causally related, his first experience of sexual intimacy having resulted naturally from the fact that he was under the spell of *Madame Bovary* (*Autour d'Emma* 34).

The origin of Chabrol's career in film, likewise, can be traced back to an unforgettable encounter. Having devoured films from an early age, active in provincial film clubs, then, during his Paris student days, a regular visitor to the Cinémathèque, Chabrol was deeply impressed when, at the age of seventeen, he met François Truffaut at a screening of Alfred Hitchcock's *Rope* (Rosenbaum).[2] After this meeting he began writing as a film critic, notably for *Cahiers du cinéma*. In 1957, when he was just 27, he collaborated with Eric Rohmer on a book about Alfred Hitchcock, the first to be devoted to the work of the Anglo-American film director. A year later, thanks to his first wife's family inheritance, he was able to produce his own inaugural film, *Le Beau Serge*, thus smoothly transitioning from critic to director. Although today he does not hesitate to mock this initial effort, confessing that he overloaded it with "toute une symbolique imbécile" [a lot of idiotic symbolism] (Braucourt 112), it was with *Le Beau Serge* that he established his credentials as a member of the iconoclastic *Nouvelle Vague*. Since then, he has been extraordinarily prolific. Indeed, some critics complain that he is *too* prolific, and that the quality of his films is uneven. Influenced in particular by the techniques of Alfred Hitchcock and Fritz Lang, the former for subjective camera angles and the latter for the abstract objectivity of Expressionism, Chabrol has made a specialty of detective movies. *Madame Bovary* was his forty-fourth film.

The evolution from New Wave filmmaker to director of a scrupulously faithful literary adaptation is not difficult to understand. For all its influence, the New Wave was in fact a relatively short-lived phenomenon, lasting from approximately 1958 until 1964, after which members of the group had "become absorbed into the French film industry [...], the characteristic New Wave form and style [being] diffused and imitated" (Bordwell and Thompson, 467). Chabrol, having made some commercial films after 1962, had fallen out of favor with New Wave purists, and his preference for the classical cinema they associated with "le cinéma de papa" completed the break. Indeed, by the mid-sixties, Chabrol was already contemplating a film version of the novel that had so impressed him in his youth. However, once he set about writing a scenario, he quickly became discouraged. This is how he described the experience to an interviewer:

---

[2] The Paris Cinémathèque, opened in the 1930s, has the world's most extensive collection of films and associated documents and realia. Films from around the world are projected daily. During the 1940s and 1950s, it became a gathering place for well-known French filmmakers.

> Very soon—after just a few pages—I saw that it was a completely
> crazy enterprise, a terrible ambition, because Flaubert's form was
> inseparable from his content and I was unable to come up with a
> cinematic equivalent of his style. (Chase 8)

Some twenty-five years later, he overcame his misgivings and tried
again. The moment was considerably more propitious than in the
sixties. The New Wave was no longer a force to be reckoned with, the
"cult of originality, of cinematic purism, and of signature filmmaking"
that defined it having held sway only until the 1970s (Millicent
Marcus, *Filmmaking* 11). At that point, according to Marcus, movie
makers quietly returned to their richest source of inspiration, the
literary text (*Filmmaking* 11). It took another ten years before the lush
productions that have been dubbed "heritage films" came to the fore
in Europe, and they would continue to be dominant throughout the
eighties and nineties. The French version of the heritage film had
certain defining characteristics:

> a French literary classic as source material; a conscientious, though
> unchallenging, rendering of the narrative; a carefully researched
> authentic period recreation; high production values with an emphasis
> on spectacle; an inherent sense of Frenchness conveyed through
> national stars and French locations; an anodyne account of French
> social history with an emphasis on aesthetic values rather than
> political content. (Cousins 35)

Supported and promoted by the socialist government then in power
(François Mitterand was President from 1981 until 1995, Jack Lang
Minister of Culture from 1981 to 1986 and then again from 1988 to
1993), such films were France's answer to Hollywood's hegemonic
hold on the film industry, a cinematic effort to combat American
influence by attracting attention both domestically and abroad to
France's rich literary patrimony. A worldwide economic recession had
not spared France, and controversial negotiations for a Europe that
would be unified economically were beginning. If the realization that
the national economy was no longer strong enough to sustain growth
without continental collaboration was painful to the French, they were
even more disheartened by the sense that their country's reputation as
a center of refinement and high culture was increasingly questionable.
Conceived and defined in opposition to Hollywood's "industrial"
output, heritage films were "cultural" products intended to restore
pride to a demoralized populace. They aimed to please an educated,

sophisticated audience, and as in England, most of the spectators who attended such films were older than the typical cinema crowd (Higson 110). The year 1990 had been a successful year for heritage films, with audience figures exceptionally healthy (Powrie 3). In this encouraging climate, Claude Chabrol chose to reclaim *Madame Bovary* for the French cinema. Although he is careful to distinguish between the honorable version of his compatriot, Jean Renoir, and the Hollywood adaptation by Vincente Minnelli, his opinion of the adaptations of his best-known predecessors, often articulated, was not high:

> Ni l'une ni l'autre ne sont fidèles à Flaubert. Celle de Renoir est assez formidable. Mais celle de Minnelli est absolument nulle. C'est un très joli film de la Metro, mais c'est une suite d'extravagances. [...] Minnelli n'a rien compris au roman. (Guérif 209)

> [Neither one is faithful to Flaubert. Renoir's is rather amazing. But Minnelli's is a complete dud. It's a very nice MGM movie, but totally over the top...Minnelli didn't understand the first thing about the novel.]

For Chabrol, then, the challenge was to do justice to Flaubert's novel while improving upon the cinematic efforts of his predecessors. The several intertextual allusions to the films of Renoir and Minnelli are playful gestures by a director fully convinced of the superiority of his product.

The idea of filming *Madame Bovary* was reborn just after the filming of *Une affaire de femmes* (1988) [*A Woman's Affair*] with Isabelle Huppert. According to Chabrol, it was Huppert who first suggested that they should not wait another ten years to make a film together again, and that perhaps they should consider filming Flaubert's masterpiece. Having previously cast Huppert as his leading lady in *Violette Nazière* (1978), the veteran director was convinced that in Huppert he had the ideal Emma Bovary, and that the opportunity would not arise again. Thus it was *he* who phoned the producer, and not the reverse, as had been the case with Renoir and Minnelli. Marin Karmitz, whose MK2 production company had already financed four of Chabrol's films (including *Une affaire de femmes*), accepted enthusiastically, and the filming began in 1990 in the same Norman town that Renoir had chosen, Lyons-la-forêt. For the other principal roles, Chabrol selected four actors with whom he had also worked previously, Jean-François Balmer (Charles), Christophe Malavoy (Rodolphe), Lucas Belvaux (Léon) and Jean Yanne (Homais). In an extraordinary interview with the literary scholar Pierre-Marc de Biasi, conducted during the montage of the film, Chabrol claimed that in selecting the cast, one of his principal requirements was that the actors have "un rapport intense au texte [du roman]" [an intense relationship with the text] (*Autour d'Emma* 47). This apparently did not require a previous familiarity with the novel, since neither Lucas Belvaux nor Isabelle Huppert recalled having read *Madame Bovary* when discussions with Chabrol began. Nevertheless, they were expected to read both novel and screenplay, and their reaction was of utmost importance to Chabrol, who had decided against his first choice for Homais, Michel Serrault, because the actor found the novel amusing.

What most sharply distinguishes Chabrol from other directors of Flaubert adaptations is his literary background and his impressive familiarity, not just with *Madame Bovary*, but with Flaubert criticism ("j'en ai lu des cargaisons"! [I've read tons of it!] (*Autour d'Emma* 36) and indeed, with all of Flaubert's work. With this in mind, one should not be surprised that Chabrol's guiding principle was to remain rigorously faithful to the novel. Flaubert, as we have seen, refused to allow illustrations for his novel and hated photographs. In a letter to Louise Colet thanking her for a portrait of herself that she had sent to him, he wrote, "Ne m'envoie pas ton portrait photographié. Je déteste les photographies à proportion que j'aime les originaux" [Don't send me a photo of yourself. My hatred for photographs is as intense as my love for the originals] (*Correspondance* 394). Chabrol was unperturbed by Flaubert's attitude. On the contrary, he was convinced that it was the fixity of the photographic image that repulsed Flaubert, and that he would have approved of moving pictures.

Given Chabrol's immense respect for Flaubert and his largely successful effort to remain as close to the novel as possible, it is thus somewhat ironic that he was denied advance funding for the film, based upon the screenplay, on the grounds that he had *added* nothing to Flaubert (Guérif 180). The amused condescension with which he recounted this minor setback contrasts sharply with the sense of indignation he displayed as he attempted to come to terms with the mixed critical reaction to the film and the somewhat disappointing box-office receipts:

C'est avec ce film que j'ai compris qu'il y avait quand même un
troupeau de cons autour de la critique de cinéma. [...] Il y a des cons à
toutes les époques, mais là, c'était vraiment formidable: je n'avais
jamais vu autant d'experts de Flaubert! C'était impressionnant. (qtd.
in Guérif 208)

[It was with this film that I began to see just how many idiots there
were among film critics...Every era has its idiots, but this was really
something; I had never seen so many Flaubert experts in my life! It
was impressive.]

Contending that the *real* Flaubert scholars—and he provided only one
name, that of Julian Barnes—"ont reconnu tout de suite le sérieux de
la démarche" [realized from the start how serious an undertaking my
film was] (Guérif 209), Chabrol was convinced that his adaptation had
merit. Legions of French high school students had been required to see
it. Moreover, in advance of its release in the United States on
Christmas Day, 1991, the film's American distributor, the Samuel
Goldwyn Company, had provided secondary school teachers and
college faculty with an eight-page study guide "intended for use by
literature, history, French and film classes from grades 11 through
college" (n.pag.) in a further effort to improve box-office
performance. An additional boost was provided by the decision of
FR3 to purchase television rights to the film. Thanks to all of this
promotion, the film was far from a commercial disaster. Yet the
mature, cultured public for whom such spectacular productions are
destined snubbed the film, and in 1999 Chabrol was no longer making
plans to adapt *L'Education sentimentale*, as he had been in 1991,
when Biasi interviewed him. To understand what went awry, it is
useful to begin with the film reviews.

Critical discussion tends to focus on two issues, the casting and
fidelity to the original. Interestingly, where the casting is concerned,
there appears to be a rather stark difference of opinion between the
French critics and their American counterparts, with most of the
former tending to approve of the cast, and the latter voicing dismay
about it. The controversy centers particularly on the choice of Isabelle
Huppert to play Emma. For *Le Monde*'s Jacques Siclier, she is
"l'interprète idéale" [the ideal actress to portray Emma], easily
eclipsing the actresses formerly cast in this role:

> Gustave Flaubert avait donné à Emma Rouault des cheveux noirs et
> des yeux bruns. Isabelle Huppert est rousse, avec des yeux couleur
> d'algue marine. Pourtant, et pour la première fois au cinéma...c'est
> bien elle, Emma, la fille du riche fermier. [...] Oui, c'est Emma, celle
> qui va attendre et rêver toute sa vie, sans jamais être satisfaite.

> [Gustave Flaubert had given Emma Rouault black hair and brown
> eyes. Isabelle Huppert is a redhead, with eyes the color of seaweed.
> Yet, and for the first time in film...it's really her, Emma, the wealthy
> farmer's daughter. ... Yes, it's Emma, the one who's going to wait and
> dream her life away, without ever being satisfied.]

In fact, Flaubert vacillated with regard to the color of his heroine's
eyes, as countless critics have noted.[3] Hence, Siclier's sense that the
details of Emma's appearance are less important than her character
seems consistent with the novelist's own perspective. Didier Roth-
Bettoni of *La Revue du Cinéma*, who considers Chabrol's film "à la
fois fidèle et éloigné de son modèle" [at once faithful to and quite
unlike its source], has no quarrels with the casting of "[la]
merveilleuse Isabelle Huppert" [the marvelous Isabelle Huppert]
whose Emma,

> quoique plus sommaire, est bien proche de celle de Flaubert, avec ses
> désirs en désordre, ses rêves de passion et de petite bourgeoise, son
> jeu de l'ennui et son vide intérieur, son égoïsme et ses blessures.

> [while less complex, is quite close to Flaubert's heroine, with her
> extravagant desires, her middle class dreams of passion, her display of
> boredom and her inner emptiness, her egotism and her pain.]

Anne-Marie Baron, whose credentials as a specialist in nineteenth-
century French literature complement her acuity as a film scholar-
critic, believes that "Isabelle Huppert incarne magnifiquement cette
héroïne dont la perversité n'est que la réponse à une situation
d'oppression" [Isabelle Huppert is a magnificent incarnation of this
heroine whose depravity is simply a reaction to her oppressive
situation] (*Romans français* 90). Joël Magny finds in Huppert an
uncanny ability to render the duality of an Emma who is "à la fois
stupide et émouvante, médiocre et pathétiquement admirable"

---

[3] See Enid Starkie, *Flaubert the Master*; Mario Vargas Llosa, *The Perpetual Orgy;*
Claude Mouchard, "En elle le noir abonde"; Claudine Gothot-Mersch, "La
Description des visages dans *Madame Bovary*."

[simultaneously stupid and moving, mediocre and pathetically admirable] (59). Similarly, Pierre Murat admires her versatility ("elle passe de la douceur à une dureté incroyable," [she goes from being sweet to incredibly harsh] (18). Summing up critical reaction a year after the film's release, the scholar Bernadette Plot notes that Huppert's role proved pivotal ("L'adhésion du spectateur au film [ou son rejet de celui-ci] semble s'être jouée essentiellement sur l'interprétation d'Isabelle Huppert") [The spectator's degree of engagement with the film seems to hinge completely on his/her reaction to Isabelle Huppert's acting], and then sounds a discordant note in the generally harmonious French symphony of praise, conceding that "l'héroïne de Flaubert nous apparaît, à la lecture, infiniment plus sensible, plus émotive aussi que celle de Chabrol" [Flaubert's heroine, in the novel, seems infinitely more sensitive and emotional than the heroine of Chabrol's film] (50).

Notwithstanding Plot's analysis of critical reaction, even those French critics who approved of the casting did not wax lyrical about the film. Quite the contrary, as we shall see. But where the principal role is concerned, there seems to be something of a consensus. When we cross the Atlantic, however, we find considerably less enthusiasm. Although some applause can be heard (*The Boston Globe*'s Matthew Gilbert believes that Huppert "seems born to play morally problematic characters such as Gustave Flaubert's adulterous heroine" and Desmond Ryan of *The Philadelphia Inquirer* considers her "the pick of screen Bovarys"),[4] most critics express displeasure with Huppert's Emma. *The Chicago Tribune*'s Dave Kehr finds that she is "without shading or sympathy ... [having] none of the bovine charm of Valentine Tessier in Jean Renoir's 1933 adaptation nor the kittenish jitters of Jennifer Jones in Vincente Minnelli's Hollywood version of 1949" and that, further, "[s]he turns the role of Emma Bovary...into a diva part, something hard, hysterical and self-absorbed" which begs the question: wasn't Flaubert's protagonist somewhat hard, hysterical and self-absorbed to begin with? (3:3). Hal Hinson, of *The Washington Post*, considers that Huppert "plays Emma as a shallow, pouty brat," and that her Emma "expresses, in microcosm, what is wrong with the movie as a whole," i.e. that it is "a colorless facsimile

---

[4] See Matthew Gilbert, "She was born to play Emma Bovary"; and Desmond Ryan, "Claude Chabrol adapts Flaubert's masterpiece for the screen".

[...] that instead of leading us to a great work, turns us away" (D2). *The New York Times*' Vincent Canby brushes aside concerns about Huppert's physical appearance: "it makes no difference that the pretty, freckled, reddish-blond Isabelle Huppert [...] appears to be too old [in fact she was 34 when the film was made] and doesn't look at all like Flaubert's dark-haired heroine whose eyes, though brown, 'seemed black under their long eyelashes.'" But he is none the less unenthusiastic: "Miss Huppert's Emma is imperious and rather frosty, so level-headed and so in command that it seems impossible that she could mess up her life with such wanton and short-sighted thoroughness" (L13). Referring to Huppert as an "ice queen," Canby laments that Emma Bovary is "missing" from the film.

Why this marked divergence of opinion along cultural lines? One might speculate that French critics, more likely not only to have read the novel, but to have studied it in school, had a more nuanced view of the heroine's character. Or that their familiarity with other roles played by a beloved film star—roles, incidentally, that have much in common with the one in question here—prejudiced them in favor of her rendition of Emma Bovary. Perhaps Huppert's culture-specific postures and attitudes were not fully understood by American film reviewers. Critics acknowledge that gestural codes are firmly anchored in a nation's culture (Hayward 12). Then too, cinematic techniques may have been a factor: did American critics respond less favorably to Huppert's Emma because of Chabrol's abstemious use of those point-of-view shots that would have encouraged audience identification with Flaubert's narcissistic heroine? Perhaps for French critics, Chabrol's enthusiasm was contagious, leading them to share uncritically the conviction of a popular film director that he had found in Huppert the ideal Emma. Whatever the case, the intriguing near-unanimity on the part of American critics that Isabelle Huppert is not a convincing Emma is highly suggestive.

Where the other roles are concerned, there is no such controversy. Nor is there a clear difference of opinion with regard to the film's overall merits. On both sides of the Atlantic, critics tend to avoid superlatives. Anne-Marie Baron considers that the film is "attachant" [captivating] but laments that it is "plus balzacien que flaubertien" [more Balzacian than Flaubertian] (*Romans français* 91). Didier Roth-Bettoni believes that "Chabrol est loin de faire preuve de la cruauté dégagée de Flaubert et de sa vision pessimiste de l'humanité" [Chabrol is far from expressing the kind of detached cruelty and pessimistic view of humanity that we find in Flaubert], whereas Joël Magny, crediting Chabrol with a "va-et-vient incessant entre le subjectif et l'objectif" [a constant back-and-forth movement between subjectivity and objectivity] that corresponds well to Flaubert's refusal to adopt the unique perspective of any character, nevertheless feels that in so doing he has fallen into a trap:

> Le spectateur finit par ne plus très bien savoir où se situe le cinéaste ni où se situer lui-même par rapport à une architecture de récit et de mise en scène qui fait songer à un mobile de Calder (Magny, 58-9).

> [The spectator ends up confused about the director's stance and about how to interpret a narrative architecture and mise-en-scène that, taken together, are reminiscent of a Calder mobile.]

In the end, Magny believes that Chabrol, having so often created characters who resembled Emma Bovary, "s'est manifestement trouvé quelque peu paralysé devant son modèle" [obviously found himself paralysed when confronted with his literary source]. Jacques Siclier's diametrically opposed opinion is that Chabrol "provoque aussi bien chez le spectateur que chez les spectatrices une identification à la seule Emma" [provokes in male and female spectators alike an identification with Emma alone]. However, Siclier studiously avoids evaluative comment about the film as a whole, concentrating instead on Huppert. Bernadette Plot, for her part, tempers her criticism through a gentle questioning:

> Dans quelle mesure le film de Chabrol est-il autre chose qu'une succession de "morceaux choisis" du livre de Flaubert? Une nouvelle "œuvre", une nouvelle "création", comme il nous semble que doit l'être toute adaptation d'un texte écrit à l'écran? (Plot, 48)

> [To what extent is Chabrol's film anything more than a series of "selected passages" from Flaubert's book? To what extent is it a new "work," a new "creation," as we believe any adaptation from a written text to the screen ought to be?]

This reproach is implicit in the reactions of many American critics. Less respectful of a cultural triad that is not their own—Flaubert, Chabrol, Huppert—reviewers, emboldened by the expanse of ocean separating them from France, sharpened their pencils mercilessly for their acerbic jabs at the film. Hal Hinson considers that, "as an exercise in literary transposition [the film] is as joyless as ditch digging." Allowing that "Chabrol's scrupulous approach to Flaubert is way ahead of Emma Bovary's flexible loyalty to her cloddish husband," Desmond Ryan considers that the movie is "too literal for the seething passions of the story," while Dave Kehr sees it as "a potboiler of a high order, but a potboiler nonetheless." Jay Carr recognizes some qualities in the film, but complains about its "suffocating literalism." Even the more indulgent Vincent Canby laments generously that the film "is so good in so many details that the wish is that it were better." However, what is most interesting about the reactions of nearly all of these critics is that they concur on the reasons for what they see as Chabrol's failure: the film, in the words of Desmond Ryan, "reduces the viewer to a dispassionate observer of Emma's doom." Whereas Flaubert allowed his reader to see Emma from within and from without, Chabrol cannot "get inside the soul of his heroine" (Hinson, D2).

I have dwelled on the tepid critical reaction to the film because it provides grist for the mill of those who would debate the importance of fidelity in the adaptation of classic literature to the screen. Not one of the critics cited questions the historical authenticity of the film. Not one accuses Chabrol of "betraying" Flaubert in the details of the plot, and even the literary critic Pierre-Marc de Biasi, who takes issue with some of Chabrol's editing, is forced reluctantly to concede that certain suppressions are "rudes mais inévitables" [brutal but unavoidable] (*Autour d'Emma* 59).

Although Chabrol, like Renoir and Minnelli before him, saw *Madame Bovary* as Emma's story and thus eliminated the entire first chapter and the bulk of the last three chapters, he spared no expense in his effort to be faithful to Flaubert's novel. This goes for the mise-en-scène, the acting, the soundtrack, even the scene-to-scene rhythm, in which Chabrol attempted to approximate the rhythm of Flaubert's prose. Thus, the scenes in which Homais is holding forth in typically pedantic fashion are often shot in long takes, as is the scene of Rodolphe's verbal seduction at the Agricultural Fair, intercut with shots of the opening ceremony taking place below. Chabrol frequently uses tracking shots to follow an Emma in seemingly perpetual motion, much as Flaubert's prose manages to center itself on the often frenzied protagonist. When Flaubert's Emma nods, Chabrol's Emma nods also. The novelistic description of the "abondante batterie de cuisine" [array of pots and pans] (71) hooked on the walls of the farmhouse kitchen at Les Bertaux has its cinematic equivalent. The phrenological head that graces Charles's desk in the novel appears in several of the film's scenes. The elegant dresses worn by Huppert are made of fabrics that were popular in the nineteenth century. When Flaubert's text alludes to the tolling of church bells (and at other times as well), they are added to the soundtrack. Over a close-up of Hippolyte's gangrenous foot, we hear flies buzzing, the director's solution for rendering Flaubert's description of "le sale oreiller où s'abattaient les mouches" [the filthy pillow crawling with flies] (287).[5] Most of the dialogues are taken almost verbatim from Flaubert.

This impressive reverence for the novel is displayed with particular force in Chabrol's use of voiceover, and it is with a discussion of this important feature of the 1991 adaptation that any in-depth analysis of the film must begin. Curiously, neither critics nor scholars have commented extensively on Chabrol's use of this technique. Vincente Minnelli, as we have seen, had elected to use voiceover back in 1949, but the voice was that of James Mason's incarnation of Flaubert, and spectators had already been introduced to the author in the opening courtroom sequence. Adopted in response to fears of censorship, the subjective, moralizing voiceover used by Minnelli would have appalled Flaubert himself, who took immense pains to remain "absent" from his novel. Chabrol's very different use of voiceover reflects not only the vastly diminished role played by censorship in the 1990s, but also the director's awareness of Flaubert criticism. The winds had shifted dramatically in the period that separated Chabrol's adaptation from that of his predecessor, and the early, "normative" criticism that decried the amorality of Flaubert's novel had given way, from about the 1970s on, to a celebration of the "indeterminacy" of the Flaubertian text.[6]

---

[5] With regard to the soundtrack, Chabrol insists on the superiority of the cinematic medium, pointing out that while Flaubert may allude to Scarlatti's sonata in his text, the reader who does not know the piece cannot fully comprehend why it makes Emma dreamy, whereas the filmmaker can actually create the mood by using it (*Autour d'Emma*). Robert Stam reiterates this point (*Literature* 180). However, although the point is well-taken, I was unable to find a reference to Scarlatti, either in the novel or its variants.

[6] Jonathan Culler's study, *The Uses of Uncertainty*, had an important part to play in this shift. See Laurence M. Porter's entry for "Critical reception" in *A Gustave Flaubert Encyclopedia*. (77-88)

It is well known that this indeterminacy results both from the *absence* of a controlling narrator who tells readers what to think and from the (complementary) exploitation of free indirect style. Through the brilliantly composite narration introduced by the pronoun "nous" of the *incipit*, Flaubert was able to access the subjectivity, not only of Emma, but of many of the other characters as well. In adapting *Madame Bovary*, Chabrol uses most of the conventional techniques to get inside the characters' heads, rendering thought as dialogue whenever possible, using extreme close-ups to reveal emotion, making judicious use of the extra-diegetic musical score to create mood. However, it is in his decision to use voiceover, not just "à cinq ou six reprises" [five or six times] as he tells Biasi (*Autour d'Emma* 50), but *twenty-six* times, that he reveals his frustration in finding a visual equivalent of Flaubert's richly evocative prose. Along with Huppert's performance, the repeated voiceovers may be the ingredient that gives the film its strongest—some would say its most unpalatable—flavor.

Unlike Minnelli, then, whose mellifluous narrator was created in response to some very specific industry imperatives, specifically, the need to appease the censors, Claude Chabrol elects to use the raspy, disembodied voice of the well-known actor François Périer, reading passages that come, for the most part, from the novel. Whether or not this voice is supposed to be that of Flaubert, as Annie Goldmann insists, is open to question (135). However, Chabrol's decision to use voiceover is in itself important. As we saw in the previous chapter, there has been some controversy among film scholars with regard to the technique of voiceover, with many theorists (and filmmakers) rejecting it because it privileges the word over the image. André Gardies, for example, pointing out that voiceover is "un mode de narration fondé sur le verbal," [a narrative mode based on words] sees it as a weakness, since "le propre du récit filmique consisterait ... en ce qu'il déploie son activité narrative en faisant usage du langage audiovisuel" [the essence of cinematic storytelling is that the story unfolds through the use of audiovisual language] (10). In defense of the technique, on the other hand, Sarah Kozloff notes that voiceover has an important place in "the grand cinematic tool chest," because it facilitates "providing exposition, condensing time, motivating flashbacks, underscoring characters' flaws, parodying other texts" (128, 26). Irony, in particular, is often communicated by voiceover, when there is a deliberate mismatch between the sound and image tracks. Kozloff concedes that when voiceover *is* used in fiction films, most directors opt for first-person narration (for obvious reasons, this is the case of Bresson's adaptation of Bernanos's novel), but finds examples of third-person voiceover narration in adaptations of novels "with indispensable narrators" (73).

In defending his decision to use voiceover, Chabrol made no mention of the famous Flaubertian irony, but emphasized rather his desire to capture "des choses qui en soi étaient sublimes [...] par la langue et le pouvoir d'évocation" [things that were in themselves sublime ... by their language and their evocative power] (*Autour d'Emma* 50). When we examine the specific instances of voiceover from the film, we see that most of them are in fact direct quotations from the text, sometimes slightly altered, and attributable to an omniscient narrator, thus confirming Guy Austin's statement that in film adaptations of works of literature, the technique serves to display the precursor text (*Contemporary French Cinema* 164). Despite their obvious foregrounding of Flaubert's prose (something that the dialogues accomplish as well), most of the voiceovers serve one of three very practical purposes: they allow us to read the thoughts of several of the characters (especially Emma); they serve to summarize plot ("Quand on partit de Tostes, au mois de mars, Madame Bovary était enceinte" [When they left Tostes in the month of March, Madame Bovary was pregnant]; they emphasize repeated past action. Occasionally, they are completely invented by Chabrol, as in the following narration that overlays a shot of Charles getting into bed beside his disconsolate wife:

> Charles s'était avisé de la langueur de sa femme. Pendant tout un temps il ne sut trop comment agir. Puis il prit une décision dans le plus grand secret, espérant que ce qui était pour lui un immense sacrifice, eh bien, permettrait à Emma de recouvrir la santé.

> [Charles had noticed that his wife was languishing. For a long while he did not quite know what to do. Then he made a decision, in strict secrecy, hoping that what would be for him an immense sacrifice would, well, allow Emma to recover her health.]

Presumably inserted in imitation of the famous free indirect style, the "eh bien" [well] seems intended to expose the slowly grinding mechanism of Charles's thought processes. But it fails to capture the mordant irony of Flaubert's prose:

> Comme elle se plaignait de Tostes continuellement, Charles imagina que la cause de sa maladie était sans doute dans quelque influence locale, et, s'arrêtant à cette idée, il songea sérieusement à aller s'établir ailleurs.
>
> Dès lors, elle but du vinaigre pour se faire maigrir, contracta une petite toux sèche et perdit complètement l'appétit.
>
> Il en coûtait à Charles d'abandonner Tostes après quatre ans de séjour et au moment *où il commençait à s'y poser.* S'il le fallait, cependant! Il la conduisit à Rouen voir son ancien maître. C'était une maladie nerveuse: on devait la changer d'air (140).

> [As she was constantly complaining about Tostes, Charles supposed that her illness was probably due to something in the area and, struck by this idea, he began to think seriously of setting up his practice elsewhere.
>
> From that moment, she drank vinegar to lose weight, contracted a dry little cough, and completely lost her appetite.
>
> It was a sacrifice for Charles to give up Tostes after living there four years, and just "when he was beginning to get somewhere". Yet if it must be! He took her to Rouen to see his old professor. It was a nervous condition; she needed a change of air.]

While it is obvious that Chabrol's rewriting achieves the goal of concision, Flaubert's humor has been sacrificed. As a result, the film does not record Charles's ironically correct diagnosis: the source of Emma's distress was indeed "quelque influence locale" ("something in the area"): *him!* Missing too is the hint that Emma was perversely manipulative, deliberately making herself ill in order to persuade Charles to leave Tostes. The suggestion that the minimally competent Charles himself needed confirmation for his suspicions from a fully qualified physician is likewise absent, as is the specification regarding the number of years he had been practicing medicine in Tostes: four. This last detail effectively precludes any possibility that he could be older than in his mid-thirties, since Tostes was his first practice.

The vast majority of Chabrol's voiceovers, however, use Flaubert's language and give us access to Emma's thoughts rather than those of Charles. Occasionally, a mildly amusing effect is achieved when the extra-diegetic voice intersects with the voice of one of the characters. For example, it is over an image of Charles and Emma at table that we hear the narrator intone one of the novel's most famous lines, "La conversation de Charles était plate comme un trottoir de rue" [Charles's conversation was as flat as a sidewalk]

(106). At this point, there is a brief pause in the narration as Charles looks up from his soup and says, "Il va pleuvoir" [It's going to rain]. The extra-diegetic voice resumes: "Et les idées de tout le monde y défilaient dans leur costume ordinaire sans exciter d'émotion, de rire ou de rêverie" [And everyone's ideas filed through it in their everyday clothes, without exciting emotion, laughter, or dreams] (106). And Charles speaks again, "Enfin, je crois" [At least I think so]. While I would not go as far as Cheryl Krueger who believes that Chabrol consciously made it seem as if Charles were agreeing with the extra-diegetic narrator's denigration of his conversational skills, the visual track and the snatches of conversation recorded as background by the soundtrack clearly illustrate—and validate—the extra-diegetic narrator's statement (Krueger 164). But herein lies a problem. In the novel, the source of this judgment is blurred, belonging as much to Emma as to the omniscient narrator. Whether Emma would have been capable of expressing her boredom with her bland husband in these terms is not at issue here, and we shall leave to others the discussion of this apparent inconsistency in Flaubert's use of free indirect style. The point is that readers *feel* Emma's exasperation. Spectators, on the other hand, hearing words that emanate from an off-screen male narrator, subjected to a show-and-tell that seems paradoxically to arrest narrative time, feel more like students at a lecture than observers of an intensely private drama. Since boredom is an expression that Isabelle Huppert's face registers easily, and banality and lack of imagination characterize Balmer's every word and action, we are left to wonder at the wisdom of referencing the text in this scene.

One might of course protest that Chabrol wanted merely to highlight the beauty of Flaubert's prose. But then how does one justify entire paragraphs of voiceover exposition, so altered that the fluid harmony of the original text has been lost, and which serve merely to describe what the spectator sees on the screen? Consider the narration that overlays a long take of an evening gathering at Homais's house. As the camera pans right to reveal the various activities taking place, the narrator explains:

> Le dimanche, c'était le pharmacien qui recevait, avec Madame Homais et leurs deux enfants, Napoléon et Athalie. Léon ne manquait pas de se trouver là. Monsieur Homais jouait à l'écarté avec Emma. Léon, derrière elle, lui donnait des avis. Puis l'apothicaire et le médecin entamaient une partie de dominos. Madame Bovary

changeait de place et Léon s'installait près d'elle. Elle lui priait de lui dire des vers. Léon les déclamait d'une voix traînante qu'il faisait expirer soigneusement aux passages d'amour.

[On Sundays, it was the pharmacist who did the entertaining, with Madame Homais and their two children, Napoleon and Athalie. Léon never failed to be in attendance. Monsieur Homais played cards with Emma. Léon, standing behind her, gave her advice. Then the pharmacist and the doctor began a game of dominoes. Madame Bovary changed places and Leon sat down beside her. She begged him to recite some poetry. Léon read the verses aloud in a drawling voice, taking care to let his voice die away to a whisper for the love passages.]

Here, voiceover is used not to get inside Emma's head but simply to describe action. Chabrol's decision to include a voiceover in this instance was probably motivated by the wish to insist on the regular recurrence of these evening get-togethers, evoked by the imperfect tense of the (altered) literary text. But more specifically cinematic means—montage, dialogue—could have been used to convey the same information. What is especially curious about these voiceovers in which soundtrack and image track are redundant is that Chabrol himself often decried such synchronicity. "[Ce] que je ne veux surtout pas, c'est faire redire l'image par le son" [What I certainly don't want is for the sound to simply repeat the image] he had told Biasi (*Autour d'Emma* 60).

Curiously, in those instances when the voiceover does *not* seem to conform to what the spectator is seeing on screen, one senses neither Chabrol's determination to be true to his conviction nor his desire to establish ironic distance. The discordance seems rather to result from inattention on the director's part. For instance, it is over a nocturnal shot of Emma running to join Rodolphe in the garden, hair flying, that we hear the grainy narrative voice: "Au bout de six mois, ils se trouvèrent l'un vis-à-vis de l'autre comme deux mariés qui entretiennent une flamme domestique" [By the time six months had passed, they were acting like a married couple, quietly tending a domestic flame]. A pause in the narration is accompanied by a close-up of Emma and Rodolphe, as Emma says breathlessly, "Je te veux, je te veux! Je veux te dévorer!" [I want you, I want you! I want to devour you!]. And then the voiceover continues: "C'est alors qu'Emma se repentit" [That's when Emma repented], as the camera cuts to a shot of Félicité and Berthe who are playing in the garden.

The camera pans left, bringing Emma into the frame. "Amenez-la-moi!" [Bring her to me!] she cries, in a seemingly spontaneous renewal of maternal interest. The narration overlaying the two frames is insufficient to explain Emma's change of heart. Furthermore, the blatant discrepancy between sound and image track (the passionate embrace hardly resembles a temperate domestic flame!) seems inadvertent, and we are led to wonder whether it resulted from the final editing, where perhaps a cut was made to the image track, while the voiceover narration that was to accompany it was retained. The celluloid Emma is given no reason to repent, whereas the novelistic heroine is reacting to Rodolphe's increasingly cruel nonchalance towards her: it is after he has "forgotten" three consecutive dates, thus after she becomes aware of his increasing indifference towards her, that she begins to regret her infidelity.

Another particularly unfortunate use of voiceover occurs towards the end of the film. Emma has just suggested to Léon that he steal the money from his law office when the voluble narrator intrudes, breaking the tension of the moment with a quotation that comes straight from the novel:

> Une hardiesse infernale s'échappait de ses prunelles enflammées et les paupières se rapprochaient d'une façon lascive et encourageante, si bien que le jeune homme se sentit faiblir sous la muette volonté de cette femme qui lui conseillait un crime. Alors il eut peur. (437)

> [Her eyes were blazing with a diabolic boldness, and she lowered her eyelids in such a lascivious and encouraging way that the young man felt himself weaken beneath the silent strength of this woman who was suggesting that he commit a crime. Then he became frightened.]

As the textual recital begins, the camera zooms in for a close-up of Isabelle Huppert whose attempt to inject boldness into her gaze is less than convincing. The camera cuts to Léon and zooms out slowly as the voiceover ends, bringing Emma back into the frame in a medium close-up with Léon, who pretends suddenly to have hit upon a solution to her financial problems. And then the scene comes (mercifully) to an end.

It has been said that unlike dialogue among the characters, on which spectators are merely eavesdropping, voiceover addresses spectators directly, making them privileged confidants and thereby pulling them into the story. If this is so, it is somewhat paradoxical that the voiceover used by Chabrol, professorial in tone and literary in content, effectively turns the theater into a classroom and distances the spectators. Chabrol's reverence for Flaubert's words is not in doubt; nor can one impugn the purity of his motives in foregrounding the literary text. However, the matter-of-fact way in which the novel's evocative language is chopped up and delivered to the viewer is unlikely to inspire respect for the text; it gives an asphyxiating, academic quality to a film that should be throbbing with passion.

Lest Chabrol's foregrounding of the novel through the voiceover technique lead one to conclude that the film is completely subordinate to the text, it is important to examine those specifically cinematic elements that function as Chabrol's signature and that prove yet again—as if proof were needed—that adaptation *is* interpretation. From the somewhat controversial casting to editing, from mise-en-scène to use of extra-diegetic sound, Chabrol's personal touch is everywhere apparent. Of principal interest are the reasons—cinematic, cultural, personal—for his decision to adopt certain strategies. Whatever their inherent value (some are more effective than others), they are part of the semiotics of this adaptation and they come to define it just as surely as the black cowboy hat defines the villain in Westerns.

Some of Chabrol's alterations are necessitated by the casting or editing. For example, since the first chapter has been suppressed, the director must find other ways to signal Charles Bovary's essential mediocrity. Aside from the casting itself—about which more in a moment—Chabrol found a way to incorporate Charles's garbled pronunciation of his own name by getting Emma to query him:

EMMA. Je voudrais savoir votre nom, docteur.

CHARLES. Charbovari.

EMMA. Pardon?

CHARLES. Charles Bovary, Mam'selle.

[EMMA. I'd like to know your name, doctor.

CHARLES. Charbovari.

EMMA. Pardon me?

CHARLES. Charles Bovary, Miss.]

Unfortunately, this brief dialogue, of which Chabrol himself was very proud, is not entirely effective, since Emma's quietly amused reaction is a poor substitute for the outburst of humiliating laughter that Flaubert's schoolboy had to endure from his classmates when he was asked to introduce himself to his new teacher. More successful in revealing Charles's awkwardness is the equally brief dialogue at the Vaubyessard Ball, when a liveried servant offers Charles a glass of champagne from a tray. "Castellane," murmurs the haughty waiter, identifying the champagne. "Bovary," responds the inexperienced Charles, believing that the waiter has introduced himself. In a medium close-up, the camera lingers on the waiter's perplexed facial expression in which just the barest hint of amused disdain shows through.

But it is above all in his choice of Jean-François Balmer to play Charles that Chabrol gives us a key to his very personal interpretation of the Flaubertian character. Critics have on the whole approved of the

Figure 5. Chabrol's *Madame Bovary* (1991).

casting of Balmer and have apparently not noticed the sharply curtailed role played by Madame Bovary Senior. (Chabrol maintains that one can tell Charles is a Momma's boy by the way Balmer plays him.)[7] Nevertheless, the choice of a slightly stooped fifty-four year old actor with coarse, doughy features, sagging eyelids, a goatee and a receding hairline poses certain very real problems for Emma's character (figure 5).[8] Although the novelistic Charles is clearly more mature than Emma (he spends several years studying for his health officer's diploma, and has been married for fourteen months when Héloïse dies), there is no indication that he is middle-aged. On the contrary, townspeople pity "ce pauvre jeune homme!" [that poor young man] (80) when his first wife dies. Nor is there any hint, despite his hangdog humility (expertly represented by Balmer), that he has the actor's aggressive plainness. With regard to the age question, Chabrol is forced to cheat a little when Charles's father dies, adding three years to his life (he's fifty-eight in the novel, sixty-one in the film), almost certainly because Balmer's Charles looks too old to have a father in his fifties. In short, it is difficult to reconcile the physical reality of the screen actor with the nubile willingness of the novelistic Emma Bovary, who reddens when Charles's chest brushes her back as they are reaching for his riding crop (74), a scene Chabrol is forced to omit. Rouault tells Charles that Emma asks after him when he stops coming to Les Bertaux, and we have no reason to suspect that he is lying; moreover, she giggles and blushes the day after the marriage agreement is sealed (84). Having been nourished during the whole of her convent years on a diet of romances featuring dashing gentlemen and swooning ladies, Emma believes at first that Charles will be the instrument of "cette passion merveilleuse qui jusqu'alors s'était tenue comme un grand oiseau au plumage rose planant dans la splendeur des ciels poétiques" [that wondrous passion which, until then, like a great bird with pink feathers, had hovered over her in the splendor of poetic skies] (105). While it is true that Flaubert's Charles is not presented as handsome (disabused, Emma thinks wistfully that "il aurait pu être beau, spirituel, distingué, attirant..." [he could have been handsome, witty, distinguished, attractive] (111)) and her father finds him puny ("gringalet," 83), something Balmer is not), Flaubert's idealistic heroine is unlikely to have agreed so quickly to a marriage proposal

---

[7] In an interview with Bernadette Plot (53), Chabrol says of Charles that "Sa simple manière de se présenter prouve qu'il a été adoré par sa mère" [Even the way he presents himself proves that he was adored by his mother].
[8] Balmer was born in April 1946.

from Jean-François Balmer's Charles.[9] The actor's age and appearance, as much any other single factor, may explain the coldness with which Isabelle Huppert plays her role, for *this* Emma never thought for a moment that she could love this dull, awkward, middle-aged health officer. (Alternatively, Balmer may have been cast in this role precisely because of Huppert's cinematic profile: she embodies world-weariness right from the first scene.) This is not intended as a criticism of Balmer's performance. On the contrary, the whiny voice in which he speaks his lines and the superbly tentative manner in which he acts, as if always seeking Emma's approval, is perfectly calibrated to suggest a lack of virility that for some is the defining characteristic of the man who is betrayed by his wife. Chabrol's representation of Charles is perfectly consistent with the traditional French representation of the cuckold as an object of ridicule, and in this cultural context, one could justifiably conclude that almost any French *auteur* (literary or cinematic) would experience difficulty in conceiving of a cuckold who is not unattractive and spineless. Chabrol was adamant about preventing spectators from identifying with Charles (*Autour d'Emma* 39), and in this, he certainly succeeded. Flaubert's Charles is the epitome of mediocrity. His lack of sophistication dismays his wife, and his lack of intelligence makes him oblivious to her suffering.[10] However, the other characteristics of the Charles presented in Chabrol's film are in the eye of the director.

Isabelle Huppert, for her part, had already proved her ability to incarnate an enigmatic and deeply troubled woman in *Violette Nazière* (1978) and *Une affaire de femmes* (1988); she was later to play a similar role in *La Cérémonie* (1995). Emma Bovary thus seemed a perfect fit for this actress who could project a powerfully willful and arrogant attitude, even when her actions betrayed her mental instability. It is hardly coincidental that Huppert saw Emma as "a survivor, a fighter... [who] goes through a lot of suffering and...wants to free herself" (Gilbert A11). Chabrol was careful to avoid anachronisms, and he insisted that he took no account of "des interprétations extérieures sur le texte" [critical interpretations of the text] (*Autour d'Emma* 38). Yet he seems to have shared Huppert's

---

[9] Jean Bouise, the actor who plays Charles in Cardinal's production is even more physically unattractive (or made to appear so) than Balmer.
[10] Genetic criticism provides fascinating insights into Flaubert's creation of this character. See Graham Falconer, "Flaubert Assassin de Charles."

view of Emma as a proto-feminist, and indeed by casting Huppert in this role, he revealed his complicity with her interpretation. In his view, "Emma Bovary est douée d'un certain héroïsme dans la mesure où elle est sporadiquement capable de prises de conscience: par éclairs, elle voit la médiocrité du monde qui l'entoure" [Emma Bovary is endowed with a certain heroism to the extent that she is capable of sporadic moments of lucidity: in flashes of insight, she sees the mediocrity of the world around her] (*Autour d'Emma* 64). Embodied in the male characters, all of whom verge on caricature, this mediocrity is displayed in stunning relief in Chabrol's adaptation.

Because the filmmaker decided to adopt a strictly linear format, avoiding flashbacks, we barely glimpse the forces that shaped the original Emma's perception of reality. Apart from a brief sequence in which Huppert's Emma first tells Charles that in convent school she often pretended to faint so as to be coddled by the nuns (a statement invented by Chabrol) and then shows him the prizes she had won for distinction in various subjects, her past is scarcely evoked. Her passing mention of her mother ("Ma pauvre maman était fière de moi quand elle me voyait avec mes couronnes. Tous les premiers vendredi de chaque mois, je vais cueillir des fleurs dans le jardin pour les porter sur sa tombe" [My poor mother was proud of me when she saw me with my laurels. On the first Friday of each month, I pick flowers in the garden and put them on her grave]) suggests that Emma is a sentimental creature, but hardly prepares the spectator for her immense capacity for illusion. Nor does the film allude to her passion for romance novels: two brief shots of Emma reading, one at the dinner table with Charles, another when, alone, she lowers her book to look dreamily into the distance, constitute fleeting references to what was in Flaubert a vital component of her character.[11] In short, these scant allusions are scarcely adequate to reveal the motivation for Emma's extravagant behavior.[12] As a result, the spectator is inclined to seek an explanation for her unquenchable yearning in the men in her (cinematic) life who, in the words of Caroline Eliacheff, "partagent tous une certaine grossièreté" [are all rather coarse] (*Autour d'Emma* 126) or in the society in which she lives, a conclusion that would be

---

[11] Robert Stam, who accurately comments that "there is little reference in the film to [Emma's] reading" (*Literature* 178) is however in error when he claims that the only shot of Huppert's Emma reading is at the dinner table (*Literature* 182).

[12] On this subject, see Goldmann 139.

entirely consistent with Huppert's own perspective. Huppert, who attributes Emma's death to the fact that she was not recognized as "une personne désirante" [a person with desires] (*Autour d'Emma* 126), has an emotional attachment to the character she plays:

> Moi, je l'aime bien Madame Bovary. Je la trouve assez courageuse et je trouve que son destin est une belle métaphore d'une certaine condition féminine et de son aliénation bien sûr. C'est une héroïne du désir. (*Autour d'Emma* 127)

> [Personally, I like Madame Bovary. I find her quite courageous and I think her story is a great metaphor for the situation in which many women find themselves, and of course for her own alienation. She is a heroine of desire.]

Clearly, the feminist criticism of the last several decades has influenced this interpretation of Flaubert's naïve adulteress. Emma Bovary's dissatisfaction may be timeless, as Huppert suggests, but it was also a response to some very specific cultural conditions, conditions that prevented middle class women from seeking employment outside the home or even from finding relief from an unhappy marriage through divorce.

To some extent, it may well be Huppert's twentieth-century reaction to the character that led her to emphasize certain aspects of Emma's character while minimizing others. Tears spring readily to the eyes of Huppert's Emma, but she does not sob and she is shown crying softly only twice. Although she sometimes displays anger, she is not generally given to hysteria. Chabrol's framing also contributes to the impression of self-control. For example, he significantly chose to put Huppert off-screen when he revealed her horror upon reading Rodolphe's letter. The camera follows her as she disappears up the steps, then stops to show a shadow playing on the wall: it is the letter, held by a trembling hand. Similarly, during her final diatribe, when Rodolphe refuses to lend her money, Chabrol's camera rests nearly as often on Rodolphe as on Emma. Those critics who have praised her mostly dispassionate performance point out that Emma's turbulence is internal and that Huppert has an admirable ability to convey her character's conflicting emotions through the tense muscles of her face. Robert Stam, noting the actress's flushed complexion at moments of passion, considers that Huppert's Emma "comes alive and radiates erotic energy when she is in love" (*Literature* 179). This may be true, but what about the eruptions of uncontrollable rage or the bouts of bottomless despair? Flaubert is explicit about Emma's fits of hysteria and about what psychiatrists might recognize today as manic-depressive tendencies or as a histrionic personality disorder:[13]

> En de certains jours, elle bavardait avec une abondance fébrile; à ces exaltations succédaient tout à coup des torpeurs où elle restait sans parler, sans bouger. (139)

> [On some days she chattered with feverish energy, and then this overexcitement would suddenly give way to a state of torpor, in which she remained without speaking or moving.]

Given Chabrol's conviction that he was being utterly faithful to the novel (and notwithstanding the discredit into which the concept of fidelity has fallen), the question here is whether Huppert's often deadpan performance really captures the character of Flaubert's impetuous, hysterical dreamer. If not, it seems reasonable to conclude that Chabrol did not consider that the mood swings and emotional outbursts of Flaubert's protagonist defined her character. In fact, both by his casting and by the filming techniques he employs, Chabrol displays his conviction that Emma's fate owed more to the patriarchal society in which she lived than to any particular character flaw.[14]

Chabrol's mise-en-scène evokes Emma's victimization at the hands of the men in her life, an emasculated Charles, a hypocritical Lheureux, a callous Rodolphe, a cowardly Léon, and a fatuous Homais. Her lack of power is underscored by the fact that in numerous frames, she is pictured seated, with the men towering over her. A number of scenes shot in deep focus feature a man—Charles, Rodolphe, Léon—in the foreground, with Emma but a small figure in the background. As she becomes progressively more willful in her rebellion, however, this perspective is reversed. In the last bedroom scene with Léon, a frame shows Emma, cigarette in hand, sitting astride a prone Léon who is at the bottom of the frame (figure 6). As the camera tilts upward, he passes out of the frame. Similarly, with Guillaumin and with Rodolphe in the humiliating scenes where she

---

[13] I owe this observation to Laurence M. Porter.

[14] Many Flaubertian scholars would disagree with Chabrol's assessment. See Laurence M. Porter, "Emma's Narcissism Revisited."

Figure 6. Chabrol's *Madame Bovary* (1991).

unsuccessfully begs for money, it is Emma who is standing in the final frame, facing her kneeling or seated suitors (Guillaumin and Rodolphe respectively) as she showers them with invective. Emma's increasing boldness is also signaled by her dresses. Chabrol is known for his color symbolism, and although he often takes his cue from Flaubert where Emma's costumes are concerned, the gradual shift from demure pastels to extravagant, revealing reds and blacks is highlighted in the film (see Austin, *Claude Chabrol* 141). The more heavily made-up Emma of the later scenes, with her plunging necklines and glittering jewels, seems a personification of wanton lust. Even her coiffures have changed, and the neat chignons and bonnets of several earlier scenes have been replaced by corkscrew curls ("les anglaises") and, finally, disheveled hair flying free. "Elle a les cheveux dénoués: cela promet d'être tragique" [She's got her hair down; this is going to be tragic] (348) the novelistic Charles had commented at the Opera, trying to persuade Emma and Léon to remain for the third act. In the end, Emma's uncoiffed hair will be one sign among many of her mental disarray and her degradation and of the tragedy that will ensue from both.[15]

Given the centrality of Emma Bovary—Chabrol has eliminated most of the scenes that do not contain her, and his camera follows her lovingly everywhere she goes, zooming in to expose every quiver of her lips, every tear that forms in her eye (it is perhaps to be expected that there are more close-ups of Huppert's Emma than of any other character)—it is unsurprising that so many reviewers focused on the actress who played her. Charles, naturally, also has a lot of on-screen time although, significantly, he is rarely shot in close-up before the deathbed scene. But there is another character who, despite the rather draconian editing required to bring a novel of the length of *Madame Bovary* to the screen, has not been diminished in the slightest by the transfer from page to screen: Homais. Chabrol has maintained nearly every scene in which Homais appears, and there are more shots of Jean Yanne's superbly annoying pharmacist than of any other character, save Emma and Charles. Moreover, he is on several occasions evoked either through his pharmacy, which figures in several exterior shots, or through his off-screen voice, a brilliant strategy that captures the essence of his bombast. One particularly notable example of this technique occurs when the desperate Emma arrives at the pharmacy, bent on suicide. Off-screen, the Homais family is at table, and Homais can be heard faintly, expatiating about the uselessness of prayer in a diatribe which, in the novel, the pharmacist had directed at Bournisien as the two men kept watch over Emma's corpse. In the film, his words overlay a close-up of Emma, her face a mask of desperate resolve. At the very moment she

---

[15] There is an historical basis for this representation, since in the nineteenth century a respectable woman always wore her hair up in public and did not go out without a hat. On the semiotics of hair, see Carol Rifelj, "The Language of Hair in the Nineteenth-Century Novel."

succeeds in persuading Justin to give her the key to the capharnaum (which Chabrol renders as "réserve") without alerting Homais, the latter shouts (again, off-screen): "Justin! Apporte-nous du chlorure de sodium!" [Justin! Bring us some sodium chloride!] Homais's pretentious use of the chemical formula for "salt," an invention of the film, encapsulates the pharmacist's insufferable affectation as effectively as the "*Saccharum*, docteur" (468) of Flaubert's Homais, who used the Latin word for sugar to impress the physician, Dr. La Rivière, in a scene omitted from the film. Chabrol's creative superimposition of a comically banal request expressed pedantically over an image of the tragic Emma manages to capture with admirable economy of means the contrast between the perpetually self-satisfied Homais and the eternally dissatisfied Emma.

Chabrol's blocking is also revealing: Homais is frequently center-frame, and in numerous scenes he is positioned between Emma and Charles. Although in this Chabrol is following the novel, which tells us that Homais, regularly arriving at dinnertime, sat down "à sa place ... entre les deux époux" [at his seat...between them] (183), the visual medium underscores what the reader may have overlooked in the text, and the symbolism of this mise-en-scène would be hard to miss. Homais's prominence is underscored in the film's final sequence, when after a long pan of Yonville's crowded public square, abuzz with conversation, the camera cuts to the pharmacy and focuses on the decorated pharmacist as he saunters across the square, stopping mid-frame to admire the ribbon of the Legion of Honor that he wears on his lapel. Whatever the personal reasons for Chabrol's decision to highlight the pharmacist's role—the director was, as we have seen, the son and grandson of pharmacists—it is worth noting that Jean Yanne's Homais is, if possible, even more abrasive and self-absorbed than the one imagined by Flaubert.

Chabrol has said that he eliminated Homais's altercations with Bournisien on the subject of religion because he no longer found the religion vs. science debate timely. The comment merits scrutiny. If the heritage genre is a means of cultural preservation, and if Chabrol's guiding principle was fidelity to the source text, this decision seems somewhat incongruous with the ostensible aims of both genre and director. In fact, this is but one of several omissions that relate to religion. In addition to reducing Emma's convent years to one brief allusion, Chabrol has evoked the renewal of Emma's religious fervor following Rodolphe's betrayal in a single snatch of conversation between Homais and Charles, and the Extreme Unction and the kiss Emma bestows on the crucifix in the death-bed scene have been suppressed completely.[16] Bournisien's speaking role has been limited to three scenes: the one in which Emma goes to see him in a vain attempt to find relief for her suffering, the brief scene at Hippolyte's bedside when the priest exhorts the stable boy to rejoice in his pain because it is a manifestion of the will of God, and the short scene that follows Emma's death when he attempts to console Charles in similar terms, prompting Charles to reply with uncharacteristic venom, "Je l'exècre, votre Dieu!" [I abhor your God!]. In other words, where the topic of religion and its ministers is concerned, Chabrol's adaptation, diametrically opposed to Minnelli's, has included only those allusions that are demeaning to religion. Whatever the reason for this selection—and most likely, Chabrol's antipathy for organized religion was a contributing factor, together with the differing socio-cultural contexts in which the films were made—the decision to discard the religious imagery (a few crucifixes scattered here and there scarcely suffice to restore it) significantly alters the personal mythology of the heroine who, in the novel, had been so entranced by the clergy's appropriation of the language of profane love to describe Christ, "fiancé...époux...amant céleste..." [fiancé...husband...celestial lover] (98) that she spent the whole of her short life in search of a lover fashioned not only on those of the romance novels that were her steady diet, but also on the Savior as He had been represented in the sermons she had heard during her convent years. While even as important a change as this may be typical of the tendency of the heritage film to emphasize aesthetics over social or political history— it has been said that such films satisfy a nostalgia for a past that never

---

[16] When Biasi interviewed Chabrol, the crucifix scene had not been definitively cut. Chabrol's comments testify to his vacillation and suggest another possible reason for his hesitation to put in the scene: "J'avais supprimé--volontairement--le baiser d'Emma au crucifix, tout à la fin. C'est-à-dire que j'avais eu un petit pépin avec les curés au moment d'*Une affaire de femmes*, et je n'avais pas trop envie que ça se renouvelle. Alors, j'avais carrément mis le baiser au crucifix entre parenthèses. Le journaliste m'a fait honte, et je l'ai réintroduit" [I had suppressed—willingly—the kiss Emma planted on the crucifix, at the end. You see, I had a bit of a problem with the priests when I made *Une affaire de femmes* and I didn't want to get into trouble again. So, I had simply put the kiss in parentheses. The journalist gave me a hard time about that, so I put it back in.] (*Autour d'Emma* 87.)

existed (Higson 113), a past characterized by prettified scenery, quaint customs, and lush costumes—the diminished role of religion in the film does seem inconsistent with Chabrol's often articulated desire to be rigorously faithful to Flaubert.

If the off-center role played by religion in the film, together with the feminist tint of Isabelle Huppert's interpretation of Emma, can be attributed to Chabrol's desire to give a modern spin to the notion of *bovarysme*, other, seemingly gratuitous alterations expose the director's ludic side or, in the case of those additions that display his vast knowledge of *flaubertiana*, his vanity. For example, the parrot that sits on a table beside Charles's desk is a playful wink to the cognoscenti.[17] Likewise, watching the scene at the Vaubyessard ball, spectators familiar with *L'Education sentimentale* can smile knowingly when they hear the guard announce the arrival of Monsieur Frédéric Moreau. The wallpaper that serves as background to Rodolphe's verbal seduction of Emma at the *mairie* features a pattern made up of fleurs-de-lys, a heraldic symbol that stands in ironic counterpoint to the democratic speeches being given in the square below. When, at the advice of her maid, the panic-stricken Emma goes in desperation to the lecherous Guillaumin to ask him to lend her money, the camera zooms in on the meal he is eating: not a cutlet, as in Flaubert's text, but a patently phallic sausage. The shot of the sausage, incidentally, is just one of several close-ups of comestible items: besides the wedding cake, there are two tarts, the (inevitable) basket of apricots, and a pot of red current jam, whimsical shots inspired perhaps by Chabrol's well-known *gourmandise*.[18] The scene that features an intensely serious Charles cutting the wedding cake as if he were performing major surgery, while wedding guests shout their encouragement with a noisy chorus of "Coupez! Coupez!" [Cut! Cut!] also appears to have ironic—and premonitory—connotations, as well as being a self-referential allusion to one of the film director's activities.

Another area in which Chabrol's stamp is indelible is that of eroticism. In the highly permissive climate of the last two decades, he could quite easily have included explicit sexual encounters, but he chose not to do so. Although he defended his decision by alluding to

---

[17] The idea to include a parrot may however have come from Minnelli. See Chapter Two.

[18] On the topic of Chabrol's love of fine food, see Braucourt 11-18.

Flaubert's subtlety in this regard, and even claimed to feel remorse for
the single fleeting shot that shows Emma and Léon embracing *inside*
the carriage, those familiar with Chabrol's work know that this
discretion is a personal preference on his part. His legendary love of
realistic detail tends to be expressed far more frequently in meal
scenes (there are ten in this film) than in passionate trysts, and it is
well-known that the erotic impulse in his work is frequently tainted
with perversity.

While it is true that in *Madame Bovary*, Chabrol exploits many
of the filming techniques that are the *sine qua non* of the heritage
genre—panoramic long shots, high angle shots, deep focus, long
takes, "pictorialist" camera work—he also continues to use a number
of the Hitchcockian and Langian techniques that characterize his *films
policiers*. Like Hitchcock, Chabrol is fond of close-ups, both of
characters and of significant objects. Semantically charged elements
of the decor that have an important function in the novel—mirrors,
windows, fireplaces—are also frequently shot in close-up. In addition,
Chabrol gives emphasis to a number of material objects that are
seemingly unimportant in the novel by filming them in close-up, not
once, but twice: the riding crop that Emma purchases for Rodolphe,
the bouquet of violets that Léon buys for her, the tarts (already
mentioned), Hippolyte's foot. In each instance, the objects draw
meaning from the context in which they are shown, thereby enriching
the narrative with a symbolism reminiscent of Lang's Expressionist
films. The symbolic use of color and the predilection for shots of
staircases ("a favorite Chabrol locale," acccording to the critic James
Monaco, 259) likewise betray the influence of Expressionism.

If certain of Chabrol's cinematographic strategies can be traced
to Hitchcock and Lang, the influence of Renoir and Minnelli on this
adaptation of *Madame Bovary* is even more pronounced. Indeed, one
could say that the film enters into dialogue with the adaptations of
these two predecessors, sometimes through direct borrowing,
sometimes through playful inversions. From Renoir, Chabrol
borrowed a favorite element of mise-en-scène, the framed painting
that has a narrative, rather than a merely decorative function. The most
obvious example in Chabrol's film is the painting of an elegant ball on
which Emma's gaze rests dreamily just after she has suffered through
the tedium of a dinner-table conversation with Charles. Besides its
importance in revealing Emma's psychology, the painting serves to

predict her presence at the Vaubyessard Ball, for it is in the very next scene that Charles returns home with the Marquis' invitation. An example of inversion is provided by the deathbed scene: whereas Renoir had shot Emma in soft focus, conferring a dreamlike quality upon her death, in Chabrol's version, the dying Emma is shot with a ruthless realism, and it is what she *sees* that is blurred. However, the most notable inversion takes place at the level of the social discourse implicit in Flaubert's novel and which Biasi has characterized as "progressiste" [progressive] (*Autour d'Emma* 82). While Renoir seized every opportunity to present the lives of the working class, Chabrol edited out all allusions to the proletariat, including even the awarding of the medal to Catherine Leroux, "ce demi-siècle de servitude" [the embodiment of a half-century of servitude] (251) at the Agricultural Fair. Presumably, a topic that was timely in the weeks and months leading up to the founding of the Front Populaire had lost its relevance by 1991.

Traces of Minnelli's influence are even easier to detect, although they more frequently take the form of inversions or distortions. We have already alluded to the fact that where religion is concerned, Chabrol included most of the scenes that Minnelli suppressed, while suppressing those Minnelli elected to retain. The warm, personal voice-over used by Minnelli is replaced by Chabrol's cold, impersonal extra-diegetic narrator. If Minnelli's male characters were all portrayed as Emma's victims and absolved of any responsibility for her behavior, every one of the male protagonists in Chabrol's adaptation contributes to Emma's demise, several of them knowingly. As Jacques Siclier has said, "[Chabrol] n'aime pas ses hommes" [Chabrol does not like his male characters] (*Le Monde*, 3 avril 1991). Moreover, the motif of prostitution, evoked repeatedly in Minnelli's version, is totally absent from Chabrol's, to the point where the novelistic Emma's statement to Guillaumin, "Je suis à plaindre mais pas à vendre" [I am to be pitied, but I'm not for sale] (445), has been changed to "Je suis à plaindre, Monsieur, pas à *prendre*" [I am to be pitied, sir, not to be *taken* (emphasis added)]. The brevity of Chabrol's dance scene at the Vaubyessard Ball is directly opposed to Minnelli's expansion of this scene in what is arguably the most famous sequence in his adaptation. Whereas Minnelli had opted to represent Emma's dizziness with his whirling camera, Chabrol's camera tracks back to record her advance as she walks across the ballroom, listening to conversations that reveal worlds and morals that are foreign to her. On the other hand—and this is perhaps the most unmistakable of Minnelli's imprints to be discovered in Chabrol's film—the camera work during the scene of Emma's first sexual encounter with Rodolphe has been directly influenced by the Hollywood director. Chabrol's lens leaves the lovers as they are about to succumb to their physical desire; he cuts to an image of Emma, sitting alone, looking dazed, then his camera climbs the trees before panning left and tilting downward to a high-angle shot of Rodolphe who is bringing back the horses. Minnelli's camera had risen all the way to the treetops before returning to the ground. However, whereas the extra-diegetic waltz music that accompanies this scene in Minnelli's version had connected Rodolphe's physical seduction of Emma with their first meeting at the Vaubyessard Ball (it will be recalled that in his version, the characters of Rodolphe and the Viscount are conflated), Chabrol has used the soundtrack to underscore the symbolism of the camerawork: over the image, the voice of a female opera singer can be heard, rising to a crescendo, then falling in a rapidly descending scale. Chabrol's use of the soundtrack in this scene, perhaps intended to evoke Flaubert's statement about Emma's dreams falling into the mud "comme des hirondelles blessées" [like wounded swallows] (293) is thus quite distinct from Minnelli's, looking forward rather than back. Nevertheless, it seems clear that a backward glance at the despised earlier version served as inspiration for Chabrol's filming of the woodland scene.

On the other hand, it would be a mistake to overemphasize the influence of his predecessors and thereby to fail to recognize the originality of Chabrol's remarkable achievement. Notwithstanding Jean-Michel Frodon's comment about "la lourdeur décorative qui corsète [la] *Madame Bovary* [de Chabrol]" [the decorative heaviness that constricts Chabrol's *Madame Bovary*] (735) there is much to like in this masterful adaptation: the playful allusions that were added by a director known for his *bonhomie*, the usually judicious editing, the rich symbolism of the mise-en-scène, the quality of the acting (whether or not one approves of the casting), the fluid camerawork, and most of all the generally scrupulous re-creation of nineteenth-century provincial life and the impressive fidelity to Flaubert's novel. In the final analysis, it is the last element more than any other that is the defining characteristic of this heritage production. Claude Chabrol has often remarked that, in making his first film, *Le Beau Serge*, he got his Catholicism "out of his system," i.e. that the experience of making a film that featured a clash between forces of good and evil and a moralistic perspective had the effect of "dechristianizing" him (Austin, *Claude Chabrol* 15). With *Madame Bovary*, Chabrol demonstrated conclusively that it is possible to abandon one's religious convictions without losing the urge to be faithful.

5

Fywell (2000): Sex in the Living Room

In its translation to the visual medium, Flaubert's classic novel has not always been granted the sanctity of the hushed and darkened theater, the awe-inspiring dimensions of the silver screen. For decades, the television production industry has been bringing classic novels to home audiences, sometimes as sharply censored made-for-TV movies, often as highly repetitious and excessively literal serial dramas, and Madame Bovary has not been exempt from this effort. Tight budgets and other constraints imposed by the medium have produced often disappointing results, of which a typical example is the 1974 Pierre Cardinal adaptation that was briefly discussed in the last chapter. Starring Nicole Courcel as a histrionic Emma and Jean Bouise as Charles, this strictly linear version, in color, is memorable mostly for its ellipses: Part I of the novel—including the initial encounter between Emma and Charles, the wedding, the Vaubyessard Ball—is absent entirely, as is the Agricultural Fair. While the simplicity of the dialogue and the bird calls and piano music that flood the sound track make it pleasant to listen to, as a visual experience this adaptation is claustrophobic and unsatisfying. Emma's thrice-repeated "J'étouffe!" [I'm suffocating!] provokes a Flaubertian "Madame Bovary c'est moi!" [Madame Bovary is just like me!] experience in the viewer.

Only slightly more successful than Cardinal was Rodney Bennett, who picked up the gauntlet for public television in 1975, directing the film for a BBC series starring Francesca Annis as Emma and Tim Conte as Charles. This was the second of three BBC attempts to adapt Flaubert's novel to the small screen; the first, starring Nyree Dawn Porter as Emma, dates from 1964. Released on videotape by

Time-Life in 2000, Bennett's English-language adaptation is divided into four 50-minute segments, entitled respectively "Marriage," "First Love," "Lost Love," and "Judgement." If the ominous allusion to punishment implied in the last subtitle suggests a cut-and-dried moralism, the adaptation's leitmotiv—a butterfly flitting around an ornate Victorian-era oil lamp that accompanies the credits at the beginning of each segment—evokes a fatal attraction with baudelairian resonances and symbolically reduces Emma's conduct to the purely instinctual.[1] Lest the viewer fail to understand the metaphor, the deathbed sequence has an intercalated scene involving two nuns, one attempting unsuccessfully to catch a butterfly in a verdant field. As the butterfly escapes her grasp, there is a fade-out, and when light returns to the screen, we see a close-up of Emma's face, now veiled but with eyes still open, a signal that she has just expired.

Most features of this production, predictably, can be traced to the simultaneously restrictive and lenient nature of the TV medium. While broadcast regulations differ from one country to the next, television movies released in Great Britain and the USA in the mid-1970s tended to present sexual encounters with discretion, thanks to government regulation but also to pressure from the public and from sponsors,[2] whereas the length of the film (two hundred minutes) permitted relatively close adherence to the novel, so that even such minor characters as the Duc de Laverdière could be included. Giles Cooper, who dramatized this version for the screen, nevertheless edited out all of Chapter 1, while adding several scenes, among them a medical visit to Bovary by Hippolyte, who has come seeking a cure for a stubborn cough. However, the adaptation's most notable feature is the heavy reliance on invented dialogue to reveal Charles's insufferable lack of imagination. "I adore big cities," says Emma dreamily to the brilliantly cast Charles, and the latter replies, "There are more people in them."

It took another fifteen years before the first truly memorable small-screen adaptation was produced. Tim Fywell's *Masterpiece*

---

[1] See Charles Baudelaire, "Hymne à la beauté": "L'éphémère ébloui vole vers toi, chandelle / Crépite, flambe et dit: Bénissons ce flambeau!" [The dazzled mayfly flutters to you, candle / Sizzles, burns and says, 'Let's bless this torch!'] (71).

[2] Television regulation is an ever-evolving phenomenon. See Silverman, Semonche, and Walker and Ferguson.

Theatre version, a co-production of BBC America and WGBH Boston, was aired on PBS in February, 2000, three months before it appeared on British TV. Shot in the French countryside, this 159-minute film was shown in two segments and presented by series host Russell Baker who cautioned viewers that Emma's "romantic encounters are portrayed with some realism" and that, therefore, "this film may not be suitable for the younger members of your family." Baker's direct address is typical of broadcast TV: besides reaching out to viewers, connecting with them and seducing them with a promise of things to come, it assumes a viewing situation that studies have shown to be largely inaccurate: the entire family gathered around the TV set (Ellis 113-5). Other features of this adaptation that make it typical of the television serial are its redundancy—Part II must be comprehensible to viewers who have missed Part I—and its tendency to melodrama. This is, after all, *Masterpiece Theatre.*

Fywell's adaptation stars Frances O'Connor, and the actress has won accolades for what Walter Goodman terms her "entirely believable Emma" (B7). Indeed, she was nominated for a Golden Globe Award for her performance and her contribution to the success of this adaptation can scarcely be exaggerated.[3] O'Connor, whose face is lovingly scrutinized by the camera lens in roughly one hundred and thirty close-ups, truly dominates this production, and while it is true that one of the features of television movies is the predominance of the close-up, the large on-screen presence of O'Connor is a defining element of this adaptation (Fischer 89; Ellis 133). In addition to privileging the protagonist's perspective, Fywell uses many of the techniques that are typical of television movies: a stripped-down mise-en-scène (i.e. the avoidance of on-screen clutter); a predilection for extreme close-ups, a sparing use of panoramic long shots, and the conscious use of the soundtrack to maintain attention and provide continuity (for example, the use of voice overlapping shots, as a sound bridge). However, the characteristics that most clearly distinguish Fywell's *Madame Bovary*, both from its small screen predecessors and from the studio adaptations, are the vastly expanded role accorded Charles's mother and the numerous graphic shots of erotic trysts, which the director defended with what may well have been a veiled

---

[3] For more on O'Connor's Golden Globe nomination, see the article "Best Performance by an Actress in a Mini-Series or Motion Picture Made for TV."

allusion to the previous BBC version: "You can't be coy about the sex. Emma is a sensual and sexual woman and you have to show that—you can't just show a bee on a flower."

In one sense, of course, the steamy *Masterpiece Theatre* adaptation is an accurate reflection of our era, with its increasingly permissive mores. There is in all likelihood a commercial factor as well, since *Masterpiece Theatre* needs rating successes in order to remain solvent, and such popular productions as *Upstairs Downstairs* have been few and far between. Certainly, the novel's ostensible subject—the transgressions of an adulterous woman—lends itself to titillating footage. Yet while it is true, as Terrence O'Flaherty points out, that "sexual promiscuity has always been acceptable to American audiences if the actors are wearing historical costumes" (18), the way in which this promiscuity is presented can vary from the discreet to the salacious. Whatever its other qualities—and there are many— Fywell's *Madame Bovary* can scarcely be deemed discreet in its representation of Emma's sexual encounters, except perhaps in comparison with the quasi-pornographic *Die Nackte Bovary*. Although Fywell's decision to highlight the erotic may well be simply a reflection of the filmmaker's interpretation of the novel (which we shall discuss in due course), there may also have been practical considerations. Torn between the desire to please the educated, upscale audience that typically responds to public television's fund-raisers and the wider public sought by the program's corporate sponsor, ExxonMobil, today's *Masterpiece Theatre* has to walk a fine line between providing high culture to the discriminating few and entertaining the masses, whose tastes run more often to the offerings of commercial TV. Although in doing so it has been accused of "undermining [the] genius [of bona fide artists, i.e. the novelists] by stooping to Hollywood-style simplicity and superficiality," it has, at least to some degree and with some productions, succeeded in its efforts (Ouellette 160). With Fywell's adaptation of *Madame Bovary*, cultural enrichment and melodramatic entertainment are skillfully blended.

As with most made-for-TV movies, this adaptation does not seem to have attracted the wide attention typically reserved for studio films, although those critics who *have* reviewed it have been generally positive in their assessment. The entertainment section of the BBC's on-line news service concedes that the explicit sex scenes "leave little to the imagination" but maintains that the movie's effect is consistent with "the shock which greeted the novel in the 19th century."[4] Steven Linan of the *Los Angeles Times* judges that Flaubert's novel has received "top-of-the-line treatment" (F15) from *Masterpiece Theatre*, and the *New York Times'* Walter Goodman considers that producer, director and actors "do justice to Flaubert" (B7). James Rampton of *The Independent* (London), paraphrasing Fywell himself, dubs this version the "sex and shopping *Madame Bovary*" and comments that "this film will certainly resonate with viewers," although he laments that it "cannot hope to reflect the intoxicating richness of Flaubert's writing." An on-line reviewer from the "Culture Vulture" website, Arthur Lazere, deems the adaptation "intelligent and respectful." In sum, the critics have been virtually unanimous in judging Fywell's version competent, but their reverence for Flaubert's masterpiece results in reviews that are timid at best. Perhaps a more compelling testimony to the success of this adaptation—or at any rate, to its popularity with viewers—is the fact that the BBC videotape (distributed by Twentieth-Century Fox) sold out long before the film became available on DVD.

Adapted for television by screenwriter Heidi Thomas, Fywell's *Madame Bovary* opens in the convent where six young novices, dressed in white, their heads veiled, are processing solemnly to the altar where they will take their final vows and renounce all worldly passions. But even before the novices appear on the screen, the religious atmosphere is established, for an ethereal plainchant fills the soundtrack as the credits fade in and out over the image of a censer swinging back and forth on its chain. The camera pans slowly to the left, leaving the censer behind and bringing a large crucifix into the frame, along with the altar boy who holds it aloft. As the camera continues its leftward movement, two candles appear, then the two young women who are carrying them. Passing behind the pillars of what one assumes to be a gothic cathedral, the six young women are momentarily hidden from the cinema spectators, if not from the on-screen spectators—nuns and laity--shown in the background, observing the ceremony from behind a partition composed of vertical bars. Following the acolyte and the priest to the altar, the novices approach the mitered bishop who waits at the altar with staff in hand.

---

[4] See "Costumed Passions Run High," an article on the *BBC News* website.

We see them fan out, drop to their knees, and raise their veils before the camera cuts to Emma, who watches the proceedings with evident emotion and yearning. A well-placed point-of-view shot shows the women prostrating themselves at the foot of the altar. The camera then tilts down to focus on their soft-soled shoes, the first of several shots of feet and footwear in Fywell's adaptation. As the ceremony begins, a male voice intones the liturgy, linking the shot of the novices with that of Emma as she is called away to see her father. The visit is not a happy one: he has come bearing news of her mother's death.

If we linger on the scene that accompanies the opening credits, it is because its romanticism conceals a rich symbolism that evokes marriage on the one hand, and female subordination and imprisonment on the other. The vertical bars behind which Emma stands, the nun's habits, the parade of novices humbly following the acolyte and the priest, the women's prostration, even the grey tones in which the sequence is filmed—all of these elements connote the drab existence of the imprisoned, an impression underscored by the fact that the actors appear to be illuminated only by the pale light coming in through the barred windows. Ironically, the spectator is invited to adopt Emma's perspective, to listen in dreamy enthrallment to the chanting nuns and to gaze, hypnotized, at the wisps of smoke rising from the censers. Against this backdrop, a ceremony takes place, and it clearly suggests a wedding: off-screen, the young Brides of Christ will promise their lives to their Heavenly Bridegroom. By introducing Emma's story with this sequence, Fywell has simultaneously found a visual equivalent of Flaubert's prose ("Les comparaisons de fiancé, d'époux, d'amant céleste et de mariage éternel qui reviennent dans les sermons lui soulevaient au fond de l'âme des douceurs inattendues" [The comparisons to fiancé, husband, celestial lover, and eternal marriage that she heard repeatedly in sermons, stirred in the depths of her soul an unexpected tenderness]) (98-99) and has evoked—for the alert spectator, at least—the theme of marriage as a prison house.

This is Fywell's version of the opening frame, and with perfect symmetry, the chanting will return at the conclusion of the film when the credits are again displayed. This time the sacred music is associated by juxtaposition with a very different sort of ceremony: the cortege, or funeral procession. In using an ecclesiastical setting to introduce Emma's story, Fywell and his writer Heidi Thomas have emphasized causality in a way usually associated with Hollywood cinema. Right from the start, the heroine's romantic longing is linked to the sensual aspects of religious practice, a connection that Flaubert emphasizes only in Chapter VI:

> Vivant donc sans jamais sortir de la tiède atmosphère des classes et parmi ces femmes au teint blanc portant des chapelets à croix de cuivre, elle s'assoupit doucement à la langueur mystique qui s'exhale des parfums de l'autel, de la fraîcheur des bénitiers et du rayonnement des cierges. (98)

> [So, leading her life without ever leaving the warm atmosphere of the classrooms, among these pale women whose rosaries had brass crosses, she was softly lulled into a state of somnolence by the mystical languor that seemed to seep out of the altar fragrances, the coolness of the holy water fonts, and the glow of the candles.]

Nearly all the elements of the literary description become props in Fywell's mise-en-scène: the incense, the anemic-looking nuns, the altar, the candles. Even the "chapelets à croix de cuivre" [the rosaries with brass crosses] (98) will be evoked when, in the following scene, Père Rouault offers Emma a religious relic: her mother's rosary.

Religion and death, death and religion. In a chiasmic (AB/BA) structure, the film's soundtrack begins and ends with plainchant, and the plainchant encloses scenes evoking death, that of the mother in the beginning and the daughter at the end. By foregrounding the death of Emma Bovary's mother, this film means to suggest that in addition to the convent life, a youthful trauma has shaped Emma Bovary's character. This episode becomes the locus of her personal transformation: Emma will rebel when her father informs her not only that her mother has died, but that she has already been buried under the plum tree. Deeply aggrieved by the discovery that the funeral has taken place without her, she cries silently, then looks her father squarely in the face and asks with a touch of defiance, "Will you bury me there when I die? Will no one be permitted to mourn me?"

In addition to the prophetic value of Emma's allusion to her own early death, this statement prepares the next scene, in which a deeply indignant Emma learns that she will not even be allowed to grieve in the convent. Following the paternal visit, the camera cuts to the altar, now empty save for a small figure viewed from a high angle. It is Emma, lying prostrate, not precisely as the novices had done in the opening sequence, for her arms are outstretched in a pose that evokes the crucifixion. Her cry of anguish to the nun who comes to get her ("There's so much agony. I can hardly bear the weight of it") is summarily dismissed. The sister tells her sternly that she must "surrender all passion" and it is at this point that a transformation seems to take place within her. No longer docile, Frances O'Connor's Emma will be marked by her rebellious nature, not in an anachronistically feminist manner, as Isabelle Huppert's Emma had been, but in her insistence upon her right to passion and pleasure. Surrender all passion? For this Emma, the nun's words are tantamount to a challenge. When she is removed from the convent by her father, she tells him that the nuns were trying to break her "like a horse." And she adds, "Jesus would have made a very tiresome bridegroom."

This comment sets the stage for Emma's quest for passion. Through its rigorously symmetrical structure, in which nearly every scene has its corollary; through its brilliant dialogue; and through its subtle exploitation of religious imagery, Fywell's adaptation represents Emma Bovary's quest as a religious pilgrimage in which the passion of the journey is associated with the suffering of Calvary. And the dialogue cleverly assigns to Emma herself the task of suggesting the connection. Showing Charles a crown of laurel leaves that she had won in a writing composition, she explains, "The title was 'What is passion?' and I furnished a pious answer hinged upon the crucifixion." It would no doubt be naive to suggest that, taken in isolation, this allusion to the Passion of Christ authorizes an interpretation of Emma as a Christ figure. However, it does evoke the etymological connection between passion and suffering. As if to drive home the point, Fywell lets us into the bedroom on Emma's wedding night. Clearly disappointed and visibly suffering pain as Charles grunts and gasps in orgasmic pleasure, Emma interrupts her husband *en pleine jouissance* (just as he is reaching a climax) to ask, "Is this passion, Charles?" She appears unconvinced by his breathless affirmation that he had never before experienced such ecstasy ("I never knew...I never knew"). Charles (played by a bearded, robust Hugh Bonneville) may know intense physical pleasure that night; for Emma, the initial taste of coitus is more akin to suffering. In a subsequent attempt to awaken in herself feelings of passion for her husband, Emma will put on a party dress, descend to the moonlit garden, and recite passages, not from Lamartine, as the novelistic heroine had done, but from the Song of Solomon. The choice of the Bible was no doubt dictated by the fact that it has a higher recognition value among the viewers of *Masterpiece Theatre* than the poetry of a French romantic. More importantly, however, it underlines the connection between religion and sensuality, a connection established in the film's opening sequence.

The wedding night scene is just the first of several graphic sexual encounters shown in Fywell's adaptation. As in the novel, Emma's first experience of sexual pleasure takes place not in the marital bed but on the dance floor at the Vaubyessard ball. It is worth mentioning that the association of the waltz with the erotic is historically accurate, since the newly imported dance was widely regarded as "immoral" in mid-nineteenth-century France. Not only were the dancers in close contact with each other, but the rapid tempo and whirling and twirling shocked those who were more accustomed to traditional dances such as the Minuet where decorum was preserved with a polite distance between partners and with slower and more precise movements.[5] In Flaubert, too, the passage describing the dance is shot through with allusions to the erotic, carefully prepared by a description of Emma's "awakening" to other sensual delights: her sensitivity to previously unknown culinary refinements, her sudden awareness of "forbidden pleasures." The film dispenses with all this and assigns to the Marquise d'Andervilliers the role of mentor. Articulating what Emma had not dared confess even to herself, the Marquise sends Charles on his way, then says conspiratorially, "He bores you." The conversation proceeds as follows:

EMMA. Oh no!

THE MARQUISE. He is your husband, and tedium is entirely proper. Do you have a bosom friend?

EMMA. A best friend?

THE MARQUISE. Somebody to confide in, label her as you will.

EMMA. I have a little dog, an Italian greyhound.

THE MARQUISE. How delightful, and such a great respecter of secrets!

EMMA. I have no secrets, Madam.

It is at this point that the Marquise swings into action: a woman with no secrets is clearly in need of assistance. Upon learning that Emma does not know how to waltz, she seizes the opportunity to

---

[5] The early waltz, known today as the Viennese Waltz, was born in Vienna in the early 1800s. For more on the history of this dance, see Sears.

serve as *entremetteuse* (go-between), beckoning to the viscount and enlisting him to teach her, because, as she informs Emma, "Gentlemen do so enjoy the opportunity to initiate one."

Fywell represents the heavily symbolic waltz as diametrically opposed to the wedding night lovemaking, with the viscount remaining in complete control while Emma's heaving breast and moist eyes suggest that for her the experience has been distinctly erotic. Unlike Minnelli, who uses a spinning camera to record the heroine's vertigo during the ball scene, Fywell keeps the focus on Emma, and her rapid breathing and languorous posture leave no doubt as to the nature of the ecstasy she has just discovered.

With Léon in his first incarnation (played by the boyish Hugh Dancy), intimacy is primarily verbal, and the only physical contact these future lovers enjoy is the suggestive way in which they press together their fingertips in a gesture that evokes hands joined in prayer. Fywell has recourse to a variation on this metonymy just before the pair become lovers: they press their fingers together as in prayer, then entwine them, recalling the novelistic description of the

Figure 7. Fywell's *Madame Bovary* (2000).

dance with the viscount, "leurs jambes entrèrent l'une dans l'autre" [their legs became entwined] (122), a phrase excised by *La Revue de Paris* and reinstated by an indignant Flaubert.[6] Besides foretelling the act that is to come, the praying hands also recall the search for a divine lover and thus link the religious and the sexual. In setting Emma's secret meeting with Léon in a church, Fywell is only following Flaubert; however, by illuminating the lovers in the carriage with light streaming through a cross-shaped opening, he is putting his own stamp on the story and suggesting the quasi-religious nature of Emma's eroticism (figure 7). Emma's question to Léon ("Is this it, Léon, is this our souls' meeting?"), ironic in view of the act that is to follow, evokes the immaterial nature of her desire and recalls the question she asked Charles on her wedding night.

It is however Emma's first fall—her woodland tryst with Rodolphe, masterfully played by Greg Wise—that most graphically (and perhaps sacrilegiously) represents the connection between religious and sexual ecstasy. The connection is no doubt prepared by the fact that Rodolphe's first attempt at seduction is set in a church (site of the patriotic discourse which, in the novel, is pronounced at the Agricultural Fair), and by his insistence, during a subsequent visit to Emma, that they will inevitably consummate their love "because the angels demand it." Nevertheless, with the forest seduction, Fywell daringly blends a scene of smoldering passion with an image that evokes, however distantly, the crucifixion. As they ride horseback through the forest with Emma in the lead, we observe Emma from the rear, as the camera tilts down to caress her body. This point-of-view shot is followed by a short scene in which the soon-to-be lovers, having dismounted, begin their flirtation. A sharp cut to a tree disorients the spectator with a steadily moving camera that reveals a half-naked Emma pinned against the bark while Rodolphe slowly unlaces her corset and kisses her buttocks as Emma gasps with anticipated pleasure. The tree here hardly brings to mind the wood of the cross, and yet, as the sequence continues, first with a graphic representation of their sexual encounter, then with a high angle shot of the couple, Emma lying face up on the ground, arms outstretched, her body covered by that of her lover, the spectator once again discovers

---

[6] See Jacques Neefs's footnote in the novel (122).

an allusion to the crucified Christ. Yet if her posture brings the crucifixion to mind, her passion (small "p") does not, for she has experienced intense pleasure. However, there is a feeling of *déjà vu* here, for the filmmaker has used similar cinematic techniques in earlier scenes displaying Emma's *pain*. The first was the high angle shot that showed Emma prostrate at the altar, the second, also shot from a high angle, had featured Emma lying on a bed, screaming in pain, her body hidden by that of Charles who is ministering to her as she undergoes the throes of childbirth. The use of similar camera angles in these three shots has a symbolic value: we have a God's eye view of Emma, whether she is in agony or in ecstasy. Indeed, the opposition collapses when Rodolphe observes that he has made her bleed—let's remember that she has already given birth, so this is an allusion not to a broken hymen but to his brutality (in his impatience, he has also cut her boot laces with his penknife)—and despite Emma's jubilant reply ("That's all right: it'll be like a second first time.") and her delight regarding her new status ("I have a lover! I have a lover!"), there are ominous signs that her pleasure will be followed by pain.

If the ubiquitous presence of religious symbolism in the erotic encounters and the association of suffering with pleasure have failed to attract critical notice, the unblinking attention to the erotic has elicited heated comment. Moreover, in addition to the five or six scenes that display human sexuality in its most conventional form, Fywell has included allusions to more "deviant" pleasures that were only implicit in the novel. Foot fetishism, masturbation, cross-dressing, prostitution, voyeurism, bestiality: all are evoked, sometimes with a wry humor, often in titillating detail. The question then arises: Why? Simply because the law no longer forbids it? I would like to suggest that in addition to the possible commercial motivation for producing a film that would keep spectators glued to their sets (we must remember that TV viewers have a remote control at their fingertips), Fywell was in fact doing what Flaubert himself would have done, had he not been hamstrung by Second Empire censorship. Flaubert was no prude, as his correspondence makes abundantly clear, and scholars have identified in *Madame Bovary* numerous veiled allusions to sexual perversions and erotic activity that would have shocked his contemporaries.[7] "Veiled" is the operative word here, for

---

[7] See Porter and Gray, *Reference Guide,* 13.

he had to exercise some self-censorship if he wanted his novel to be published. From this perspective, one might even say that Fywell was avenging Flaubert, for the filmmaker routinely and somewhat perversely included most of the scenes with which the public prosecutor took issue at the obscenity trial, as well as those (in most cases the same ones) that Minnelli carefully excised from his adaptation. On the other hand, he had no need for the finger-pricking scene or the sexually symbolic liqueur drinking scene, for obvious reasons, and they have been edited out of this adaptation. One might object, of course, that by focusing so narrowly on the physical nature of Emma's relationships, Fywell reduces her desires to nymphomania and her disillusionment to post-coital depression. To do so would be to underestimate the role of Madame Bovary Senior.

The remarkable expansion of the role of Charles's mother is consistent with the internal logic of this adaptation. However, this alteration also speaks volumes about ideological presuppositions on the cusp of the twenty-first century. The current tendency to pathologize unacceptable behaviors finds expression in the foregrounding of the death of Emma's mother. An implicitly causal relationship is thus established between maternal deprivation and Emma's inability to find happiness within the domestic sphere of her marriage. But in a film as shaped by antithesis as this one is, this absence must be balanced by a corresponding presence, and the presence too becomes part of the etiology of Emma's "illness." This "presence" takes the shape of the acidic Madame Bovary Senior, played by Eileen Atkins whose scornful condescension is diluted by the fact that her blistering rebukes are delivered in a Midlands accent. The mother-in-law/daughter-in-law antipathy is of course timeless, but its prominence in this adaptation is both a function of the medium (for it intensifies the domestic drama which is the specialty of the small-screen film) and a product of our time, in which, according to conventional wisdom, a mother is to blame for almost every psychological affliction.[8] Of course, practical considerations no doubt also motivated this shift in emphasis, since Charles is widowed when we meet him. By inflating the role played by Charles's mother, Fywell dispenses with that of Héloïse, whose jealous carping is reassigned to Madame Bovary Senior. Moreover, since Homais is stripped of his

---

[8] See, for example, Nancy Friday's *My Mother/My Self*.

ambition in this adaptation, his role being reduced to that of insufferable know-it-all who plays no role in Emma's downfall, Fywell needs to find another antagonist, and that antagonist is Madame Bovary Senior. Whereas Chabrol had if anything expanded the pharmacist's role, Fywell, wisely judging that the long-winded expatiations of the novelistic character Homais would not hold audience interest—unlike cinema spectators, TV viewers are easily distracted—opted for the crisp, acrimonious dialogue that pitted mother-in-law against daughter-in-law.

Even before she has met the young woman from the Rouault farm, Charles's mother takes a disliking to her. Sensing that her son is returning to the farm more often than Rouault's condition necessitates, she admonishes him that he needs to "attract a better class of invalid." Indeed, she has gathered information about the Rouaults:

> I have heard things about that family. And her. Nothing as prosperous as they make out, for all she's been washed and buffed up by the Ursulines. There was a cousin of theirs, had up in the country assises. Sheep came into it.

Notwithstanding her allusion to bestiality (an exemplary display of wit by screenwriter Heidi Thomas), Madame Bovary Senior's principal objection to the match she suspects her son may be about to make is that the family is insufficiently affluent. The pecuniary interests of the novelistic character, who marries Charles to his first wife Héloïse because she believes her to be wealthy, are thus intact in this adaptation. However, the irony is more pointed, since Emma too is concerned with class. But while both women can be described as social climbers, Emma's manners have been refined in the convent, whereas the elder Madame Bovary betrays her proletarian origins at every turn. Once the marriage takes place, she focuses her attacks on Emma's extravagance, starting with the netting and bows of her wedding dress ("She'll never wear it again," she says acidly to Père Rouault, a prediction that proves false when Emma is buried in her wedding gown). The older woman's concern with money is diametrically opposed to the fiscal irresponsibility and insouciance that eventually provoke Emma's downfall, and in the magnificently ironic scene in which Mme Bovary Senior, having surprised the maid's male visitor in the house, complains about Félicité's morals, Emma retorts: "Truly well-bred people don't give a fig about how domestics conduct themselves. If I hadn't been told otherwise, I would think that you were working class." This outburst pits the two women against each other somewhat more dramatically than in the novel, when Emma had said simply to her mother-in-law, "De quel monde êtes-vous?" [What class do you belong to anyway?] (302) and had uttered her most insulting comments, "Ah! quel savoir-vivre! quelle paysanne!" [Oh! What manners! What a peasant!] (302), only after she had fled the company of the older woman.

Whereas the petty-minded mother-surrogate represented by the meddling Madame Bovary Senior cannot not possibly fill the gap left by Emma's mother, there are at least two other characters in the novel who try—unsuccessfully as it turns out—to lavish maternal care on Emma. The first is the Marquise d'Andervilliers, who briefly serves as a mentor to Emma in a way diametrically opposed to that of her mother-in-law.   The other is Charles. In Fywell's brilliantly witty transposition of the novelistic character to the screen, the bovine traits of Flaubert's character have been reduced to a single gesture: Charles gives milk. During one of the many scenes added in this adaptation, Charles comes upon Emma and Léon who are enjoying a moment of innocent intimacy, Emma at the piano, Léon standing beside her, singing robustly in German. Charles interrupts this carefree moment when he enters the room with a tray, announcing: "Milk time, Sweetheart." His solicitude with regard to his wife's health, here motivated by his concerns regarding her pregnancy, is a leitmotif of this version, where it repeatedly takes the form of an injunction to drink. "Have a sip of water, Sweetie," he suggests when she chokes on an apricot from the basket delivered by Rodolphe's servant. "Here, you must drink this milk now," he begs, as Emma is convulsed with cramps on her death bed, "please, please...drink it! Good girl, good girl!" Quite apart from the parental tenor of his endearing address to his wife, the cinematic Charles is a caregiver by nature, whence his excitement when he discovers that Emma is pregnant. Once the baby is born, it is he, not Emma, who is shown repeatedly attending to her—feeding her, playing with her, holding her in his arms, reading to her—that is, playing a role that nineteenth-century society would have assigned to women.[9] Moreover, he often reminds Emma of her

---

[9] In this respect, the cinematic Charles is true to his novelistic source because Flaubert's character takes the duties of fatherhood just as seriously.

maternal duties ("You were exhausted last night. Berthe doesn't like it when you go straight to your room"; "Berthe wouldn't go to bed without you"). Emma, for her part, although she is sporadically capable of maternal feelings and intends to take Berthe with her when she runs off with Rodolphe, unlike the egotistical Emma played by Jennifer Jones in Minnelli's adaptation, does pawn a sterling silver rattle that she steals from her daughter so that she can treat Léon to an evening at the carnival.

Despite its significance as a measure of Emma's desperation, this theft (absent from the novel) has the effect of distancing the viewer from Emma, who at least temporarily joins the ranks of the film's deviant mothers. From the diagnosis of her pregnancy to the quickening, the preparation of the layette, the labor and delivery, every step of Emma's maternity is charted by this adaptation in such abundant detail that her betrayal of her maternal calling is not a mere footnote to the story. Maternal negligence, maternal abdication, maternal disapproval, maternal severity, maternal death, finally, all the variants of maternal deprivation are represented in a film that is inhabited by a longing for the good mother. It is a longing that nothing else can satisfy, not physical intimacy, not marriage, not material wealth. "Did you make your mother proud?" Emma asks Léon when she meets him on the steps of the Rouen opera house, and one senses that this question is central to the film's interpretation of the novel. However timeless the need for the mother's approval, it has particular relevance to the viewer for whom this film is targeted, the twentieth-century viewer whose psyche may have been poked and prodded by a therapist's weekly questions, the viewer saturated with stereotypes from pop psychology, the typically affluent viewer of *Masterpiece Theatre*.

A parallel effort to update Flaubert's novel can be seen in the film's tendency to shy away from the religion vs. science debate, perhaps deemed irrelevant in the year 2000, as it was in the Chabrol adaptation eight years earlier.[10] Indeed, in addition to shrinking Homais's role, this film eliminates Bournisien altogether. Nevertheless, the four scenes that take place inside a church (in three of which the church becomes the locus of an illicit rendezvous), the

---

[10] One might speculate whether this omission would have occurred had the film been an exclusively American production, given that the proponents of creationism and intelligent design keep the religion vs. science debate timely in the U.S.A.

ubiquitous presence (symbolic or literal) of crosses and crucifixes, and the foregrounding of the convent, together with the numerous allusions to religion in the dialogue, suggest that this is a distinctly religious interpretation of Emma's suffering. If, as she lies dying, this Emma does not plant a passionate kiss on the effigy of the crucified Christ, it is not only because she has explicitly rejected Christ as a bridegroom, judging him "boring," but because such a gesture would be incongruous, given that she herself has been assimilated to the Christ of the Passion. Small wonder, then, that the deathbed scene, like the other scenes of intense pleasure or pain, features a crane shot. Nor should the spectator be surprised that on one occasion in the film, Emma strikes the classic pose of Christ immortalized in paintings of the pieta (figure 8). The scene follows Rodolphe's betrayal and a

Figure 8. Fywell's *Madame Bovary* (2000).

hysterical attack that the film presents as a choking incident. The angle of the head, the languid posture of the body, the pallor of the skin, all evoke the paintings of Christ's body in the arms of his mother. Perhaps not coincidentally, a similar pose is struck by Huppert's Emma in the deathbed scene of Chabrol's adaptation.

To present the vagaries of an adulterous woman as the agonizing steps of a human Calvary is to flirt with the ridiculous, and Fywell's film is rife with techniques that suggest an ironic perspective. In this film's grammar, shots are often juxtaposed in such a way as to evoke that ironic distance from the characters—including Emma, and in spite of all the close-ups—that was a hallmark of Flaubert's prose. A perfect illustration of this technique is the cross-cutting that is used in the scene of the amputation of the stable boy's leg. Canivet has arrived, "Paul" (the screenwriter has performed her own amputation, robbing Hippolyte of all but the second syllable of his name) is screaming in pain, while Emma, within earshot, is wracked with mental suffering and regret. The camera cuts back and forth between close-ups of Paul, whose contorted facial expression and inarticulate cries need no interpretation, and Emma, who is shot in medium close-up, her thoughts echoing on the soundtrack. Her words ("What have I done? I must be insane to have sacrificed so much!") are a succinct expression of her self-absorption. Paul, whose screams provide a catalyst for her thoughts, has sacrificed a leg to her ambition. This collapse of distinctions between physical and psychological pain, between the material and the immaterial may, it is true, be intended merely to emphasize the intensity of Emma's mental anguish, but it is difficult not to find some irony in the situation as it is presented here.

The confusion that links the physical with the psychological is most famously evoked in the novel when Emma goes to see Father Bournisien in search of relief for her emotional pain. The priest, misinterpreting the young woman's obvious distress, surmises that she is suffering from digestive problems and advises her to return home and have a cup of tea: "ça vous fortifiera, ou bien un verre d'eau fraîche avec de la cassonade" [that'll pick you up, either that or a glass of cold water with some brown sugar] (203). Since Fywell's adaptation has eliminated the role of Bournisien, other means must be found to highlight the connection between physical and psychological suffering. Often, dialogue becomes the vehicle for the juxtaposition, as when Emma, reading from the Song of Solomon in the garden at midnight, attempts to awaken passion in herself and in Charles. "My lover put his hand onto the door," she recites. "His fingers were scented with oil. I opened the door unto my lover." Placing Charles's hand on her thigh, she continues, "I trembled at the perfume of him."

The discomfited Charles cautions Emma that his mother, sleeping in a bedroom overlooking the garden, might awaken. The dialogue continues as follows:

> EMMA. Well, go back inside then! Put on your cotton nightcap! Roll over, go to sleep and dream of nothing!
>
> CHARLES. You're getting overexcited. Would you like me to make you a tincture of anise?
>
> EMMA. But I want to be excited! Don't you understand? You can't mix me up a potion to prevent it!

The parallels between this scene and the novelistic visit to Bournisien are unmistakable.[11] But in the film, an even earlier scene had provided a more patently ironic illustration of Charles's inability to comprehend his wife's psychological needs. Shortly after they are married, Emma expresses dismay when Charles, cutting short their pillow talk, makes ready to leave on his daily rounds. However, go he must, for a patient's carbuncle needs lancing. "But I miss you when you're gone!" protests Emma. Charles replies, "That's easily remedied" and the camera cuts to a rear shot of Emma, standing in the window. Another cut, and we see her in profile: she's holding an Italian greyhound puppy in her arms. According to the logic of Charles's very literal mind, one warm body is as good as another. However, the juxtaposition of shots in this sequence, specifically the substitution of a canine for a human, reflects not only the prosaic nature of Emma's husband but sets up an equation: Charles and the puppy are interchangeable. In the novel, it is Emma who eventually makes this connection, but only after she has, through a predictable anthropomorphism, projected her own misery upon the dog:

> —Allons, baisez maîtresse, vous qui n'avez pas de chagrins.
> Puis, considérant la mine mélancolique du svelte animal qui bâillait avec lenteur, elle s'attendrissait, et, le comparant à elle-même, lui parlait tout haut, comme à quelqu'un d'affligé que l'on console. (112)

---

[11] One could also point to the novelistic passage: "Elle pâlissait et avait des battements de coeur. Charles lui administra de la valériane et des bains de camphre. Tout ce que l'on essayait semblait l'irriter davantage" [She was growing paler and was having palpitations. Charles gave her some valerian and camphor baths. Everything they tried seemed to make her more irritable] (139).

["Come on, give your mistress a kiss, you who have no worries."
Then, noting the melancholy face of the graceful animal, who yawned
slowly, she was touched, and mentally comparing the animal to
herself, she spoke to her aloud as you would speak to somebody in
pain whom you were consoling.]

Djali thus becomes the confidant that Emma so needs, a stand-in for
Charles in his absence, and Charles's role is correspondingly
diminished:

car, enfin, Charles était quelqu'un, une oreille toujours ouverte, une
approbation toujours prête. Elle faisait bien des confidences à sa
levrette! (134)

[for, after all, Charles was somebody to talk to, always ready to listen
and to give his approval. She confided lots of things to her greyhound,
after all!]

Whereas in the novel the puppy had been a gift from one of Charles's
patients, thus a testimonial to at least some professional competence,
however limited, and whereas it is the novelistic Emma who
assimilates Charles ("une oreille toujours ouverte" [an always open
ear; 123]) to a canine companion, the film assigns to Charles himself
the responsibility for his own belittlement, for it is he who assumes
that his company can be replaced by that of a puppy.

Fywell's Emma comes increasingly to recognize Charles's
literalism, while her own flights of fancy continue to be a mystery to
him. The role of confidant played by Djali, who here, as in the novel,
escapes from the carriage en route to Yonville, is assumed in the film
by Léon, and Emma wastes no time in sharing with him her disdain
for Charles's inability to understand her emotional needs. When Léon
speculates that "in his innermost heart," Charles wants "to live by the
laws of love and not by the laws of nature," Emma retorts, "I don't
think Charles has got an innermost heart. Just a plaster model of one.
He keeps it on his desk. At medical school, they told him the heart
was just another muscle and he believed them." Notwithstanding the
cruelty of Emma's putdown of her husband, Charles's prosaic nature
finds visual support throughout the film. In one particularly illustrative
sequence, the camera focuses on Charles as he paints the woodwork
inside their house, using broad brush strokes, then cuts quickly to a
shot of Emma at her easel outside, delicately applying color to her
canvas. Here, the image track alone is effective in suggesting that

there can be no meaningful communication between this terre-à-terre husband and his more refined and artistic wife.

In addition to being simple and irremediably practical, Charles is characterized by a lack of spontaneity that is depicted as a preoccupation with time. The novelistic heroine's lament that Charles's lovemaking was always on schedule, "une habitude parmi les autres, et comme un dessert prévu d'avance, après la monotonie du dîner" [a habit among others, like a dessert that could be counted on, after the monotony of dinner] (110) has its cinematic equivalent. On several occasions in the film we observe Charles taking out his pocket watch. One scene in particular illustrates his excessive concern with punctuality: as he enters the conjugal chamber one evening, he discovers that Emma has drawn a bath. Ignoring her seductive pose, he admonishes her, "It's ten o'clock. We go to bed at ten o'clock!" Even his wife's prophetic retort ("Habits, Charles, are like promises and pie crusts—made to be broken") and her romantic gesture of strewing rose pedals into the bath water do not awaken his desire. His decision to go downstairs "until you've prepared yourself" underscores a lack of spontaneity that is in direct opposition to the sentiments expressed in Rodolphe's romantic discourse. Writing of their planned departure, Emma's lover promises that in "only seven days, only six sleepless nights, the tyranny of the clocks will be forever overturned."

Indeed, this is not the only case in which this adaptation uses words rather than images to reinforce the opposition that pits Charles against Emma's extra-marital lovers. The clichéed amorous discourse in which Rodolphe, Léon and Emma herself indulge is often presented through a voiceover technique that differs sharply from the one used by Minnelli and Chabrol. Whereas both Minnelli and Chabrol had used extradiegetic narrators (James Mason's Flaubert in the first instance, a disembodied voice in the second), Fywell overlays close-ups of the characters with a voice in echo that represents their thoughts. Sometimes the voice is their own; at others, the voice of someone else—typically, a lover—is echoing in their head. For example, over two shots, the first showing Rodolphe gazing out a window, the second, Emma lying in bed next to her husband, the spectator hears, in Emma's voice, the words of a letter that the heroine has written to Rodolphe: "I feel no remorse, suffer no guilt, fear nothing. You have poured yourself into my heart and love comes streaming out. The heavens have been torn open. Passion has been spilt everywhere." Emma's lack of originality is suggested by the fact that in an earlier scene, Léon had said to her, as he pressed his fingers to hers, "I'm pouring myself into you." But what is more significant for our present purposes is the way the real world intrudes on her thoughts. The dreamy extra-diegetic music stops abruptly as Emma becomes aware that Charles is making ready to leave. "Are you going out? It's early," she remarks, and his reply offers yet another example of the immaterial/material juxtaposition that is part of this adaptation's irony: "I have to ride halfway to Rouen. Big emetic needed." The juxtaposition of the romantic discourse with the medical could scarcely be more pointed. Charles deals, not with "spilt passion" but with vomitus, and his words remind Emma of the gulf that separates her from the country physician she has married. While Rodolphe tells her that he wants to make her blood "sing in her veins like a river of milk," a poetic, almost baudelairian phrase rich with sexual innuendo that echoes on the soundtrack of her mind throughout the second half of the film, Charles attempts to cure her through a therapeutic blood-letting.[12]

Yet, for all this, there's a certain tenderness about Bonneville's Charles. Those spectators who protest that Fywell's scenes of eroticism reduce Emma's desires to the purely physical do not take into account the fact that this director has cast in the role of the cuckold an actor who, while perhaps not handsome in a canonical way, is attractive and virile. Far from the inarticulate bumbler of Flaubert's character, Bonneville's Charles, despite his down-to-earth pragmatism, can at times be both passionate and romantic. In fact, in what may well be a wink to the cognoscenti, i.e. those viewers aware both of Flaubert's foot fetishism and the large role played by feet and footgear in the novel, Fywell endows Charles with a particular fondness for feet.[13] In one especially moving scene, Charles takes Emma's foot in his hands and kisses it tenderly, murmuring, "Do you

---

[12] In the novel, this image is attributed to an impersonal narrator who embraces the heroine's perspective: "Le silence était partout; quelque chose de doux semblait sortir des arbres; elle sentait son coeur, dont les battements recommençaient, et le sang circuler dans sa chair comme un fleuve de lait." [Everything was silent; something soft and sweet seemed to emanate from the trees; she felt her heart beating again, and the blood seemed to flow in her veins like a river of milk] (264).

[13] On the role of feet and footgear in Flaubert's work, see Florence Emptaz.

remember when I used to kiss your feet? That perfect little place just inside the hollow of your instep? Oh, I cannot resist you." There are different ways to interpret this scene, of course. One might point out Emma's obvious discomfiture: this is a heroine more easily seduced by the classic *baise-main* [hand kissing]. One might recall the scene of the woodland lovemaking with Rodolphe, when Emma's lover had brutally cut the laces of her delicate boot with his pen knife and ripped it off, while leaving his own long riding boots firmly in place. Whatever one's interpretation, it seems clear that antithesis is the organizing device here.

And where antithesis is concerned, there is probably no more eloquent an expression of this director's fondness for oppositional structures than the way in which he incorporates the organ grinder into the film. Unlike the other adaptations we have considered here, Fywell's version makes of the barrel organ a veritable leitmotif. Whereas in the novel, the street musician grinds out tunes "que l'on jouait ailleurs sur les théâtres, que l'on chantait dans les salons, que l'on dansait le soir sous des lustres éclairés" [that were being played in other places, in the theatres, tunes that were sung in drawing rooms and danced to in the evening, under lighted chandeliers] (137), in this adaptation the tune heard over and over again is the very waltz music played by the orchestra at the Vaubyessard ball. Furthermore, while the novel's barrel organ had been decorated with many tiny replicas of dancers "femmes en turban rose, Tyroliens en jaquette, singes en habit noir, messieurs en culotte courte" [women in pink turbans, Tyrolians in jackets, monkeys in black frock coats, gentlemen in knee breeches] (137), the film has reduced the dancers to two, a waltzing couple in formal dress who, both for the protagonist herself and for the viewer, evoke Emma and the Viscount. Fywell has conflated two of the novel's characters (the organ grinder and the beggar) to create his blind street musician, and just as the blind beggar of the novel seems possessed of a symbolic importance that has been the object of numerous studies, the organ grinder here comes to represent the banality and the triviality of Emma's desires.[14] The street organ appears four times in the film, and except for the first appearance, which is unaccompanied by music, it is generally associated with

---

[14] On the blind man, see articles by Max Aprile, Sheila Bell, Mary Donaldson-Evans, Murray Sachs, William Bysshe Stein, P. M. Wetherill, and Michael J. Williams.

reminiscences of the Vaubyessard ball, its tinny, hurdy-gurdy waltz music a vulgar imitation of the music that had accompanied Emma's "initiation" to sensual pleasure and thus a taunting reminder that what she considered the most perfect moment of her life is gone forever. Whereas in the novel, the street musician disappears when the couple moves to Yonville-L'Abbaye, this organ grinder follows the couple to the larger town, cranking out his music throughout the entire film. If at first Emma is hypnotized by the twirling dancers atop the barrel, by the time the organ grinder makes his penultimate appearance, she has been disabused, and she notices for the first time the condition of the organ grinder himself. Stopping en route to the pawn shop in one of the novel's last scenes, she rings his bell and says to him, "You ought to get something done about your eyes. I have a magnificent doctor in Yonville."

Notwithstanding the visual wordplay—the organ grinder puts his hand out for a tip, but the tip he gets is not monetary—the scene is not merely playful. Emma's perverse recommendation of Charles's services provides an apt parallel with the novelistic scene in which Homais tells the blind beggar that he should be following a diet rich in meat and wine: like the pharmacist, Emma offers a patently ludicrous solution to the vagrant's problem. In addition, this scene marks an "awakening" of sorts: unlike the organ grinder, she is no longer "blind," for she now "sees" the ugliness of reality, the music having lost the power to hypnotize her. This signals the new depths of despair to which she has descended. However, the most poignant representation of the barrel organ is the last. As the funeral cortege, shot from a high angle, rounds a corner, the organ grinder comes into view, and with him the dancing figurines. In a transition from the sublime to the ridiculous, the plainchant and tolling church bells that had accompanied the first part of the funeral procession is replaced by hurdy gurdy waltz music. Suddenly, the camera cuts to the ball, in a flashback that establishes an unmistakable parallel between the mechanically revolving miniatures and the human dancers formed by Emma and the Viscount. As the romantic ball scene is replayed, with its close-ups and dissolves and the orchestral waltz, the viewer hears Emma's words in voiceover echoing on the soundtrack: "It was the most perfect moment of my life." And it is precisely at this point that the camera cuts back to the present, the street musician and his barrel with the tiny couple turning endlessly on top of it. The shift is accompanied by the subtle blending of the street music with the strings and brass, until the former drowns out the latter. This is the ultimate trivialization of Emma's dreams, and it is on this image that the film ends. When the credits roll, now over a black background devoid of images, they will be accompanied by plainchant.

The contrast between the mechanically-produced street music and the orchestral waltz requires no commentary. Nevertheless, the significance of Fywell's foregrounding of the barrel organ can be more fully appreciated when one puts the instrument into its historical context. Despite the fact that the name by which it is known in French (*l'orgue de barbarie*) has nothing to do with barbarism, "barbarie" being a corruption of "Barbieri," the name of the instrument's Italian inventor, the instrument was associated with the primitive and the uncouth. (See Ord-Hume 233) Street musicians, many of whom were foreigners, were often disabled and thus unable to seek other forms of work. Blindness was common. Because they ground out their music relentlessly, barely noticing if their instrument was out of tune, they came to be regarded as a nuisance, and it was not unusual for people to pay them to *stop* playing. Aristocrats in particular had little tolerance for them. That Fywell's adaptation has reduced Emma's desires to the mechanically produced music and the slowly revolving figurines of a barrel organ is all the more ironic in that the instrument and its player were associated with Italy, the country to which she dreamed of escaping. Emma will go nowhere, and the tiny dancers, turning rhythmically in the circumscribed space of the barrel top, evoke the circular movement of Binet's lathe and become, like it, a metaphor for her eternal claustration.

It is also possible to see in Fywell's organ grinder a self-referential irony. Like the director of made-for-TV movies, the street musician is an entertainer, and his entertainment involves the vulgarization of high art. The barrel organ, not in fact a new invention, but an adaptation of a more respected musical instrument, the pipe organ, can be likened to television's small screen, itself an "adaptation" of the silver screen of cinema theatres. Pipe organ and silver screen, in turn, occupy an intermediate rung on the ladder leading up to the full orchestra and the novel, respectively. Just as the organ grinder, with his mechanically produced melody and the spinning dancing figures, provides for Emma a reductive, simplistic, but ultimately haunting reminder of her life's only epiphany, so does the TV film director interpret her story with the limited means he has at his disposal. Viewed in this perspective, the scenes in which the organ grinder appears might be considered examples of what Millicent Marcus terms "umbilical scenes," i.e. scenes "which make explicit the relationship between parent text and filmic offspring" (Marcus, "Umbilical Scenes" xx).[15] The retention of only the middle syllable of Hippolyte's name might similarly be regarded as a metaphorical allusion to the filmmaker's activity, since the first and last sections of Flaubert's novel have also been amputated.

Before we draw this discussion of Fywell's adaptation to a close, a word must be said about intertextuality, "text" in this instance referring to film texts. Although it would undoubtedly be an exaggeration to see in this film a parodical montage of scenes from previous adaptations of *Madame Bovary*, there can be no doubt that this director was aware of earlier efforts to adapt Flaubert's novel to the screen, and that he referenced them in a very self-conscious way. Now, film parody is notoriously difficult to identify, since it depends upon the visual literacy of the viewer.[16] Nevertheless, there are many revealing examples of interfilmic allusions in Fywell's adaptation, of which I shall discuss only three. From Renoir, who framed Emma and Charles in the doorway of the Rouault farmhouse and overlaid the shot with the whinnying of horses on the soundtrack, Fywell took the idea of associating the couple's first meeting with the horse. However, in the *Masterpiece Theatre* adaptation, the animal is introduced on the image track: between Emma and Charles, framed in profile in the doorway, chatting to each other, one sees, in the lower third of the frame, a horse's hindquarters. If this mise-en-scène will undoubtedly fail to resonate for those who are not intimately familiar with Renoir's adaptation, the cognoscenti will experience it as a jab in the ribs, impossible to ignore.

From Chabrol, this film borrows technique. One example in particular is the use of voice in continuity editing. Whereas in Chabrol's film, it is Homais's voice that drones on, even when the

---

[15] One could probably extend this discussion of the self-referentiality of the organ grinder to the music itself. As Julie Sanders has observed, "it is perhaps in music and musicology that some of the most enabling metaphors for the kinetic process of adaptation might be sought" (39).

[16] See François Jost, "La Parodie audio-visuelle dans quelques-uns de ses états" and "La Parodie au cinéma".

camera has moved away from him and he is no longer visible to the spectator, in Fywell, the grating, nagging tones of Madame Bovary Senior are often used as a sound bridge. Fywell also seems to take from Chabrol the use of color symbolism, but while the former had dressed his heroine in fiery reds that were emblematic of her passionate nature, Fywell has a predilection for yellow gowns that distinguish her from the faded colors that compose her world, a spot of sunshine against the drab grays of her environment.

However, it is undoubtedly Minnelli's influence that echoes the most loudly in this adaptation. At the first and most obvious level, the representation of sexuality, Fywell appears to have set out deliberately to produce a film that is the polar opposite of Minnelli's strictly self-censored version. In fact, given Fywell's penchant for wordplay (about which more later), one might speculate that the *censer* which is shot in close-up as the film begins may be intended to evoke the homophonic *censor*. Like the incense burner which is quickly left behind by the panning camera, the legal guardians of morality, who had featured so prominently in Minnelli's opening frame, will be ignored by this camera. Other reminiscences of Minnelli's film range from the anecdotal to the essential. An example of the former is the scene during which Emma is shown practicing scales on the piano. In Minnelli's version, the shot is part of a montage of scenes from Emma's convent life that includes several shots of Emma turning the pages of "forbidden" books. Intended collectively to display the co-existence of discipline and transgression, this montage is deconstructed by Fywell, who, with subtle humor and admirable economy of means, uses the monotonous piano scales across shots, linking an image of Emma at the piano with one of two nuns walking together, within earshot. One of the nuns has just reported to the other that she has "found the most shocking piece of literature in [Emma's] chemise drawer" and has added that although she "cannot dwell upon details," the offending work "involves a gondolier." As soon as they leave Emma's field of vision, and as if in response to the next snatch of dialogue, a question provoked by the revelation of Emma's forbidden reading ("Are you not confident of her vocation, Sister?"), the scales are abandoned and Emma pounds out a jaunty ragtime tune, a surprising anachronism, perhaps, but an effective device for suggesting the young girl's insubordination. Fywell also appears to take his inspiration from Minnelli in his predilection for the pan in general and the swish pan in particular. The spinning camera movement which, in Minnelli's justly famous ball scene, captured Emma's dizziness, is used by Fywell to evoke the heroine's perspective, not at the ball, but at the carnival she attends, in trousers, with Léon. When the camera cuts back to show her, we see her as a whirling dervish, twirling out of control with arms raised, her avowed intention ("I want to lose myself") on the point of realization. Fywell teeters on the brink of intertextual parody here, violating the 180-degree rule in imitation of Minnelli but to a very different effect. Rather than experience Emma's almost delicious disorientation as had been the case in Minnelli's lengthy ball scene, this adaptation's viewer is swept up in the horror of an ominous realization: like the other problems that beset her, her vertigo is self-inflicted.

One way in which Fywell's film appears, not to mock Minnelli's adaptation but to emulate it, is in the casting. Related to this is a certain indulgence towards the male leads in the film. As in Minnelli, Charles is played by an actor who, while no Adonis, has a certain avuncular appeal. In both cases, the country doctor is pleasant looking, earnest, kindly, and aware of the limits to his medical competence. Unlike Minnelli's Charles, Fywell's country doctor (Hugh Bonneville) will operate on the club foot, but will be made to seem a victim of his wife's ambition and insensitivity. Although in the context, it may seem a feeble excuse, his lament that "everybody makes mistakes" resonates with viewers. Furthermore, he shows considerable strength of will in his dealings with his domineering mother. As for Rodolphe, played by Greg Wise, an actor whose physical appearance alone makes him a natural in the role of the consummate cad, he is a gambler "besieged by creditors" and thus unable to rescue Emma *in extremis.* Léon, played by the boyish-looking actor Hugh Dancy, is a miserable law clerk who has his reputation to look out for and who cannot grant Emma's every whim ("You ask too much of me," he tells her when she suggests he steal from his firm). Homais (David Troughton) is bumptious but innocuous in his diminished role, and, among the male characters, the only true villain is Lheureux (Keith Barron) who encourages Emma to assume ever greater debts, then breaks his implicit promise not to pass them along to others for collection ("I only said such a thing would be ungentlemanly"). In tandem with this near-exoneration of the males, the montage of the conclusion, in which only Léon is denied a flashback to happier times, recalls Minnelli's film, which shows, one after another, the people whose lives had been affected by Emma as the extra-diegetic Flaubert-Mason intones: "And so it was. A woman had been born into this world and had died young. She touched on numerous lives. Some lightly, some not so lightly. Some despised her. Some mourned her ... a little. Some profited by her. And then of course there were those she had ruined, who would never cease to love her."

This chapter would be incomplete were we not to treat in closing the linguistic playfulness of Fywell's adaptation, for it is here that the director and the screenwriter demonstrate their sensitivity to the language of Flaubert's novel. Chabrol, too, had been highly reverential towards Flaubert, but his decision to employ an actor who would read, in voiceover, entire passages from *Madame Bovary*, slowed the action and deadened the imagination. In this adaptation, on the contrary, both soundtrack and image track bear witness to a preoccupation with language as theme. Some of the examples of this preoccupation have already been cited, as for instance, the implicit allusion to the etymology of the word "passion" or the amputation of the first and last syllables of Hippolyte's name, or, finally, the censer on the image track, evoking perhaps the homophonic "censor." There are also numerous *double entendres,* a prime illustration being the word "prologue" that one can see clearly on the sheet music from which Emma is playing during the early scene of innocent intimacy with Léon to which we alluded earlier. This scene will indeed be a prologue to the serious love affair that develops later. Homais's reaction to the sight of Paul's gangrenous foot provides another example of the *double entendre.* Suggesting that the screws be tightened in the apparatus clamped on the stable boy's foot and leg, he adds, "That might hasten the process." The dialogue also provides instances of *quid pro quos*, in some cases, visually reinforced. When Canivet, called to Paul's bedside, expresses indignation that medical practitioners could have reduced the stableboy to such a sorry state, he asks angrily, "Who did this?" and then adds, "He wants shooting!" Paul, thinking the surgeon is referring to him, lifts his head and moans, terror etched into his face. "Not you!" says the doctor, aware of the misapprehension. The comment about shooting serves as a subtle allusion to the stableboy's association with the horse, an association weakened when the name Hippolyte was abandoned.

In addition to wordplay, the dialogue often serves a metatextual function, referring repeatedly to the poverty of language to express emotion or even to communicate humble realities. "I had not the words," explains Rouault when Emma protests that his letters had not informed her of the gravity of her mother's illness. "What language do you call that?" he asks Charles who, examining his leg, proffers a diagnosis in Latin. "Do you think it's easy to discuss such matters?" asks Emma when Léon reproaches her for having kept her pregnancy a secret. And when Léon attempts to express his feelings for Emma, she stops him: "Must you say them aloud? We haven't been in the habit of saying things aloud." Even Lheureux, alluding to the price of fabric he wishes to sell to Emma, refers her to the back pages of the catalog where she will see "the matters of which we must not speak." "I thought we understood each other," objects Emma to him later, after he has passed her debt on to a collector. "I'm not allowed to tell you," insists Justin when Emma asks him the location of the key to the cupboard where the arsenic is kept. "Could you not have confided in me?" whimpers Charles to his dying wife.

In a remarkable tour de force, Tim Fywell and his screenwriter Heidi Thomas have used the medium of television to create a film that is at once a compelling melodrama and a subtle interpretation of a classic of world literature. Like a Maupassant story, simple on the surface, while possessed of hidden complexities, this adaptation of *Madame Bovary* has something for everyone. In this respect, it becomes a perfect solution to the frequently cited problems besetting public television. As an erotically charged domestic drama, it has popular appeal, seducing casual viewers and causing channel surfers to linger. As a respectable adaptation of a literary classic, eager to capture on screen the nuances of the written page, it generates excitement among the more discriminating viewers that public television seeks to please. Depending upon their cultural literacy, viewers can peel away the layers of meaning in order to appreciate the richness of a film made with limited financial resources, or they can sit back and enjoy sex in the living room, gazing dreamily at the moving pictures much as Emma looked down from her window at the twirling figurines of the barrel organ.

6

Adaptation and its Avatars

In 1999, producer Jonathan Demme approached screenwriter Charlie Kaufman with a proposal: would he be interested in writing the screenplay for Susan Orlean's 1998 novel, *The Orchid Thief*? Demme had already made the offer to at least two other screenwriters, Stephen Schiff and David Henry Hwang, and they had declined it. As Schiff tells it, he had read the novel and loved it, but despite the widespread belief that "in every terrific book there's a terrific film wildly signaling to be let out," he could simply not find the movie in Orlean's novel (28). Kaufman, still flushed with the success of *Being John Malkovich*, accepted the offer. He was to spend the next several months in a mood of utter despair and crippling depression as he wrestled with the project, until he finally hit upon an unlikely strategy: to write himself and his travails into the movie. The result of his effort, a script that deftly melded the novel's narrative and the tale of his personal anguish, was enthusiastically accepted by the studio chiefs, and the film *Adaptation*, directed by Spike Jonze, was released in 2002. Unstinting in their praise, critics lauded this film not only as an adaptation but as a meditation on the very art of adaptation.[1]

Dubbed "the 'I' cure for writer's block" by *The New York Times*, Kaufman's solution to his creative paralysis is instructive to those who study the process of adaptation. (Zalewski 1+) While the cure is banal—there is hardly a writer's manual that fails to advise neophyte novelists to write about what they know best, i.e. to draw upon their own life experiences in the creation of their narratives—the

---

[1] For a more detailed discussion of the film *Adaptation*, see Stam and Raengo, *Literature and Film*, 1-2.

process of creating a film script out of someone else's ready-made narrative would seem to be incompatible with the autobiographical impulse. And yet, among those involved in the business of film adaptation, Kaufman had company, both in his struggle and, relatively speaking, in his solution. One after the other, the adaptations of *Madame Bovary* that we have examined in detail have offered up their secrets, disclosing the presence of the filmmakers, both directors and screenwriters, within visual narratives that claim to be objective.[2] Like the cameo appearances that Hitchcock made in his own films, the sometimes nebulous signs of the filmmakers' self-referentiality are easy to miss. Without engaging in facile and ultimately pointless speculation about Renoir's problematic relationship with his father, Minnelli's troubled marriage to Judy Garland, Chabrol's conflicted rejection of Catholicism, or Fywell's sense of the limits of the TV medium in which he was forced to work, it is nevertheless possible to identify autobiographical elements in each of the adaptations of *Madame Bovary* that we have examined in detail. Whether conscious or unconscious, such elements shape the films subtly, and if we acknowledge their importance, we can enhance our understanding of the films and of the process of adaptation.

In the preceding chapters, we have focused on the ways in which the *Madame Bovary* adaptations have been inflected, not only by their creators' life experiences (experiences that gave rise to what Robert Stam terms "auteurist predilections" ["Beyond Fidelity" 69]), but above all by technology, censorship, national ideology, budget, and the limits and possibilities of the film and TV media. We have seen how Renoir's adaptation was influenced by early film techniques and technologies and by industrial pressures, yet also bore witness to his reverence for Flaubert and his ambivalence with regard to an artist of Flaubert's generation, his own father, Pierre-Auguste Renoir. In his foregrounding of the lower classes, we have also found evidence of Renoir's populist sympathies. Minnelli's adaptation, informed by a cleverly simulated adherence to the Hays Code, not only bears the imprint of official censorship but reveals the hegemony of public opinion in the moralistic era that followed the Second World War. Chabrol's extravagant production offers ample proof of its director's

---

[2] It is important to point out that both Renoir and Chabrol did double duty as screenwriters *and* directors for their adaptations.

respect for a cultural icon and his infatuation with a beloved actress as well as his ardent desire to restore French film to the prominence it enjoyed in the heady days of New Wave Cinema. It is also inhabited by a feminist bias that makes it truly a film of the late twentieth century. Fywell's *Masterpiece Theatre* adaptation, finally, seemingly uncomplicated and melodramatic, as befits a film produced for television, testifies both to the permissive mores of its era and to a sophisticated understanding of Flaubert's novel that is consistent with that of contemporary critics. Like the novel, Fywell's film playfully thwarts expectations.

In its analysis of four of the eighteen adaptations of *Madame Bovary*, this study has been inspired by Dudley Andrew's suggestion that the time has come "for adaptation studies to take a sociological turn" ("Adaptation" 458). What remains is to attempt a response to Andrew's related question: "How does adaptation serve the cinema?" The standard answers to this question—that it takes advantage of a tried-and-true narrative formula, that it capitalizes on the existence of a ready-made public (the book's readers), that (in the case of adaptations of classic novels) it borrows the prestige of its source—all relate to the economic imperatives of filmmaking. To play the devil's advocate by continuing in this somewhat negative vein, one might speculate about the failure of the imagination and the malady of an industry that depends increasingly for its survival on the production of remakes, sequels, adaptations, and even reworkings of TV sitcoms. One might say, with Jacqueline Nacache, that the Seventh Art will reach maturity only when it decides to abandon adaptation and to dedicate itself to original subjects "faits pour ses moyens et *son* style" [suited to its techniques and its *own* style] (34). But is it not possible to put a more positive spin on the art of adaptation, one that does not relegate the film to an inferior position, in need of the inspiration provided by literature? Is it not possible—limiting ourselves now to the adaptation of canonical works of literature—to see a more noble purpose, that of bringing high culture to the wider public that typically frequents the movies? Spectators who have not previously read the novel on which a film adaptation is based are in fact often led to the novel from the movie. Indeed, the phenomenon of novelization—producing a novel from a screenplay—relies on this practice. Is it not possible to see in the desire to film classic literature a parallel with the desire to give visual representation to history, a desire that Maurice

Samuels finds expressed in the early nineteenth-century's panoramas, dioramas and theatrical productions? If history can be rendered more digestible by turning it into spectacle, why not cultural history, of which literature is a part? Is it not possible, given the now widely accepted notion that adaptation is interpretation, to consider the film adaptation as a democratic act of literary criticism, designed to reach an audience of non-specialists? Provided that they are not fixated on the fidelity issue, spectators who have read the novel from which a film is adapted may be guided to a greater appreciation of the novel by their viewing, indeed, may experience what Linda Hutcheon terms "the palimpsestic pleasures of doubled experience" (173). As Morris Beja wrote nearly three decades ago, "What a film takes from a book matters; but so does what it brings to a book" (88). Beja was referring to the truly masterful adaptation that "relates to the book from which it derives yet is also independent, an artistic achievement that is in some mysterious way the 'same' as the book but also something other: perhaps something less but perhaps something more as well" (88).

Leaving aside the broader issues raised by Andrew's question and reframing it for the purposes of this study, how do the adaptations of *Madame Bovary* serve the cinema? To respond to this question is to recognize that films, in addition to being the product of various influences, also have a transforming power of their own (Goldmann 133). What lessons does *Madame Bovary* impart, what ideologies does it serve? Here again, the answer is culture-bound and time-specific. *Madame Bovary* can be used to decry the corruption of Western Civilization (Mehta); to warn of the dangers of inter-class marriage (Ray), to protest the backward-looking conservatism of modern-day Portugal (Oliveira), to evoke France's collaboration with Hitler in World War II (Schott-Schöbinger), to draw attention to the plight of women in a patriarchal society (Chabrol), to inspire reflection on the role of the artist and the effects of censorship (Minnelli), or simply, and most frequently, to warn of the dangers of allowing fiction and fantasy to gain pre-eminence over reality.

As might be expected, the French adaptations of *Madame Bovary* have treated the novel with the greatest reverence. Unwilling to tamper with a masterpiece of their own culture, Renoir and Chabrol shot their films on location in Normandy, lifted dialogues straight from the novel, strove for historical authenticity in the mise-en-scène, and incorporated as many of the novel's characters and plot elements as budget and time would allow. The adaptations made outside of France, on the other hand, take considerable liberties with Flaubert's novel. Less respectful of a cultural icon that is not their own, the directors of these adaptations focus more on creation than on re-creation. As a result, their films are often less "literary" but more successful in cinematic terms.

Given the relative sense of freedom that British and American directors exhibit with respect to the novel, it is curious that among the Anglo-American adaptations of *Madame Bovary* there has been no attempt—at least not since 1932 (*Unholy Love*)—to set the story in the twentieth century in a way similar to the updating of Jane Austen's *Emma* in *Clueless* or that of Choderlos Laclos' *Dangerous Liaisons* in *Cruel Intentions*. In both of these films, the basic plot and principal characters of the source novel are retained and dressed in modern garb, their dilemmas brought into conformity with life in the twentieth century. While there have been notable efforts in other countries (India and Portugal, for example) to do this, neither England nor the United States has submitted *Madame Bovary* to a similar updating. Why? Considering only the novel's narrative framework, one might of course respond that Emma Bovary's plight is specific to the nineteenth century, that in contemporary American or British society, an unhappily married woman has a number of options open to her, both legally and practically. No longer necessarily dependent upon her husband in economic terms, she may divorce and remarry or divorce and remain single, supporting herself with income from the wide array of career opportunities enjoyed by contemporary women. She may even elect to remain married and to seek marital counseling in order to learn how to communicate more effectively with her husband. Thus, the sense of despair and longing felt by women living in a patriarchal society that imprisoned them in their domestic duties, a society in which marriages were still often arranged and divorce was illegal, may not be seen as translatable to modern times, at least not in American or British culture.[3] But is not *Madame Bovary* more than its plot? Is not the drama at the heart of Flaubert's novel far more timeless and complex than one would assume, given the reductive

---

[3] Permitted by the liberal law of 1792, divorce was restricted in 1803 and completely abolished in 1816. It was not legalized again until passage of the Naquet Law in 1884.

tendency to equate it with the disillusionment of the unhappily married woman?

To judge by a 51-minute documentary made by "Films for the Humanities and Sciences" in 1999, one would think not. The videotape jacket presents the documentary as follows:

> This program examines Flaubert's masterpiece in its historical context, deftly interweaving film excerpts and dramatized scenes of Flaubert at work. Commentary on the author, Emma Bovary, bourgeois society, the Romantic movement, and marital discontent— both then and now—is provided by professors from Princeton, Cornell, and Wesleyan Universities; Erica Jong; and Dalma Heyn, author of *Marriage Shock: The Transformation of Women into Wives*.

Narrated by Donald Sutherland, the documentary features numerous shots of nineteenth-century French paintings and stock footage from the two BBC mini-series, aired in 1964 and 1975 respectively and currently housed in the BBC Film Archives. The novel's plot is summarized, with many scenes being illustrated by clips from the two BBC adaptations. Talking heads from academe (Eric Le Calvez, Victor Brombert, and Ann-Louise Shapiro), all respected scholars, provide a fairly standard literary critical interpretation of the novel and lend *gravitas* to the discussion through their contextualization of the plot, while novelist Erica Jong and author Dalma Heyn provide a lighter touch, often through a then-and-now comparison. Dramatized scenes of modern infidelities enliven what might otherwise come across as a rather dry academic presentation, and the emphasis throughout is on romanticism. The voiceover narrator informs us that Gustave Flaubert was "a nineteenth-century romantic author at war with his own romantic obsessions," and that these obsessions were exorcized through the writing of *Madame Bovary*, a novel created "to explore the contradictions of his heart." Although an attempt is made to define the Romantic Movement (a blend of "eroticism and transcendence ... sensation and escape"), the documentary's emphasis is on a more common perception of the romantic: "Above all, romanticism is about following one's heart."

The documentary opens with a clip from the 1965 *Madame Bovary* mini-series. It features Emma sitting on her bed, as the voiceover narrator tells viewers that "it's time for bed, but this woman is not ready for sleep. After years of unhappy marriage, she has discovered feelings that have never been awakened before." The universality of Emma's situation is quickly underscored: "The temptation to be unfaithful is age-old. We know that we should be content but we long for more." A somewhat questionable statistic, with neither context nor documentation, is provided as proof: roughly 50 to 70 per cent of married people have been unfaithful in their marriages. Why? Because they're bored: "Locked in the humdrum routine of daily life, couples long for passion and intimacy." Dalma Heyn's research (hopefully not funded) has revealed to her that many people enter marriage with illusions. The camera cuts to a young wife, presumably real, who recalls her first post-wedding "awakening": "I remember sitting on the porch and thinking 'Omigod, I have made a mistake." Another wife, having decided to have an affair after six years of married life, exudes "I have discovered that I have within myself an entire galaxy of erotic energy." Does she feel guilty about her erotic trysts with a married man met on the Internet? An emphatic "no"! "Something that has made me feel so much better isn't something I'm going to be feeling guilty about."

Although the documentary does return to a reverent consideration of the novel as a classic of world literature—this is, after all, a "Great Books" series—it ends as it began, with an allusion to the transgressive erotic that it implicitly sees as the very *raison d'être* of the novel:

> A century and a half later, *Madame Bovary* is a cautionary tale. Emma ruined her life chasing dreams that could never come true. Flaubert reminds us that in a modern society driven by fantasy and desire, our longings can be our downfall. We must choose our dreams wisely.

Aside from its erroneous characterization of Flaubert as a romantic author, this documentary errs not in its facts but in its neglect of the subtleties of *Madame Bovary*, its overly simplified Cliff Notes pitch to the impatient undergraduate, and its insistence on giving "relevance" to the novel by engaging in popular psychology and reducing the suffering of Flaubert's heroine ("who thinks self-esteem can come from without") to the ennui of the twentieth-century American woman disappointed by married life. Although it does pay lip service to Flaubert's criticism of bourgeois society, and although it does allow that "there is more freedom today than in the nineteenth century," it does not burden itself with the problematics of Flaubert's novel, does not, for example, recognize the characters' repeated failures or the (related) insufficiencies of language (Schehr 210). Perhaps this is inevitable, given the nature of the documentary genre and the implicit goal of the series to which it belongs, specifically that of introducing "great books" to a diverse public. Unfortunately, the resultant production, awash in clichés, turns one of the most celebrated classics of world literature into an eminently forgettable work of pulp fiction. Yet with all that, it serves a useful purpose by throwing into sharp relief the theme of adultery, one of the greatest motors not only of novels, as Tony Tanner has shown, but of film.

Ironically, the documentary's focus seems to legitimize the connection that many spectators establish between Flaubert's novel and films that seem to be related to it only marginally through the fact that its protagonist is an adulteress. These are in no way conventional adaptations, and they generally deviate substantially from the novel's plot, yet they are frequently linked with the novel. In most cases the resemblance centers on their protagonist, the quintessentially unhappy married woman who seeks satisfaction outside her marriage. That the adulteress should feature prominently in film is certainly not surprising, given that practitioners of the Seventh Art have historically been as entranced by infractions against the Seventh Commandment as have their literary forebears. Indeed, what Robert Stam terms "the guilty pleasures of cinephilia" have often been associated with sinful sexuality, among others by François Truffaut (*François Truffaut and Friends* 31). What is perhaps more bewildering is the reductive identification of such a wide array of films as *Madame Bovary* spin-offs, often in the absence of convincing proof that they were in any way derived from the novel. Some light may be shed on the phenomenon of what I shall call the "false positive" by consideration of the well-known principle according to which readers tend to have a much longer recall for character than for plot. Years after a novel has been read, the details of the narrative will have been forgotten, but the principal traits of the protagonist will remain etched in one's memory. And what are the salient traits of Flaubert's adulteress, a character who has achieved mythic dimensions, although, unlike Don Juan (for example), she does not yet figure in dictionaries of myth? What is it about Emma Bovary that causes us to find her avatars in so many celluloid creations? I should like to suggest that the answer to these questions lies less in her personal weaknesses (her naïveté, her unrealistic expectations, her narcissism) than in the simple fact that she betrays her marital vows. A brief look at three of the "false positives" will suffice to illustrate my point.[4]

Bette Davis's Rosa Moline, in King Vidor's *film noir, Beyond the Forest* (1949), is trapped in a small Wisconsin town. Married to a physician for whom she has little respect, Moline yearns to live in Chicago with a millionaire industrialist met during one of his visits to his nearby hunting lodge, because for her, living in the suggestively named Loyalton is "like living in a funeral parlor and waiting for the funeral to begin [...], like lying in a coffin and waiting for them to carry you out." Considered "the ultimate portrait in Bette Davis's long gallery of evil dames," this adulteress cheats, lies, and even murders to get what she wants, yet in the end she, like Emma Bovary, dies an untimely death. Created the same year as Jennifer Jones's Emma Bovary, Bette Davis's cruel, conniving Rosa Moline inspires horror, not pity, and if as been suggested, the wellspring of this film is Flaubert's novel, one can only marvel at the creative transformation that made a monster of truly mythical proportions out of Flaubert's self-pitying, deluded heroine. Given this highly unsympathetic portrayal of the adulteress, eloquent testimony to the way in which adultery was conceived in 1949, there is a mordant irony in the fact that this film was condemned by the Legion of Decency whereas Minnelli's *Madame Bovary*, with its more [sym]pathetic heroine, was not.

A German film that has sometimes been seen as a perverse re-working of *Madame Bovary* is Rainer Werner Fassbinder's *Bolwieser (The Stationmaster's Wife)*, released in 1977. In fact, Fassbinder's film is an adaptation of a novel of the same title published in 1931 by Oskar Maria Graf, and although there is no proof that Graf had been inspired by *Madame Bovary*, there are a few provocative parallels between his novel—at least as adapted by Fassbinder—and Flaubert's. Hannerl ("Hanni," played by Elisabeth Trissenaar) quickly tires of her doting husband, Xaverl (Kurt Raab), a heavy-drinking station master,

---

[4] Marshall Olds has called to my attention yet another *Madame Bovary* spin-off, the recently released *Le Passager de l'été*. The film features a direct reference to the novel and a shot of the novel's 1936 edition. Flaubert's novel features as a prop in another recent release, *Little Children* (dir. Todd Field, 2006) in which an adulteress played by Kate Winslet identifies with Flaubert's heroine. This film, adapted from a novel of the same name by Tom Perrotta, includes a book club scene in which suburban housewives debate whether Emma is a "slut" or a "feminist." See A. O. Scott, "Playground Rules."

and seeks to relieve her boredom by having an adulterous liaison with a butcher (Merkel). Indeed, so trusting is her husband that he agrees when his wife proposes lending a large sum of money to Merkel so that he can buy a local pub. When tongues begin wagging in the fictional Bavarian town where this story is set, Hanni and Merkel decide to take the "slanderers" to court, and they persuade the naive Xaverl to testify on their behalf. In order to save his wife's reputation, the loyal Xaverl perjures himself in court. The adulterers prevail, and the "slanderers" are fined 300 marks. Later, Merkel, who has lost favor with Hanni and has been served notice that he must repay his debt to her and her husband, tells authorities about the perjury and Xaverl is thrown into jail while his wife gallivants around with her second lover, the hairdresser, Shafftaler. The novel's last scene takes place in jail. Xaverl, having learned that his wife is filing for divorce, signs the requisite papers and is led back to his cell. The perversity and cynicism of this early twentieth-century tale of an adulterous woman who, unlike Flaubert's hapless heroine, is nothing but an unscrupulous pleasure-seeker, an illustration of the songline according to which "girls just want to have fun," are inscribed in its conclusion. Not surprisingly, given his preoccupation with the theme of the unfaithful wife, Fassbinder has also made a film adaptation of Fontane's *Effi Briest*, a novel inspired by *Madame Bovary*.

A more recent film that has been cited as a stepchild of *Madame Bovary* and for equally questionable and reductive reasons (the protagonist is an adulteress) is Miguel Arteta's *The Good Girl* (2002) with Jennifer Aniston as Justine Last. The wife of Phil Last (played by John C. Reilly), a pot-smoking house painter with a low sperm count and too many rain-drenched hours to fill, Justine finds her escape in the arms of a fellow employee at Retail Rodeo, the discount store where she works. A melancholic and an aspiring writer who takes very seriously the fact that he was named after Holden Caulfield, the protagonist of J. D. Salinger's *Catcher in the Rye*, her lover promises to write her story, and when, following his suicide, she discovers his notebook, her narrative is complete. Although this treatment of the unhappily married woman who resorts to adultery to cure her boredom is more compassionate than King Vidor's *Beyond the Forest*—in the end, Aniston's character becomes the "good girl" of the title by turning in her lover who has embezzled money from the store in order to flee with her—it is similar in its preoccupation with the sorry consequences of infidelity. Once again, this is slim evidence for a *Madame Bovary* intertext, although Flaubert's novel was lurking in the wings, so to speak, through Phil's reference to a street named Bovary on which he has a painting job. "Bovary" is hardly a classical American street name.

Based upon this brief survey, one is tempted to theorize that adultery in the *sine qua non* of the *Madame Bovary* spin-offs and consequently that, for the vast majority of readers, Flaubert's "book about nothing" is indeed about *something* and that this "something" is adultery. If this is the case, the translation of the novel currently on sale in Iran is difficult to imagine: having been vetted by the Ministry of Culture and Islamic Guidance, this translation excludes all allusions to Emma's adultery![5] Ironically, perhaps, the *Madame Bovary* film spin-off that engages most profoundly with the novel also does away with the heroine's actual adultery. The film in question is Woody Allen's *The Purple Rose of Cairo* (1985). While, like the other films discussed in this chapter, this film is not really an adaptation in the strict sense of that word, we may well characterize it as an "appropriation," a category that Julie Sanders establishes to describe a text that "affects a more decisive journey away from the informing source into a wholly new cultural product and domain" (26). Like Allen's short story, "The Kugelmass Episode," in which the lines separating fiction from reality are playfully erased, the film is pure fantasy. However, unlike the story, the film does not specifically reference Flaubert's novel. Nevertheless, because the parallels are not limited to the basic narrative situation, that of an unhappily married woman who seeks relief for her dissatisfaction in extra-marital relationships (here only *virtually* adulterous), the film merits a more ample discussion than *Beyond the Forest*, *The Stationmaster's Wife* and *The Good Girl*.

Mocking the clichés of romantic fiction in a way that recalls *Madame Bovary*, Allen's film updates the theme of the young woman taken in by the illusions of fiction by making the protagonist Cecilia (played by Mia Farrow) an addict of romantic movies rather than a reader of romantic literature. Cecilia works at a diner to support her unemployed husband ("Monk," played by Danny Aiello) who cavorts with other women, drinks, gambles, and beats her when she "gets out

---

[5] See Azadeh Moaveni, 27.

of line." To escape the tensions of her conjugal nightmare and the realities of life during the Great Depression, she goes to the movies, and her preference for romance is known even to the personnel at the Jewel Theater which she frequents assiduously. When movies appeal to her sensibilities, she sees them repeatedly, and it is during her fifth viewing of *The Purple Rose of Cairo* that one of the characters in the movie, Tom Baxter, spies her in the audience and steps out of the movie screen and into the "real world" (i.e. the real world of Woody Allen) to court her. (One is reminded here of Emma Bovary's conviction that the tenor Edgar Lagardy is looking straight at her as he performs his role in *Lucie de Lammermoor*.)[6] Since Baxter's experiences are limited to those of the role he plays, that of "poet, adventurer, explorer" who has traveled to Manhattan after a fruitless search in Cairo for a legendary purple rose, he knows nothing of sexual congress (in the movies, there's a fadeout after the kiss), nothing of prostitution, nothing of the Great War, old age, and sickness, nothing, in short, that does not figure in the movie— including the popcorn the audience is munching on. Thus, while the world of the film is in complete disarray without one of the principal actors, Baxter pursues his dream to win the heart of the enthralled Cecilia. The situation becomes more complicated when Gil Shepherd, the actor who plays Baxter, is dispatched to the New Jersey town at the behest of the executives of his Hollywood studio in order to find his character and return him to the screen, for complaints from disgruntled audiences and theater managers are flooding the studio and his acting career is threatened. In the hope that she will lead him to his character, he too courts Cecilia, promising her that he will take her back to Hollywood with him, demonstrating all of the advantages of his "reality" to seduce her away from the cinematic character he plays. He eventually succeeds, but not before Cecilia has had her own brief experience of life in the movies. In the novel's last scene, Cecilia, having been betrayed by Gil Shepherd, who has escaped to Hollywood without her once Baxter has been safely restored to the

---

[6] Robert Stam believes that the novel's opera scene anticipates this sequence in the film (*Literature* 186). Stam writes that "Mia Farrow *imagines* (emphasis added) that the film star is addressing her directly"; by "Mia Farrow," I assume he means "Cecilia" (the character that Farrow inhabits), but in my understanding of the film, the actor "really" does step out of the screen. The "imagining" takes place in the mind of Woody Allen himself.

screen, is again at the movies, this time watching with evident delight as Ginger Rogers and Fred Astaire dance cheek-to-cheek in *Top Hat*.

At the surface level of plot, *The Purple Rose of Cairo* has little in common with *Madame Bovary*. Indeed, the basic "givens" of the novelistic plot are overturned one by one in the film. While it is true that the narrative revolves around an unhappily married woman who seeks happiness outside her marriage, Cecilia has been mismatched, not to a mediocrity like Charles Bovary, but to an abusive, alcoholic philanderer. Rather than create her illusions, as in the novel, romantic fictions provide her with a means to escape her woes. Until she in turn loses her job, she is the breadwinner of her household, not the spendthrift. Although she is willing to betray her husband, circumstances do not allow her to consummate her love affairs. Finally, when given the choice between fiction (Tom Baxter) and reality (Gil Shepherd), she chooses reality. While the novel's basic structure can be seen as an "x" (the intersecting lines figuring the rise of Homais and the fall of Emma), the film's structure is circular. In the end, Cecilia is exactly where she was at the beginning: at the movies, caught up in the world of illusion.

It is impossible to know whether Allen had *Madame Bovary* in mind when he made his film. However, given his intimate knowledge of the novel, demonstrated in "The Kugelmass Episode"; given the large number of parallels and oppositions that connect the film and the novel (and for that matter, the film and the story); given the presence in the film of a character named Emma; given, finally, that Allen's lyrical comedy is in its essence a meta-film that comments on the power of cinema to create believable illusions, much as Flaubert's novel can be seen as a meditation on the power of literature to do likewise, it does not seem unreasonable to posit a connection. Examined more closely, Allen's film appears almost iconoclastic, mocking not only Flaubert's novel but the literary criticism devoted to it, and in particular the type of literary criticism that would treat fictional characters as real people.[7] The fanciful premise that the film shares with "The Kugelmass Episode," i.e. that transmigration between fiction and reality is possible, decisively removes it from the

---

[7] See Woody Allen's "The Purple Rose of Cairo" in *Three Films of Woody Allen*, the man who likes the movies because he is "a student of the human personality" (374).

realist category.[8] But it also enables Allen to engage in a sophisticated meditation on the freedoms afforded by life in the "real" world. Cecilia is not the only Emma Bovary avatar in this film. Through the character Tom Baxter, we are made aware of the limits of a fictional existence, limits symbolized by the fact that the film within the film is in black and white, whereas the world outside the silver screen is in color. In the imbedded film, Tom is enthralled with an on-stage performer, Kitty, much as Emma Bovary is enthralled with Edgar Lagardy. But Tom, breaking the cardinal rule of narrative cinema (in which the on-screen characters can neither see nor even pretend to see the spectators), spies Cecilia and steps out of the movie.[9] His excitement upon escaping from the world of the embedded film ("I'm free! After two thousand performances of the same monotonous routine, I'm free!") stems from his impatience with the deterministic existence of a fictional character ("I want to be free to make my own choices"). He may not get hurt or bleed in his cinematic life, but the champagne bottles are filled with ginger ale, and his "life" is contrived, the product of artifice. Tom's desire to inhabit the "real world" identifies him *a contrario* with Emma Bovary, as does his naïveté, brilliantly exposed in his confrontation with the most cynical character in that real world, a prostitute named Emma who will do "anything that'll make a buck," and for whom being in love is a quaint illusion. The Emma Bovary of the last pages of Flaubert's novel, at last truly cynical, has in fact attempted to prostitute herself.

This multiplication of characters who recall Emma Bovary—an unhappily married woman whose dreams are nourished by fiction, a fictional character defined by naïveté and seduced by life in a parallel universe, a cynical prostitute—make this film a remarkable *tour de force*. By giving the same name (*The Purple Rose of Cairo*) both to his film and to the film within the film, Allen further plays with the notion of *mise-en-abyme*: his embedded narrative reflects the containing narrative not only in its message but in its status as fiction. However, if *Madame Bovary* is a novel about the danger of reading

---

[8] In "The Kugelmass Episode," a "real person," bored with his life and aided by a magician, "enters" a novel (*Madame Bovary*); this is a perfect counterpart to the action of *The Purple Rose of Cairo*, in which a film character, tired of endlessly repeated scenarios, "exits" the screen.

[9] This rule distinguishes narrative cinema from documentaries and from TV broadcasts in which a speaker often addresses the viewing audience directly.

novels, *The Purple Rose of Cairo* is not really a film about the danger of seeing films. Ultimately, Hollywood is validated and the film's worth as a means of escapism affirmed, provided that the escapism is recognized for what it is.

For those *Madame Bovary* fetishists who are obsessed by the novel and disdainful of any effort to claim it for the cinema, there is a lesson in Allen's movie. Films, like novels, are the product of art and artifice, and as such, they provide a means of escape from the often mundane realities of our daily existence. The brilliance of Flaubert's achievement should not blind us to the fact that what he authored was a work of *fiction*. To realize that film directors, in seeking to create their own version of that fiction, can neither destroy the novel nor take anything *from* it is to gain the freedom that allows us to enjoy the illusion of the silver screen in general and the *Madame Bovary* adaptations in particular. Flaubert's cast of characters will not step off the page to join our "reality" and to decry the "fictional" nature of their celluloid reproductions.

Conclusion

Whether we're dealing with films loosely based upon *Madame Bovary*, perhaps "suggested by" or "inspired by" Flaubert's novel but so divergent in the details of their plots that they do not even acknowledge it as a source, or films that are truly adapted from the novel, it is clear that Flaubert's perennially youthful classic will continue to seduce image-makers throughout the world. There is, however, mordant irony in this phenomenon, for whereas Flaubert took immense pride in the "impersonality" and "objectivity" of his novel, it has inspired a series of very personal, ideologically-based recreations, a phenomenon, incidentally, that is not limited to the cinematic hypertexts, as Elizabeth Amann has shown. Even more bitingly ironic is the fact that, in adapting *Madame Bovary* to the screen, directors demonstrate that they have been infected with their own brand of *bovarysme*: they are attempting to do what Emma Bovary could not: i.e. to join the linguistic sign (signifier and signified) to its real-life referent. If, throughout the space of her paper existence, Flaubert's protagonist failed to accomplish this feat, the filmmakers have, to varying degrees, succeeded in rendering "real" (as "real" as the indexical medium of cinema can be) the word on the page. The problem is that their reality will always be pitted against that of the spectators familiar with the novel who, in watching their adaptations, may suffer the same disconnect as Emma. Just as Charles Bovary did not correlate to the knights in shining armor that Emma imagined as she devoured romantic prose, so also may the celluloid Emmas created by Valentine Tessier, Jennifer Jones, Isabelle Huppert, and Frances O'Connor fail to live up to the protagonist as she was imagined by *Madame Bovary*'s readers. Yet as spectators they are forced to accept the "reality" before them, for, as Morris Beja points out, "the relationship of signifier to signified in a picture seems undeniably more direct than in the case of a word" (55).

But what of spectators whose first contact with Flaubert's narrative is visual? The German-born filmmaker Ernst Lubitsch was once reputed to have said, "I've been to Paris, France, and I've been to Paris, Paramount. Paris, Paramount is better" (quoted in Hohenadel 2:11). Notwithstanding Lubitsch's preference for the world of illusion over the "real" world—a preference he shares with Emma Bovary— millions of people throughout the world have traveled to foreign lands that they first encountered on the silver screen. Is it not reasonable to assume that the same phenomenon might obtain with film adaptations of classic novels, i.e. that spectators who first encounter a classic novel on-screen may well be tempted to visit the "real thing," the work of literature, afterwards? Mario Vargas Llosa, who became acquainted with *Madame Bovary* through Minnelli's adaptation, went on not only to read the novel but to write *A Perpetual Orgy*, a highly personal exploration of the novel, its author and its genesis, and although he denies that the film led him to the novel (indeed, seven years elapsed between viewing and reading), experiencing the film first may well have led to one of his important insights. Llosa contends that by effacing the narrator, Flaubert freed both his characters and his readers:

> Flaubert was the first novelist to realize that, if he was to convince his readers that his fiction had a life of its own—something that all good stories achieve—then his novel had to be seen by them as a sovereign, self-sufficient reality, not in any way parasitic on life outside itself, real life. ("Flaubert, Our Contemporary" 221)

While, as we have seen, Minnelli's film set up "Flaubert" as narrator of Emma's story, the historical Flaubert, for his part, eschewed the practice of inventing an intrusive narrator who gave his own opinions (thus influencing the reader's perspective) and "knew everything—always much more than one character could possibly know about another character" (Llosa 220), thus limiting his characters' freedom, "turning them into puppets" (221). In other words, Flaubert succeeded in achieving the "reality effect" that is the specialty (Minnelli's conceit notwithstanding) of narrative cinema.

At the conclusion of this exploration of a select number of the *Madame Bovary* adaptations, it is important to acknowledge that the canonical status of Flaubert's novel rests not on its trivial plot, but on its impeccable marriage of form and subject, that is, on the way in which the stylistic perfection of Flaubert's prose redeems the banality of his topic, gives it artistic value. If by definition the camera cannot hope to capture the beauty of that marriage, it can, in the hands of a talented director, create another. Besides increasing our appreciation for the literary text by showcasing Flaubert's genius, the story of that often renewed act of creation—in all its permutations—provides us with compelling evidence of the versatility and power of the Seventh Art.

Appendix A

Synopsis of the Novel[1]

Madame Bovary is divided into three parts. Part I opens in a study hall where a new pupil, not yet in school uniform, is arriving. The child is Charles Bovary, a simple country boy whose awkwardness makes him the laughing stock of his class. The first chapter traces his path from youth to adulthood, schoolboy to Health Officer (a grade inferior to that of fully licensed medical doctor), emphasizing his mediocre intelligence and his submission to the will of his domineering mother (who will continue to meddle in his affairs throughout the novel). By the end of the chapter, he is married to Héloïse, an emaciated forty-five year old widow hand-picked by Madame Bovary Senior who had mistakenly believed her to be wealthy. Charles leads a dull life until, early one morning, he is summoned from his home in Tostes to the Rouault farm ("Les Bertaux") some eighteen miles away to attend to the owner, who has broken a leg. It is here that Charles (and simultaneously, the reader) first meets Rouault's daughter, Emma. Héloïse conveniently dies in Chapter 2, and by the end of Chapter 3, Charles is marrying Emma, not at midnight, by torchlight, as the romantic young woman would have liked, but in the afternoon, at a raucous country wedding. Emma Rouault thus becomes the novel's third Madame Bovary, after Charles's mother and his first wife. In contrast to Charles, who is for a long time deliriously happy in his marriage, Emma is soon bored. Chapter 6 is given entirely to the young woman's reminiscences about her school days, when romantic novels smuggled into the convent by

---

[1] For a more detailed plot summary and for a wealth of other information relevant to the novel, see the excellent reference guide by Laurence M. Porter and Eugene F. Gray.

an old seamstress nourished her dreams and the Church's representation of Christ as heavenly bridegroom stimulated her imagination. Except for this flashback, which gives the reader the background information necessary to understand the depth of her unhappiness as the wife of an unimaginative health officer, the narrative is relentlessly linear as it moves forward through her successive illusions and disillusions.

Emma is delighted when she and Charles receive an invitation to a ball given by a local nobleman, the Marquis de la Vaubyessard, whom Charles has treated for a gum boil. The social event gives the young woman a tantalizing glimpse of the aristocratic existence of which she had read, and even the sight of the decrepit old Duke de Laverdière makes her heart skip a beat: he was rumored to have slept with Marie-Antoinette! Cinderella-like, Emma attracts the attention of a handsome viscount who asks her to dance. The sensuous waltz in which they engage awakens her to physical pleasure, but when the ball is over, she must return to her dull life. Waiting in vain for another invitation the following year, she is afflicted by a seemingly intractable depression and lethargy.

Part II begins with a description of Yonville-L'Abbaye, a larger town to which Charles has moved his now pregnant wife in the hope that her melancholy will be cured by a change of scenery. The couple encounters financial problems here, not only because Homais, the bumptious village pharmacist, practices medicine illegally in his back room and Charles never succeeds in building a respectable clientèle, but also because the unctuous and unscrupulous cloth merchant, Lheureux, begins tempting Emma with wares that she can ill afford. Another temptation comes in the form of Léon Dupuis, a handsome young law clerk, met the very day of their arrival in Yonville. Although Emma and Léon appear right from the start to be kindred spirits, the relationship between them is slow to develop, for Emma is preoccupied with preparations for the impending birth of her baby, an event in which she loses interest when she discovers that she and Charles cannot afford the layette she wishes to purchase. She is, however, eager to be delivered, and she ardently desires a son who, unlike her, would be free to follow his dreams. Flaubert maliciously entrusts Charles with the news that "C'est une fille!" (153) [It's a girl!] The child will be called Berthe, a name Emma had heard at the Vaubyessard Ball.

After her convalescence, Léon begins to lavish attention on Emma, but their unconsummated love becomes a source of more anguish than pleasure when the young woman, although burning with passion, plays the role of virtuous housewife. In her misery, Emma seeks guidance from the village priest, Bournisien (whose name evokes the French *borné*, narrow-minded), but he is too obtuse to understand her suffering, which he assumes to be purely physical. Emma's depression deepens when Léon, thoroughly discouraged by his lack of success, leaves town to complete his studies.

It is not long thereafter that a local notable, Rodolphe Boulanger, brings his servant to Charles to be bled, and spies the pretty young woman. When the agricultural fair comes to town soon afterwards, Rodolphe makes his move, guiding Emma to the second floor of the town hall, where they find themselves alone in the council chambers. Against the sonorous backdrop of lowing cows and bleating sheep, through which one can hear the Prefect's deputy droning on about the dignity of agriculture, Rodolphe pursues his verbal seduction of the gullible Emma, spouting a seemingly endless supply of romantic clichés that stand in ironic counterpoint to the vapid political speech heard below.

After a strategic delay designed to stimulate Emma's impatience, Rodolphe makes Emma his mistress in the course of a "therapeutic" horse ride through the woods. The love affair is an all-consuming preoccupation for Emma until the wealthy playboy tires of his demanding mistress, and she turns back to her husband. Believing that she could love Charles if he became famous, she colludes with the ambitious Homais, an apostle of progress, to persuade the health officer to perform an operation on the club-footed stableboy, Hippolyte. However, Charles, unqualified to perform this surgery, bungles the operation and Hippolyte's leg becomes gangrenous and must be amputated by a physician from nearby Neufchâtel, Dr. Canivet. Humiliated by her husband's incompetence, Emma seeks refuge in Rodolphe's arms. The relationship ends definitively when Emma insists that they run away together. After writing her a "Dear Emma" letter, Rodolphe skips town to avoid carrying out the plan. Emma collapses with "brain fever" (a well-known strategy for temporarily immobilizing a character in a Victorian-era novel). As her condition slowly improves, Charles sinks more deeply into debt. The deplorable state of his finances does not, however, stop him from taking the pharmacist's suggestion that he buy tickets for an opera performance in Rouen in order to distract Emma and thereby complete her recovery. It is at the performance of Donizetti's *Lucie de Lammermoor* that chance again brings Emma face to face with Léon Dupuis.

In Part III, Emma begins a love affair with Léon when the young man persuades her to take a ride with him in a hansom cab in broad daylight. In one of the novel's most celebrated scenes, Flaubert describes the carriage's hours-long passage through the streets of Rouen, with shades lowered, bouncing and rocking to the rhythm of its passengers' love-making, as the exhausted coachman wipes the sweat from his brow and passers-by look on in amazement.

To keep the affair alive, Emma needs a pretext to return to Rouen. A first opportunity is given to her when, having managed to get power of attorney to look after Charles's finances, she offers to consult Léon, now a lawyer, about the estate of Charles's father, who has just died. Subsequent visits require more ingenuity. Emma, who had played the piano when Charles first knew her, thus develops a sudden interest in resuming piano lessons, insisting that there are no teachers worthy of her talent in Yonville. Charles acquiesces to her plans for weekly visits to Rouen, and the trysts with Léon begin in earnest. At first passionate, these meetings become increasingly less satisfying, even as her debts are mounting. Having signed one promissory note too many, Emma is horrified when Lheureux submits her bills to a collector who wastes no time in sending a bailiff to her home to make an inventory of her possessions. En route home from Rouen where she has unsuccessfully sought the aid of Léon, she throws her last five-franc coin to a blind beggar in the street whose grotesque song and dance, observed on a previous trip, had overwhelmed Emma with sadness. Upon arriving in Yonville, she sees a poster advertising an auction of her furnishings and, at the suggestion of her maid, Félicité, rushes to the home of Maître Guillaumin. The old roué is willing to give her financial assistance, but only in return for sexual favors. Aghast, she refuses his advances: "Je suis à plaindre, mais pas à vendre!" (378) [I am to be pitied, but I'm not for sale!]. In desperation, she runs to the château of her former lover, Rodolphe, who has now returned, and throws herself on his mercy. Moved at first by her emotional distress, Rodolphe cools quickly when he realizes that she has come for a loan. He refuses to aid her. Suicide is her last resort, and she stumbles toward the pharmacy. Homais's young helper, Justin, whose infatuation with Emma has been evoked throughout the novel, reluctantly gives her the key to the dispensary where the arsenic is stored when she insists that she needs it to kill rats. He watches in horror as Emma scoops the white powder out with her cupped hand and ingests it.

Flaubert describes with medical precision the physical symptoms (excruciating pain, nausea, chills, perspiration) caused by arsenic poisoning. Emma's suffering makes a mockery of her romantic belief that she would die peacefully ("je vais dormir, et tout sera fini!" 390) [I'm going to sleep, and everything will be over.] Neither Charles nor Homais can save her; Canivet's treatment is ineffectual, and even the distinguished physician Larivière, called to her bedside *in extremis*, merely shrugs when he sees her. Just after the priest has administered the sacrament of Extreme Unction, the blind beggar passes beneath her window, singing his obscene ditty. Upon hearing him, she sits up, galvanized, emits a hysterical burst of laughter, then slumps back on her pillow, dead.

The novel's last chapters describe the wake, the arrangements for Emma's funeral, Rouault's arrival, the burial. While the grieving Charles allows himself to be exploited by Emma's debtors, the insensitive Homais goes about his own business, struggling to silence the blind beggar, who has begun spreading rumors about the inefficacy of his treatment. He succeeds in having him institutionalized. One day, Charles discovers love letters written by Léon and Rodolphe. During a chance encounter with Rodolphe soon afterwards, he tells his late wife's erstwhile lover that he doesn't hold it against him: "C'est la faute de la fatalité!" 424 [It was decreed by Fate!]. Charles's tritely romantic statement elicits the silent scorn of the impenitent playboy. The following day, Charles quietly dies of a broken heart (an ironic allusion to the archetypally romantic death). In the novel's final paragraphs, we learn that Charles's mother too has succumbed and that Berthe, who had been entrusted to her care, has been lodged with an aunt who sends her to work in a cotton mill. The novel's supremely ironic last sentence informs the reader that the self-satisfied and unscrupulous Homais, the epitome of bourgeois ambition who has been indirectly responsible for much of Emma Bovary's unhappiness, has just been awarded the Cross of the Legion of Honor.

Appendix B

Filmography

Jean Renoir
Madame Bovary
(Nouvelle Société des Films, 1934)

Language: French
Producer: Gaston Gallimard
Screenplay: Jean Renoir
Photography: Jean Bachelet
Music: Darius Milhaud and Donizetti
Running Time: 102 minutes, B/W

Cast

Valentine Tessier .... Emma Bovary
Pierre Renoir ....Charles Bovary
Daniel Lecourtoios...Léon Dupuis
Fernand Fabre .... Rodolphe Boulanger
Alice Tissot .... Charles's mother
Héléna Manson ....Charles's first wife
Pierre Larquey...Hippolyte
Max Dearly .... Homais
Robert le Vigan.. Lheureux
Maryanne .... Madame Homais
Léon Larive..the prefect
Florencie... Bournisien
Romain Bouquet .... Guillaumin
Georges Cahuzac ....Rouault
Henry Vilbert .... Canivet
Georges Denebourg .... Le Marquis de Vaubyessard
Edmond Beauchamp .... Binet

Vincente Minnelli
Madame Bovary
(MGM, 1949)

Language: English
Producer: Pandro S. Berman
Screenplay: Robert Ardrey
Photography: Robert Planck
Music: Miklos Rozsa
Running Time: 114 minutes, B/W

Cast

Jennifer Jones .... Emma Bovary
Van Heflin .... Charles Bovary
Louis Jourdan .... Rodolphe Boulanger
Christopher Kent .... Léon Dupuis
Gene Lockhart .... Homais
James Mason .... Flaubert
Frank Allenby .... Lheureux
Gladys Cooper .... Madame Dupuis
John Abbott .... Mayor Tuvache
Henry Morgan .... Hippolyte

Claude Chabrol
Madame Bovary
(MK2 Productions, Compagnie Européenne de Droits, FR3, 1991)

Language: French
Producer: Marin Karmitz
Screenplay: Claude Chabrol
Photography: Jean Rabier
Music: Matthieu Chabrol
Running Time: 140 minutes, Color

Cast

Isabelle Huppert .... Emma Bovary
Jean-François Balmier ....Charles Bovary
Christophe Malavoy... Rodolphe Boulanger
Lucas Belvaux..Léon Dupuis
Jean Yanne .... Homais
Christiane Minazzoli.. Madame LeFrançois
Jean-Louis Maury .... Lheureux
Jacques Dynam .... Bournisien
Jean-Claude Bouillaud.. Rouault
Dominique Zardi...the blind man
François Périer .... the narrator

Tim Fywell
Madame Bovary
(British Broadcasting Corporation, WGBH Boston, 2000)

Language: English
Producer: Tony Redston
Screenplay: Heidi Thomas
Photography: Chris Seager
Original Music: John Lunn
Running Time: 159 minutes, Color

Cast

Frances O'Connor... Emma Bovary
Hugh Bonneville ....Charles Bovary
Greg Wise .... Rodolphe Boulanger
Keith Barrow.. Lheureux
David Troughton .... Homais
Hugh Dancy ....Léon Dupuis
Eileen Atkins...Charles's mother
Trevor Peacock ....Rouault
Jessica Oyelowo...Félicité
Thomas Wheatley .... Canivet
Mary Macleod... Madame Lefrançois
Joe McGann ....Paul (Hippolyte)
Barbara Jefford ....la Marquise d'Andervilliers
Adam Cooper ....le Vicomte
Willie Ross...Hurdy Gurdy Man
Stanley Lebor .... Binet
Roy Macready ....Vinçart

Appendix C

Glossary of Film Terms

180° rule: a convention of continuity filming according to which an imaginary line must not be crossed by the camera within a single scene, i.e. the objects and people filmed must have a stable right/left relationship to each other so that the spectator doesn't become disoriented. Also called "axis of action."

background projection: a technique that allows the filmmaker to combine an action in the foreground with background action that has been filmed earlier. The filming of the foreground action is done in a studio, in front of a screen, while behind it, the previously filmed background action is projected onto the screen either from behind it ("rear projection") or from in front of it ("front projection").

blocking: the positioning of actors on a set and the coordination of their movements; also the planning of camera movements.

close-up: a shot in which the object—often (but not always) a human face—is quite large, nearly filling the screen. This can be done by placing the camera near the object or by using a zoom lens.

continuity editing: a system of editing a narrative film for ease of comprehension. Observing the 180° rule, for example, is an element of continuity editing.

cross-cutting: an editing technique that alternates between two or more scenes taking place simultaneously but in different places.

cut: (vb.) in filmmaking, to stop the camera; in the finished film, the joining of two shots; (n.): the transition between two shots. A simple cut creates the impression that the first shot is instantaneously replaced by the second.

deep focus: method in which everything in front of the camera is shot in sharp focus, regardless of its distance from the camera (i.e. which plane it's on). Deep focus gives the spectator more freedom to choose what to look at.

dissolve: a means of connecting shots in which the first image slowly disappears while the second image appears over it. For a brief moment, the spectator sees the two images superimposed.

double feature: a film industry phenomenon in which two feature films were shown for the price of one. Double features fell out of popularity by the 1980s.

editing: the assemblage of a film by selecting and joining camera takes and sound tracks.

establishing shot: a long shot, usually at the beginning of a scene, which shows the spatial relationship among objects that will later be shown in more detail.

extradiegetic: something that is not part of the world represented by the film's story or diegesis . Hence, extradiegetic music (used to create mood) would be heard by the spectator but not by the characters on screen. (This should not be confused with theme music which can sometimes be heard by the characters if it emanates, say, from an instrument shown on screen.)

fade: a means of connecting shots. There are two varieties of fades, the fade-in, in which a dark screen gradually lightens, and the fade-out, in which the screen fades to blackness.

film noir: a French term (literally "black film") which describes a certain type of American film, usually characterized by a dark mood and low lighting to match; often a detective or ganster film.

frame: a single photograph on a strip of film

heritage film: a term that came into use to refer to certain British films of the 1980s but which can be employed to describe any expensively produced costume drama that represents a past era with attention to authentic recreation of period details and visual perfection. The heritage film, meant to inspire pride in a country's cultural heritage, is often characterized by lavish sets, panoramic long shots and deep focus.

high angle shot: the position of the object filmed in relation to the camera is low.

image track: everything that is seen on the screen, as opposed to the soundtrack which refers to everything that is heard (voices, sounds, music, etc.).

intertitle: a title card or subtitle, usually superimposed on an image that appears any time during the film (i.e. after the opening credits and before the tail credits).

long take: a shot that has an exceptionally long duration before the camera cuts to the next shot.

medium close-up: a framing in which the object shot is quite large, filling most of the screen, but less large than for a close-up. A medium close-up of a person would show the person from the chest up.

medium shot: a framing in which the object shot is moderately large, but less so than for a medium close-up. A medium shot of a person would show the person from the waist up and would fill most of the screen.

mise-en-scène: A French word that means, literally "putting on stage." It refers to all of the items placed in front of the camera before the filming begins: decor, costumes, lighting, etc.

montage: a French word derived from the verb monter, to set up or mount, referring to the assemblage of a film (in this sense it is synonymous with editing).

montage sequence: a segment of a film in which a series of shots, often linked by dissolves or fades, is juxtaposed to summarize a topic or suggest repeated action over a period of time or simply to evoke the passage of time.

out-takes: a take which is not used in the finished production.

pan: (vb) to rotate a stationary camera horizontally (on a vertical axis); (n.) a stationary camera's horizontal rotation.

pictorialist camera work: a kind of photography that emulates painting, especially that of the Impressionists (with the use of soft focus, for example). Emphasis on "the pretty" and the artistic.

point-of-view shot: a shot taken with the camera placed where the character's eyes would be, so that what the spectator sees is what the character sees. It is usually preceded by a shot of the character looking.

post-synchronization: the process of adding sound (e.g. noises, diegetic music, voices) to the image track after it has been assembled.

production values: a term that refers to the degree to which a filmmaker has been able to pay attention to details in props, costumes, etc., usually in accordance with the film's budget. Thus a film with high production values is generally one that is expensive to produce.

shot/reverse shot: a technique often used for filming dialogues, in which the camera adopts in turn the perspective of the characters who are speaking (although they may be merely looking at one another). One character is shown looking (often off-screen) at another character, and then the other character is shown doing the same. The spectator assumes they're looking at each other, since they're in facing opposite directions.

soft focus: slightly hazy effect that results from shooting out of focus.

sound bridge: the technique of carrying sound over from one scene to the next, either forwards or backwards (i.e. the sound of one scene can still be heard at the beginning of the next, or the sound of the new scene can already be heard at the end of the first).

swish pan: an extremely rapid horizontal movement of a stationary camera on its vertical axis which produces a blurring effect.

tilt: a camera movement in which a stationary camera tilts upwards or downwards on its support. (tilt refers to vertical movement, unlike pan which refers to horizontal movement.

track: (vb.) to move the camera forward, backward or sideways, usually on a moving vehicle. A picture taken in this way is a tracking shot.

voiceover: the technique of placing an off-screen voice over the images shown on the screen. Often, the voice emanates from a narrator and is used to comment on what is being shown; at other times, it may be employed to render the thoughts of a character shown in the scene but not speaking aloud.

zoom in: (vb.) to use a lens of variable focal length in order to enlarge the image, giving the impression that the camera has moved towards the object.

zoom out: (vb.) to use the same kind of lens used for zooming in, but to do the opposite (i.e. to give the impression of moving away from the image, enlarging the space but making the object smaller).

Bibliography

Abbot, Waldo and Richard L. Rider. *Handbook of Broadcasting*. New York: McGraw-Hill, 1957.

Allen, Woody. "The Purple Rose of Cairo." In *Three Films by Woody Allen*. London and Boston: Faber and Faber. First published in the USA in NY: Randomhouse, 1987.

Altman, Rich. *Film/Genre*. London: British Film Institute, 1999.

Amann, Elizabeth. *Importing* Madame Bovary: *The Politics of Adultery*. New York: Palgrave Macmillan, 2006.

Andrew, Dudley. *Mists of Regret: Culture and Sensibility in Classic French Film*. Princeton: Princeton UP, 1995.

———. "Adaptation." In *Film Theory and Criticism: Introductory Readings*. 5th Edition. Ed. Leo Braudy and Marshall Cohen. New York: Oxford UP, 1999. 452-60.

———. and Steven Ungar. *Popular Front Paris and the Poetics of Culture*. Cambridge, MA: Harvard University Press, 2005.

Aprile, Max. "L'Aveugle et sa signification dans *Madame Bovary*." *Revue d'histoire littéraire de la France* 76 (1976). 385-92.

Asheim, Lester. "From Book to Film: Simplification." *Hollywood Quarterly* 5.3 (1951): 289-304.

———. "From Book to Film: Mass Appeals." *Hollywood Quarterly* 5.4 (1951): 334-49.

———. "From Book to Film: The Note of Affirmation." *The Quarterly of Film Radio and Television* 6.1 (1951): 54-68.

———. "From Book to Film: Summary." *The Quarterly of Film Radio and Television* 6.3 (1952): 258-73.

Assouline, Pierre. *Gaston Gallimard*. Trans. Harold J. Salemson. San Diego: Harcourt Brace Jovanovich, 1987.

Astruc, Alexandre. *Ecrits (1942-1984)*. Paris: L'Archipel, 1992.

Austin, Guy. *Contemporary French Cinema: An Introduction*. Manchester, UK: Manchester UP, 1996.

———. *Claude Chabrol*. Manchester, UK: Manchester UP, 1999.

Autour d'Emma. Collection Brèves Cinéma. Directed by Gilles Jacob. Paris: Hatier, 1991.

Axelrod, Mark. *I Read It at the Movies. The Follies and Foibles of Screen Adaptation*. Portsmouth, NH: Heineman, 2007.

Barnes, Julian. *Something to Declare*. New York: Knopf, 2002.

Baron, Anne-Marie. "De Flaubert à Chabrol, ou la fidélité des adaptations." *Cinéma 91*, No. 476, April 1991.

———. *Romans français du XIXe siècle à l'écran. Problèmes de l'adaptation.* Clermont-Ferrand: Presses universitaires Blaise Pascal, 2008.

Barsamian, David. *The Decline and Fall of Public Broadcasting*. Cambridge, MA: South End Press, 2001.

Battison, John H. *Movies for TV*. New York: MacMillan, 1950.

Baudelaire, Charles. "Hymne à la beauté." *Les Fleurs du mal*. Ed. John E. Jackson. Paris: Livre de Poche classique, 1991. 70-71.

Bazin, André. *Qu'est-ce que le cinéma*? Paris: Les Editions du Cerf, 1987.

Beja, Morris. *Film and Literature*. New York: Longman, 1979.

Bell, Sheila. "Un Pauvre Diable: The Blind Beggar in *Madame Bovary*." In *Studies in French Fiction in Honor of Vivienne Mylne*. Ed. Robert Gibson. London: Grant & Cutler, 1988. 25-39.

Bernard, Claudie, "Monsieur Bovary." *French Forum* 10.3 (Sept. 1985): 307-24.

Bertin, Celia. *Jean Renoir: A Life in Pictures*. Trans. Mireille Muellner and Leonard Muellner. Baltimore: Johns Hopkins UP, 1991.

"Best Performance by an Actress in a Mini-Series or Motion Picture Made for TV." 2001 Golden Globe Awards <http://us.imdb.com/title/tt0212318/awards>.

Blandford, Steve, Barry Keithgrant and Jim Hillier. *The Film Studies Dictionary*. London: Arnold, 2001.

Bluestone, George. *Novels into Film*. Berkeley: U of California P, 1971.

Bordwell, David and Kristin Thompson. *Film Art. An Introduction*. Fifth edition. New York: McGraw Hill, 1997.

Bouillaguet, Annick. *L'Ecriture imitative. Pastiche, Parodie, Collage*. Paris: Nathan, 1996.

Boyum, Joy. *Double Exposure: Fiction into Film*. New York: New American Library, 1989.

Brady, Ben. *Principles of Adaptation for Film and Television*. Austin, TX: University of Texas Press, 1994.

Braucourt, Guy. *Claude Chabrol*. Paris: Editions Seghers, 1971.

Braudy, Leo and Marshall Cohen. *Film Theory and Criticism: Introductory Readings*. 5th Edition. New York: Oxford University Press, 1999.

Buisine, Alain. "Emma c'est l'autre." In *Emma Bovary*. Ed. Alain Buisine. Paris: Editions Autrement, *Figures mythiques*, 1997. 26-59.

Buss, Robin. *The French through their Films*. New York: Ungar, 1988.

Canby, Vincent. "From Claude Chabrol, a *Madame Bovary* with Isabelle Huppert." *New York Times* 25 Dec. 1991: L13+.

Chase, Donald. "A Day in the Country." *Film Comment* 27.6 (1991): 7-14.

Chatman, Seymour. "What Novels Can Do That Films Can't and Vice Versa." *Critical Inquiry* 7 (1980): 121-41.

Cléder, Jean. "L'Adaptation cinématographique." <http:www.fabula.org/atelier.php?Adaptation>.

Cole, Barry G., ed. *Television: A Selection of Readings from TV Guide Magazine*. New York: The Free Press, 1970.

Cook, Pam, ed. *The Cinema Book*. New York: Pantheon Books, 1985.

"Costumed Passions Run High." *BBC News* 7 Apr. 2000. 6 Oct. 2004 <http://news.bbc.co.uk/1/hi/entertainment/701429.stm>.

Cousins, Russell. "The Heritage Film and Cultural Politics: *Germinal* (Berri, 1993)." In *French Cinema in the 1990s: Continuity and Difference*. Ed. Phil Powrie. Oxford, UK: Oxford UP, 1999. 25-36.

Crisp, Colin. *Genre, Myth, and Convention in the French Cinema, 1929-1939*. Bloomington: Indiana UP, 2002.

Culler, Jonathan. *Flaubert: The Uses of Uncertainty*. Ithaca, NY: Cornell UP, 1974.

Curot, Frank, ed. *Renoir in France*. Cahiers Jean Renoir 1. Montpellier: U Paul Valéry, 1999.

Donaldson-Evans, Catherine. "Ratings Debate Peaks Again with 'Brokeback'." *Foxnews.com*. 9 December 2005. <http:// www.foxnews.com/0,3566,178156,00.html>

Donaldson-Evans, Mary. "*Madame Bovary*'s Blind Beggar: A Medical Reading." *Medical Examinations*. Lincoln: U Nebraska P, 2000. 22-40.

———. "A Medium of Exchange: The *Madame Bovary* Films." *Dix-Neuf* 4 (2005): 21-34.

———. "Teaching *Madame Bovary* Through Film." In *Approaches to Teaching Flaubert's* Madame Bovary. Ed. Laurence M. Porter and Eugene F. Gray. New York: The Modern Language Association of America (1995): 114-21.

Durgnat, Raymond. *Jean Renoir*. Berkeley: U of California P, 1974.

Duszynski, Fabienne. "La volte-face d'Emma." *Vertigo* 22 (October 2001): 85-6.

Eisenstein, Sergei. *Film Form: Essays in Film Theory*. Ed. and trans. Jay Leyda. New York: Harcourt, Brace & Co., 1995.

Ellis, Jack C. *A History of Film*. Englewood Cliffs, NJ: Prentice Hall, 1979.

Ellis, John. *Visible Fictions: Cinema, Television, Video*. Rev. ed. New York: Routledge, 1992.

Emptaz, Florence. *Aux pieds de Flaubert*. Paris: Grasset, 2002.

Ezra, Elizabeth and Sue Harris, eds. *France in Focus. Film and National Identity*. New York: Oxford UP, 2000.

Falconer, Graham. "Flaubert assassin de Charles." In *Langages de Flaubert*. Ed. Michael Issacharoff. Paris: Lettres Modernes, 1976. 115-41.

———. "*Madame Bovary* and the Translators." In *Significations*. Toronto: Canadian Scholars Press, 1997. 41-50.

Faulkner, Christopher. *The Social Cinema of Jean Renoir*. Princeton, NJ: Princeton UP, 1986.

Fischer, Edward. *The Screen Arts*. New York: Sheed & Ward, 1960.

Fiolet, Annick. "Val Abraham." *L'Art du cinéma* 3 (1993). <http://www.imaginet.fr/secav/adc/n3va.html>.

Flaubert, Gustave. *Correspondance*. Ed. Jean Bruneau. Bibliothèque de la Pleiade. Paris: Gallimard. Vol. II, 1980. Vol. III, 1991.

———. *Madame Bovary*. Ed. Jacques Neefs. Le Livre de Poche classique. Paris: Librairie Générale Française, 1999.

———. *Madame Bovary. Trans*. Lowell Bair. New York: Bantam, 1987.

———. *Madame Bovary*. Ed. Margaret Cohen. Trans. Eleanor Marx Aveling and Paul De Man. New York : Norton, 2004.

———. *Madame Bovary*. Trans. Margaret Mauldon. Oxford & NY: Oxford UP, 2004.

Friday, Nancy. *My Mother/My Self: The Daughter's Search for Identity*. NY: Dell Publishing, 1977.

Frodon, Jean-Michel. *L'Age moderne du cinéma français*. Paris: Flammarion, 1995.

Gardies, André. *Le Récit filmique*. Paris: Hachette, 1993.

Genette, Gérard. *Palimpsestes, la littérature au second degré*. Paris: Seuil, 1982.

Gilbert, Matthew. "She Was Born to Play Emma Bovary." *Boston Globe* 22 Dec. 1991: A11.

Gilliatt, Penelope. *Jean Renoir: Essays, Conversations, Reviews*. New York: McGraw-Hill, 1975.

Goldmann, Annie. "Madame Bovary vue par Flaubert, Minnelli et Chabrol." *CinémAction* 65 (1992): 132-41.

Goodman, Walter. "That Bovary Woman, Making Trouble Mostly for Herself." *New York Times* 5 Feb. 2000, late ed.: B7.

Gothot-Mersch, Claudine. "La Description des visages dans *Madame Bovary*." *Littérature* 15 (1974): 17-26.

Griffith, James. *Adaptations as Imitations*. Newark, DE: U Delaware P, 1997.

Guérif, François. *Conversations avec Claude Chabrol: Un Jardin bien à moi*. Paris: Denoël, 1999.

Harvey, Stephen. *Directed by Vincente Minnelli*. New York: Museum of Modern Art, 1989.

Hayward, Susan. *French National Cinema*. London: Routledge, 1993.

Higson, Andrew. "Re-presenting the National Past: Nostalgia and Pastiche in the Heritage Film." In *Fires Were Started: British Cinema and Thatcherism*. Ed. Lester Friedman. Minneapolis: U Minnesota P, 1993. 109-29.

Hinson, Hal. "Wayward *Madame Bovary*." *Washington Post* 25 Dec. 1991: D2.

Hohenadel, Kristin. "Paris for Real vs. Paris on Film: We'll Always Have the Movies." *New York Times* 25 Nov. 2001, sec. 2: 11.

Horton, Andrew and Joan Magretta, eds. *Modern European Filmmakers and the Art of Adaptation*. New York: Frederick Ungar Publishing Company, 1981.

Hutcheon, Linda. *A Theory of Adaptation*. New York: Routledge, 2006.

Jayot, Delphine. "Les Adaptations cinématographiques de *Madame Bovary*." Diss. Université de Paris IV, 1992.

Jarvik, Laurence. *PBS. Behind the Screen*. Rocklin, CA: Prima Publishing Company, 1997.

———. "PBS and the Politics of Quality: Mobil Oil's *Masterpiece Theatre.*" *Historical Journal of Film, Radio and Television* 12, no. 3 (1992): 253-74.

Jeancolas, Jean-Pierre. *15 Ans d'années trente*. Paris: Editions Stock, 1983.

Jost, François. "La Parodie audio-visuelle dans quelques-uns de ses états." In *Dire la Parodie: Colloque de Cerisy*. Ed. Clive Thompson and Alain Pagès. New York: Peter Lang, 1989. 312-28.

———. "La Parodie au cinéma." In *Dire la Parodie: Colloque de Cerisy*. Ed. Clive Thompson and Alain Pagès. New York: Peter Lang, 1989. 361-71.

Kehr, Dave. "Emma the Charmless." *Chicago Tribune* 25 Dec. 1991, sec. 3:3.

Konigsberg, Ira. *The Complete Film Dictionary*. Second Edition. London: Penguin, 1997.

Kozloff, Sarah. *Invisible Storytellers: Voice-Over Narration in American Fiction Film*. Berkeley: U of California P, 1988.

Kroeber, Karl. *Make Believe in Film and Fiction: Visual vs. Verbal Storytelling*. New York: Palgrave Macmillan, 2006.

Krueger, Cheryl. "Being *Madame Bovary*." *Literature Film Quarterly* 31.3 (2003): 162-68.

LaCapra, Dominick. *Madame Bovary on Trial*. Ithaca, NY: Cornell UP, 1982.

Ladenson, Elizabeth. *Dirt for Art's Sake. Books on Trial from* Madame Bovary *to* Lolita. Ithaca, NY: Cornell UP, 2007.

Lazere, Arthur. "Madame Bovary." *CultureVulture.net*. <http://www.culturevulture.net /Television/MadameBovary.htm>.

Lagny, Michèle, Marie-Claire Ropars and Pierre Sorlin. *Générique des années trente*. Saint-Denis, France: PU de Vincennes, 1986.

Leprohon, Pierre. *Jean Renoir*. Trans. Brigid Elson. New York: Crown, 1967.

Le Calvez, Eric, ed. *Gustave Flaubert: A Documentary Volume. Dictionary of Literary Biography*, Vol. 301. Detroit: Thomson Gale, 2004. 67-82.

———. "Génétique scénarique : les scénarios de la scène du fiacre dans *Madame Bovary*." In *La Création en acte. Devenir de la critique génétique*. Ed. Paul Gifford and Marion Schmid. Amsterdam, New York: Rodopi, "Faux Titre" 2007. 67-82.

Levin, Harry. *The Gates of Horn*. New York: Oxford UP, 1963.

Linan, Steven. "The Fire of Desire in *Madame Bovary*." *Los Angeles Times* 5 Feb. 2000: F15.

Lindgren, Ernest. *The Art of the Film*. London: George Allen and Unwin, Ltd., 1963.

Lloyd, Rosemary. *Madame Bovary*. London: Unwin Hyman, 1990.

Lotman, Jurij. *Semiotics of Cinema*. Trans. Mark E. Suino. Ann Arbor: University of Michigan, 1976.

MacKillop, Ian and Alison Platt. "'Beholding in a Magic Panorama': Television and the Illustration of *Middlemarch*." In *The Classic Novel from Page to Screen*. Ed. Robert Giddings and Erica Sheen. Manchester, UK: Manchester UP, 2000.

MacLeay, Daniel A. "*Madame Bovary* on Screen." *Publications of the Missouri Philological Association* 21 (1996): 38-44.

Magny, Joël. "Caméra-Plume." *Cahiers du cinéma* 442 (1991): 58-9.

Marcus, Fred. *Film and Literature: Contrasts in Media*. Scranton, PA: Chandler Publishing Company, 1971.

Marcus, Millicent. *Filmmaking by the Book: Italian Cinema and Literary Adaptation*. Baltimore: Johns Hopkins UP, 1993.

———. "Umbilical Scenes: Where Filmmakers Foreground their Relationships to Literary Sources." *Romance Languages Annual* X (1999): xix-xxiv.

Mayne, Judith. *Private Novels, Public Films*. Athens, GA: U of Georgia P, 1988.

McElhaney, Joe. "Vicente Minnelli." Senses of Cinema. 14 Aug. 2008. <http://www.sensesofcinema.com/contents/directors/04/minnelli.html>.

Metz, Christian. *Film Language. A Semiotics of the Cinema*. New York: Oxford UP, 1974.

———. *Le Signifiant imaginaire. Psychanalyse et cinéma*. Paris: C. Bourgeois 2002.

Miller, Jeffrey S. *Something Completely Different. British Television and American Culture*. Minneapolis: U of Minnesota P, 2000.

Miller, Jonathan. *Subsequent Performances*. New York: Viking, 1986.

Minnelli, Vincente. *I Remember It Well*. London: Angus and Robertson, 1975.

Moaveni, Azadeh. "Letter from Tehran: Seeking Signs of Literary Life." *The New York Times* 27 May 2007, sec. 7:27.

Monaco, James. *The New Wave: Truffaut, Godard, Chabrol, Rohmer, Rivette*. Oxford, UK: Oxford UP, 1976.

Mouchard, Claude. "En elle le noir abonde." *Autour d'Emma.* 149-59.

"The Motion Picture Production Code of 1930." *ArtsReformation.com*. 7 Sept. 2004 <http://www.artsreformation.com/a001/hayscode.html>.

Murat, Pierre. *Télérama* 3 Apr. 1991: 18.

Nacache, Jacqueline. "La Plume et la Caméra." *La Revue du cinéma* 471 (1991): 32-34.

Naremore, James, ed. *Film Adaptation*. New Brunswick, NJ: Rutgers UP, 2000.

Neil, Sinyard. *Filming Literature: The Art of Screen Adaptation*. London: Croom Helm, 1986

O'Flaherty, Terrence. *Masterpiece Theatre: A Celebration of 25 Years of Outstanding Television*. San Francisco: KQED, 1996.

Ord-Hume, Arthur W. J. G. *Barrel Organ: The Story of the Mechanical Organ and Its Repair*. South Brunswick: A.S. Barnes, 1978.

Orr, Christopher. "The Discourse on Adaptation." *Wide Angle* 6.2 (1984): 72-76.

Orr, Mary. *Flaubert: Writing the Masculine*. Oxford and NY: Oxford UP, 2000.

O'Shaughnessy, Martin. *Jean Renoir*. Manchester, UK: Manchester UP, 2000.

Ouellette, Laurie. *Viewers Like You? How Public TV Failed the People*. New York: Columbia UP, 2002.

Pauly, Rebecca. *The Transparent Illusion: Image and Ideology in French Text and Film*. New York: Peter Lang, 1993.

Plot, Bernadette. "'Madame Bovary' à l'Ecran." *Le Français dans le monde* 247 (1992): 46-53.

Porter, Laurence M., ed. *Approaches to Teaching Flaubert's* Madame Bovary. Edited with Eugene F. Gray. New York: The Modern Language Association of America, 1995.

―――. "Critical Reception." *A Gustave Flaubert Encyclopedia*. Ed. Laurence M. Porter. Westport, CT: Greenwood, 2001. 77-88.

―――. "Emma Bovary's Narcissism Revisted." In *kaleidoscope*. Ed. Graham Falconer and Mary Donaldson-Evans. Toronto: Centre d'etudes romantiques Joseph Sablé, 1996: 85-98.

―――. *Gustave Flaubert's* Madame Bovary: *A Reference Guide*. Edited with Eugene F. Gray. Westport, CT: Greenwood, 2002.

Powrie, Phil, ed. *French Cinema in the 1990s: Continuity and Difference.*
    Oxford, UK: Oxford UP, 1999.
————. "Heritage, History, and 'New Realism': French Cinema in the
    1990s." In *French Cinema in the 1990s: Continuity and Difference.*
    Ed. Phil Powrie. Oxford, UK: Oxford UP, 1999. 1-21.
Premier Plan. "Jean Renoir." Special Issue: Nos. 22-23-24. May 1962.
Rampton, James. "The Sex and Shopping *Madame Bovary*." London: *The
    Independent.* 7 April 2000. Features: 9.
    <http://proxy.library.upenn.edu:8167/universe/document>.
Rapping, Elayne. *The Movie of the Week: Private Stories/Public Events.*
    American Culture 5. Minneapolis: U of Minnesota P, 1992.
"Réquisitoire, Plaidoirie et jugement du procès intenté à l'auteur devant le
    Tribunal correctionnel de Paris (6e chambre), du 29 janvier au 2 février
    1857." Reproduced in Gustave, Flaubert. *Madame Bovary.* Ed.
    Bernard Ajac. Paris : Garnier-Flammarion, 1986 : 437-519
Renoir, Jean. *Ma Vie et mes films.* Paris: Flammarion, 1974.
Richardson, Robert. *Literature and Film.* Bloomington, IN: Indiana UP,
    1969.
Riemer, Willy. "Tracking K.: Michael Haneke's Film Adaptation of Kafka's
    Das Schloß." *Journal of the Kafka Society of America*, Nos. 1-2
    (June/December 1997), 47-53.
Rifelj, Carol. "The Language of Hair in the Nineteenth-Century Novel."
    Nineteenth-Century French Studies 32.1-2 (Fall-Winter 2004): 83-103.
Rifkin, Benjamin. *Semiotics of Narration in Film and Prose Fiction.* New
    York: Peter Lang, 1994.
Ropars-Wuilleumier, Marie-Claire. *Ecraniques: le film du texte.* Lille:
    Presses universitaires de Lille, Collection "Problématiques," 1990.
Rosenbaum, Jonathan. "Both Sides Now." *On Film.* 1997. Chicago Reader.
    <http://www.chireader.com/movies/archives/0297/02147.html>.
Roth-Bettoni, Didier. *La Revue du cinéma: La Saison cinématographique.*
    1991. Hors série xxxix.
Rousset, Jean. "*Madame Bovary* ou le livre sur rien." In Rousset, *Forme et
    signification: Essai sur les structures litteraires de Corneille a
    Claudel.* Paris: Corti, 1962. 109-33.
Ryan, Desmond. "Claude Chabrol Adapts Flaubert's Masterpiece for the
    Screen." *Philadelphia Inquirer* 25 Dec. 1991: D6.
Sachs, Murray. "The Role of the Blind Beggar in *Madame Bovary.*"
    Symposium 22 (1968): 72-80.
Salt, Barry. *Film Style and Technology: History and Analysis.* 2nd ed.
    London: Starword, 1992.
Samuels, Maurice. *The Spectacular Past. Popular History and the Novel in
    Nineteenth-Century France.* Ithaca, NY: Cornell UP, 2004.
Sanders, Julie. *Adaptation and Appropriation.* New York: Routledge, 2006.

Santoro, Patricia J. *Novel into Film*. Newark, DE: U of Delaware P, 1996.

Schehr, Lawrence, "Flaubert's Failure." In *The Cambridge Companion to Flaubert*. Ed. Timothy Unwin. Cambridge, UK: Cambridge UP, 2004. 208-19.

Schiff, Stephen. "All Right, You Try: Adaptation Isn't Easy." *New York Times* 1 Dec. 2002, sec. 2:28.

Scott, A. O. "Some Material May Be Inappropriate or Mystifying, and the Rating May Be as Well." *New York Times on the Web*. <http://movies2.nytimes.com/2006/09/01/movies/01rate.html>

———. "Playground rules: No Hitting, No Sex." Review of *Little Children*. *New York Times* 29 September 2006: E1+.

Sears, Harold and Meredith. *Some Waltz History*. <http://members.isp01.net/hfsears/drdc/DRDC-WaltzHist.html>.

Semonche, John. *Censoring Sex: A Historical Journey Through American Media*. NY: Rowman and Littlefield, 2007.

Serceau, Michel. *L'Adaptation cinématographique des textes littéraires*. Liège: Editions du Céfal, 1999.

Sesonske, Alexander. *Jean Renoir: The French Films, 1924-1939*. Cambridge: Harvard UP, 1980.

Siclier, Jacques. "Isabelle Bovary." *Le Monde* 3 April 1991.

Silverman, David. *You Can't Air That*. Syracuse, NY: Syracuse UP, 2007.

Slide, Anthony. *The New Historical Dictionary of the American Film Industry*. Lanham, Maryland: Scarecrow Press, Inc., 2001.

Spiegel, Alan. *Fiction and the Camera Eye. Visual Consciousness in Film and the Modern Novel*. Charlottesville: UP of Virginia, 1976.

Stam, Robert. "Beyond Fidelity: The Dialogics of Adaptation," In *Film Adaptation*, Ed. James Naremore. New Brunswick, NJ: Rutgers UP, 2000. 54-76.

———. *François Truffaut and Friends: Modernism, Sexuality and Film Adaptation*. New Brunswick, NJ: Rutgers UP, 2006.

———. *Literature through Film: Realism, Magic, and the Art of Adaptation*. Oxford: Blackwell, 2005.

Stam, Robert and Alessandra Raengo, eds. *Literature and Film: A guide to the theory and practice of film adaptation*. Oxford: Blackwell, 2005.

Stark, Steven D. *Glued to the Set*. New York: Free Press, 1997.

Starkie, Enid. *Flaubert the Master: A Critical and Biographical Study (1856-1880)*. New York: Atheneum, 1971.

Stein, William Bysshe. "*Madame Bovary* and Cupid Unmasked." *Sewanee Review* 73 (1965): 197-209.

Stern, Lesley. "Fiction/Film/Femininity—Paper Two." *Australian Journal of Screen Theory* 9-10 (1981): 51-68.

"Study Guide for Chabrol's *Madame Bovary*." Distributed by Samuel Goldwyn Company. New York: New York Council of the Arts, 1991.

Tanner, Tony. *Adultery in the Novel: Contract and Transgression*. Baltimore: Johns Hopkins UP, 1979.

Thibault, Bruno. "La transposition dans *Prénom Carmen* de Jean-Luc Godard et dans *La Belle Noiseuse* de Jacques Rivette." *French Review* 79.2 (2005): 332-42.

Thiher, Allen. *The Cinematic Muse. Critical Studies in the History of French Cinema*. Columbia, MO: U of Missouri P, 1979.

Thomson, Clive and Alain Pagès, eds. *Dire la parodie*. New York: Peter Lang, 1989.

Thomsom, David. *A Biographical Dictionary of Film*. Third Edition. New York: Knopf, 1995.

Ukff-Móller, Jens. *Hollywood's Film Wars with France*. Rochester, NY: U of Rochester P, 2001.

Unwin, Timothy, ed. *The Cambridge Companion to Flaubert*. Cambridge, UK: Cambridge UP, 2004.

Vargas Llosa, Mario. *The Perpetual Orgy. Flaubert and Madame Bovary*. Trans. Helen Lane. New York: Farrar, Straus, Giroux, 1986.

———. "Flaubert, our Contemporary." In *The Cambridge Companion to Flaubert*. Ed. Timothy Unwin. Cambridge, UK: Cambridge UP, 2004. 220-24.

Wagner, Geoffrey. *The Novel and the Cinema*. Rutherford, NJ: Fairleigh Dickinson UP, 1975.

Walker, James R., and Douglas A. Ferguson. *The Broadcast Television Industry*. Boston: Allyn & Bacon, 1998.

Walter, Klaus-Peter, "Réalisme littéraire et réalisme cinématographique: *Madame Bovary* au cinéma. Renoir, Minnelli, Chabrol." In *Modernité de Flaubert*. Warsaw: Editions de l'université de Varsovie, 1994), 93-105.

Waterhouse, Keith. "The Celluloid Collar." *The Listener* 119. 3058 (April 14, 1988): 12-13.

Wetherill, P. M. "*Madame Bovary*'s Blind Man: Symbolism in Flaubert." *Romanic Review* 61 (1970): 35-42.

Williams, Alan. *Republic of Images: A History of French Filmmaking*. Cambridge, MA: Harvard UP, 1992.

Williams, Michael J. "The Hound of Fate in *Madame Bovary*." *College Literature* 14.1 (1987): 54-61.

Williams, Michael A., S. J. "The Director's Eye: *Madame Bovary* on Film." <http://ntserver.shc.edu/www/Scholar/williams/ williams.html>.

Zalewski, Daniel. "The 'I' Cure for Writer's Block." *New York Times* 1 Dec. 2002, Sec. II (Arts & Leisure): 1+.

Index